Praise for *Comebacks*

"This exciting and discerning collection sheds light on those stars who are sensitively described as 'post-peak.' *Comebacks: The Return of the Aging Film Star* constructs a conceptually rich framework within which to examine the comeback of a star in terms of when and how it happens, and also how the returning star relates to their younger screen self and their aging body. These diverse and perceptive essays are not only a fascinating read but also a prompt to reconsider the reappearances of older stars in their moving and courageous complexity."

—Lucy Bolton, professor, Queen Mary University of London

"This innovative book brings a fresh and exciting perspective to bear on film studies. At a time when cultural representations of aging are hotly contested, *Comebacks* is a vital intervention in the debate about what it means to grow old on-screen."

—Melanie Bell, professor, University of Leeds

"This is a fascinating and entertaining collection of essays about older stars' comebacks. It offers original and inspiring readings of often-neglected or critiqued films and sheds new light on older stars' performances and careers, besides contributing prominently to the study of cinema, visibility, and aging."

—Anne Jerslev, professor, University of Copenhagen

COMEBACKS

Contemporary Approaches to Film and Media Series

A complete listing of the books in this series can be found online at wsupress.wayne.edu.

COMEBACKS

THE RETURN OF THE AGING FILM STAR

EDITED BY
GLORIA MONTI
AND
MARTIN SHINGLER

Wayne State University Press
Detroit

ISBN 9780814350621 (paperback)
ISBN 9780814350638 (hardcover)
ISBN 9780814350645 (ebook)

Library of Congress Control Number: 2025931227

On cover: Publicity still of Joan Crawford and Bette Davis in *What Ever Happened to Baby Jane?* (1962). Courtesy of Wikimedia Commons. Cover design by Elke Barter.

Published with the assistance of a fund established by Thelma Gray James of Wayne State University for the publication of folklore and English studies.

Wayne State University Press rests on Waawiyaataanong, also referred to as Detroit, the ancestral and contemporary homeland of the Three Fires Confederacy. These sovereign lands were granted by the Ojibwe, Odawa, Potawatomi, and Wyandot Nations, in 1807, through the Treaty of Detroit. Wayne State University Press affirms Indigenous sovereignty and honors all tribes with a connection to Detroit. With our Native neighbors, the press works to advance educational equity and promote a better future for the earth and all people.

Wayne State University Press
Leonard N. Simons Building
4809 Woodward Avenue
Detroit, Michigan 48201-1309

Visit us online at wsupress.wayne.edu.

CONTENTS

Part III. Departing from the Younger Screen Self

Part IV. Aging Star Bodies

ACKNOWLEDGMENTS

First and foremost, we would like to thank our contributing authors for making this enterprise so rewarding for us. We owe you all a huge debt of gratitude for your intellectual work, patience, persistence and flexibility. We are grateful to Barry Grant for accepting this book for the Contemporary Approaches to Film and Media series at Wayne State University Press and for his suggested improvements and endorsement. The comments and recommended revisions of our two anonymous readers have similarly been instructive and beneficial, enabling us to hone and refine the book, especially the introduction. Thanks are also due to Marie Sweetman and her colleagues at Wayne State University Press for their diligence, advice, and numerous skills in bringing this project to fruition.

Gloria would like to thank California State University, Fullerton, for granting her a sabbatical leave, making it possible to pursue this book project. She also thanks Richard Day Gore, who provided assistance and encouragement at every stage; her best friend, colleague, and ally since graduate school, Robert Cagle; her students, too many to mention, who make every writing effort worthwhile. Thanks also to Giancarlo Concetti of the Biblioteca Luigi Chiarini at the Fondazione Centro Sperimentale di Cinematografia and Davide Badini of the Biblioteca Renzo Renzi at the Cineteca di Bologna for providing invaluable research materials on Alida Valli. She extends special thanks to her coeditor, Martin Shingler. "Coeditor" only begins to describe Martin's impact on this volume, as she might call him copilot and consultant. His knowledge of academic publishing and his flawless skills as a writer and researcher contributed vitally to this volume, while his tireless enthusiasm made completing this book a rewarding experience.

Martin would like to thank former colleagues and mentors, as well as existing friends and loved ones for their inspiration, encouragement, advice and support over many years, chiefly Cynthia Baron, Melanie Bell,

Colin Cruise, Richard Dyer, Thomas Elsaesser, Christine Gledhill, Anna Raeburn, Simon Rushton, and Ulrike Sieglohr. His greatest thanks, however, are to Gloria Monti for the invitation to coedit this unique volume of studies on aging stardom, for her trust in his judgment, for her forensic attention to detail and, most important of all, for taking on the larger share of the administration, management, and coordination of this ambitious project.

While Martin dedicates this book to his great friend Jules A. Sykes, Gloria dedicates it to all the actors who didn't get a chance to have a comeback.

INTRODUCTION

Gloria Monti and Martin Shingler

Some Different Kinds of Comeback Film

Sunset Boulevard (Billy Wilder, 1950), one of the most famous comeback films of all time, made a deep impression on audiences and critics upon its original release and subsequently remained popular with film fans, critics, teachers, and scholars. There can hardly be a better example of an aging star returning to the global spotlight than this. Gloria Swanson's performance as an increasingly delusional fifty-year-old former silent film diva was nothing short of magnificent: astonishing and almost shockingly self-revelatory in the way it evoked aspects of the star's own life, career, and persona. Swanson's characterization of Norma Desmond as she makes a desperate bid for a cinematic comeback was so accomplished, sincere, and brave that it earned her an Academy Award nomination for Best Actress for the first time in twenty years, along with a Golden Globe Award.[1] Moreover, vast numbers of people purchased tickets to see it in cinemas around the world, making this Swanson's first box-office hit since 1929.

There is no disputing the fact that *Sunset Boulevard* was a comeback film, given that it was not only about an aging star trying to make a comeback in the entertainment business but that it also succeeded in delivering a box-office hit for an aged and faded star performer after a

1. Swanson's last Academy Award nomination was for *The Trespasser* (Edmond Goulding, 1929).

period of absence from the big screen.[2] *The Star* (Stuart Heisler, 1952) can also be considered a comeback film due to the fact that it features Bette Davis as a middle-aged, bankrupt, alcoholic, and unemployed film actor trying to rebuild her career. However, this wasn't designed as a vehicle to return Davis to prominence after an absence.[3] Consequently, *The Star* only functioned as a comeback in terms of the plot. Bette Davis actually made her greatest career comeback twelve years later playing an unhinged former child star of vaudeville opposite Joan Crawford as her persecuted, wheelchair-bound sister in the low-budget psychothriller *What Ever Happened to Baby Jane?* (Robert Aldrich, 1962). Here, Davis's Jane subjects Crawford's Blanche to a succession of increasingly cruel pranks, humiliations, and torture, in between attempts to resuscitate her juvenile stage act long after her fame has faded, and her name has been forgotten. In addition to becoming a massive box-office hit, this black comedy/horror film earned Davis an Academy Award nomination for Best Actress in 1963, while propelling its two veteran stars back to prominence, profitability, and employability in their mid-fifties after a period of decline in their film careers, making it one of the most successful and best-known comeback films of all time.[4]

Unlike the previous three examples, *A Star Is Born* (George Cukor, 1954) is not about an aging actor trying to regain her stardom. On the contrary, the plot revolves around a young female singer (Judy Garland) who becomes a Hollywood star after meeting and marrying a washed-up, alcoholic film actor (James Mason). Yet *A Star Is Born* is a comeback film by virtue of the fact that the thirty-two-year-old former child star Judy Garland returned to the big screen in a blaze of glory as the film's main protagonist some four years after being dropped by her studio, Metro-Goldwyn-Mayer, due to her erratic behavior.

2. Until she made *Sunset Boulevard*, Swanson hadn't appeared in a feature film since *Father Takes a Wife* (Jack Hively, 1941).
3. Davis was a familiar presence on the big screen in 1952. Following her Oscar-nominated headline role in Joseph L. Mankiewicz's hit comedy in *All About Eve* (1950), she starred in *Payment on Demand* (Curtis Bernhardt, 1951) and *Another Man's Poison* (Irving Rapper, 1951).
4. For more details, see Shingler's chapters on Joan Crawford and Lucy Fischer's on Bette Davis in this volume.

With an Oscar nomination for her role as an idealistic and idealized singer-turned-Hollywood star, Garland reasserted her credentials as a talented screen performer. However, *A Star Is Born* failed to break even at the box office, despite earning over six million dollars in receipts, consequently failing to restore Garland's bankability, which is partly why she secured no more starring roles until 1963.[5] Of course, a comeback film doesn't necessarily have to result in its star regaining marquee value—an example would be the critically and commercially unsuccessful film *The Comeback* (Donald Wolfe, 1970). What makes this a comeback in more than just name is the fact that its original intention was to restore the stardom of one of Hollywood's most vivacious actors of the 1930s, Miriam Hopkins, with her daring portrayal of an aging, alcoholic, and reclusive retired film star, as Gabrielle Stecher explains in the first chapter of this volume.

As the above examples show, there are a variety of reasons why a film can be conceived of as a comeback. Some are about an actor trying to regain a prominent position in the entertainment industry (*What Ever Happened to Baby Jane?*). Some of these may succeed in delivering a box-office hit for an aged and faded star performer after a period of absence from the big screen (*Sunset Boulevard*), while others fail to do so (*The Comeback*). Other comeback films do not involve protagonists attempting to make a comeback in show business and yet do succeed in restoring a faded star to fame and glory (the 1954 production of *A Star Is Born*). A notable example of this is *The Spider's Stratagem* (Bernardo Bertolucci, 1970), which not only restored Alida Valli's status as a preeminent Italian film star in 1970 but also revitalized her career by expanding her repertoire of characters and extending her working life as a screen actor into her fifties, sixties, and seventies, as Gloria Monti explains in this volume. In many respects, *The Spider's Stratagem* is one of the greatest comebacks of all time, given that it had such a profound and lasting impact on Valli's career more than thirty years after she had made a name for herself in Italian popular cinema and two decades after she had become a Hollywood star.

Comebacks: The Return of the Aging Film Star testifies to the fact that actors around the world have regained fame, popularity, marquee value, and box-office success after a period of decline or absence from the cinema

5. Garland's next starring role was opposite Burt Lancaster in *A Child Is Waiting* (John Cassavetes, 1963).

screen in all kinds of parts (as a main protagonist or in a supporting role, even a cameo) and in all types of films. Our anthology demonstrates that numerous star actors have achieved commercial or critical success after their peak by skillfully managing the limited opportunities open to them in an ageist and sexist film industry. Orbiting around both a fear of old age and the tyranny of youth at the heart of popular culture, our authors reveal how aging stars have resurrected abandoned or stalled careers in various ways, in different eras and countries.

To understand this process better, a range of scholars were invited to produce short case studies on comeback films and slightly longer ones on post-peak film stardom.[6] What this has revealed is a whole range of possibilities for aging star actors who return to the big screen after a significant absence. While it is true that some have been cast in low-budget exploitation films (some of which deride and degrade them), other veterans have had the chance to display a much greater set of performance skills in their comeback films than in star vehicles made at the height of their careers. Notable examples include Viveca Lindfors in Sweden and Burt Reynolds in the United States, as discussed, respectively, by Saki Kobayashi and Jennifer Louise Field in this volume.

As this collection of essays suggests, there is no single means by which actors have gained major or artistically significant comebacks after their popularity and marquee value have declined. This means that a comeback vehicle is often serendipitous, occasionally proving successful against the odds and even against all expectations. Some films that are strategically designed to restore a star's popularity and bankability deploy elements from earlier successful comebacks, notably *Sunset Boulevard* and *What*

6. Rather than commissioning authors to produce case studies of the most well-known and documented comebacks, such as Gloria Swanson's *Sunset Boulevard* and Judy Garland's *A Star Is Born*, we sought to promote new research on films that have so far received little academic attention (e.g., Miriam Hopkins's *The Comeback*), as well as others that have rarely, if ever, been considered as comeback films—most notably, *The Bridge on the River Kwai* (David Lean, 1957), which is discussed at length in Daisuke Miyao's case study of Sessue Hayakawa. The major exception is *What Ever Happened to Baby Jane?*, which is discussed in Martin Shingler's chapter on Joan Crawford and Lucy Fischer's on Bette Davis, although it doesn't constitute the only or main case study in these chapters.

Ever Happened to Baby Jane?[7] Yet many films that share recycled elements with these two films have failed to achieve critical or commercial success, indicating that there is no formula for guaranteeing a successful comeback.

Nevertheless, some of the films that were commercially or critically unsuccessful are worth watching and studying, especially those derided by reviewers as tasteless and tacky or exploitative and derivative. Indeed, as several chapters in this anthology note, many once-denigrated comeback films can be reclaimed as major achievements for has-been stars. Consequently, several of the comeback films analyzed in this book involve a radical reassessment of their strengths even when also acknowledging their weaknesses, notably Joan Crawford's *Trog* (Freddie Francis, 1970), Mae West's *Sextette* (Ken Hughes, 1977), and Viveca Lindfors's *Tabu* (*Taboo*, Vilgot Sjöman, 1977). In the process, *Comebacks: The Return of the Aging Film Star* offers new ways of understanding and evaluating films featuring post-peak stars.

Adding Something Unique to Studies of Aging Film Stars

Comebacks: The Return of the Aging Film Star contributes to debates within the field of film studies specifically concerned with issues of aging and longevity in relation to stardom and stars. These age-old issues date back at least as far as 1957, when Edgar Morin published his book *Les stars*. Here, the French sociologist highlighted a double standard in Hollywood before 1940, one that commonly restricted female stardom to performers in their early-to-mid-twenties while enabling male stars to prosper well into middle age (Morin [1957] 2005, 36). Some fifty years later, this situation appeared to have been transformed, notably with a succession of age-affirmative hits such as *Mamma Mia!* (Phyllida Lloyd, 2008), *The Best Exotic Marigold Hotel* (John Madden, 2011), and *Philomena* (Stephen

7. For instance, aspects of *What Ever Happened to Baby Jane?* have been recycled many times, creating a slew of schlocky horrors (also known as "hagsploitation" films) such as *Hush . . . Hush, Sweet Charlotte* (Robert Aldrich, 1964), starring Bette Davis and Olivia de Havilland, and *What Ever Happened to Aunt Alice?* (Lee H. Katzin and Bernard Girard, 1969), starring Geraldine Page and Ruth Gordon. For other examples, see Leon Hunt's chapter on Carroll Baker's Italian thrillers and Gabrielle Stecher's analysis of *The Comeback* in this volume. For more on hagsploitation films, see Peter Shelley's *Grande Dame Guignol Cinema: A History of Hag Horror from "Baby Jane" to "Mother"* (2009).

Frears, 2013), all of which were built around hugely popular international female stars such as Meryl Streep, Maggie Smith, and Judi Dench, women well over the age of fifty when the films were made. Responding to the popularity and success of these mature female stars, Niall Richardson's *Ageing Femininity on Screen: The Older Woman in Contemporary Cinema* (2019) examines the aesthetic and ideological strategies at the heart of seemingly age-affirmative vehicles for middle-aged and elderly star actors. Richardson's book is just one of many publications to focus specifically on cinematic representations of aging.[8]

Since Deborah Jermyn edited a special issue of *Celebrity Studies* (2012), "Back in the Spotlight: Female Celebrity and Ageing," and coedited the anthology *Women, Celebrity, and Cultures of Ageing: Freeze Frame* with Su Holmes (2015), academic studies of aging female stardom have proliferated, along with research on aging stardom more generally.[9] These works now constitute a rich seam of scholarship that productively extends across disciplinary boundaries, including media and cultural studies, celebrity and star studies, sociology and gerontology. Amid academic research on aging in the mass media, the persistence of film stars has been explored in Lucy Bolton and Julie Lobalzo Wright's coedited collection *Lasting Screen Stars: Images That Fade and Personas That Endure* (2016). This wide-ranging set of essays examines the diverse ways in which stars have, on the one hand, remained in public circulation long after their careers have ended or, on the other, disappeared almost entirely from public consciousness after achieving extraordinary levels of success and popularity. More recently, film scholars have pursued the matter of aging stardom in conference papers, journal articles, book chapters, and monographs.[10] *Comebacks: The Return of the Aging Film Star* adds something unique to this important body of film literature by focusing specifically on examples

8. See, for instance, Desjardins 2015; and Bielby, Bardo, and Harrington 2014.

9. The debate sparked by Jermyn's guest editorship of *Celebrity Studies* was significantly expanded when Anne Jerslev and Line Nybro Petersen edited a subsequent special issue, "Ageing Celebrities, Ageing Fans, and Ageing Narratives in Popular Media Culture" (2018). This volume not only included studies of male stars and celebrities but also older audiences and fans across a wider range of media.

10. See, for example, Purse 2017; Dolan 2017; McKenna 2019; and the final five chapters of Redmond 2021.

of films that herald the reappearance—and sometimes maintain the public visibility—of a well-known actor after a period of absence from the screen.

A Four-Part Investigation into Comebacks

Comprised of sixteen original essays written by established and emerging film scholars from different parts of the world, *Comebacks: The Return of the Aging Film Star* includes case studies from Brazil, Britain, France, India, Italy, Sweden, and the United States. Rather than provide a chronological history of the comeback film, this volume explores some of the key facets of aging star comebacks across a sixty-two-year timespan, extending from *The Bridge on the River Kwai* (David Lean, 1957) to *Terminator: Dark Fate* (Tim Miller, 2019). These studies are not arranged in chronological order but instead are grouped into four separate sections under headings that clearly indicate the main focus of chapters: "Camp and the Veteran Star," "Connecting to the Younger Screen Self," "Departing from the Younger Screen Self," and "Aging Star Bodies." These headings also constitute the four principal themes of our book.

The case studies contained within these four discrete but overlapping sections mostly employ a research method that involves close textual analysis of film moments, either key scenes or segments of scenes, although some authors also draw upon critical reception, such as analysis of reviews in newspapers that accompanied a film's original release, along with other forms of audience data. Both of these methods have become widely used within film studies, with the combination of close textual analysis and reception/audience data being recognized as a distinguishing feature of the "New Film History," as described by James Chapman, Mark Glancy, and Sue Harper in their introduction to *The New Film History: Sources, Methods, Approaches* (2007, 7–8). On the one hand, these film readings are nuanced and sensitive, responding directly to the aesthetic (visual and aural) strategies of filmmakers. On the other hand, they acknowledge that certain audiences actively read, decipher, and understand differently from others, interpreting film texts in culturally and historically specific ways according to their own distinct needs, wants, desires, and ideologies. Consequently, by combining close textual analysis with audience research, our authors remain alert to the intricacies of both cinematic signification (i.e., how cinema signifies) and reception (i.e., how audiences use films and extracinematic materials such as publicity and promotional matter to create meaning and pleasure for themselves).

The "Camp and the Veteran Star" section analyzes how an aging female star's late career or comeback vehicle incorporates aspects of camp in order to either mock her earlier image, roles, and films or to reposition her for more niche audiences, most notably gay men, once she has been widely considered to be a fading or faded star. Interestingly, while camp is generally considered to be a gay sensibility (Babuscio 1999), instances of camp can also be found in films aimed at mainstream and primarily straight audiences. All three chapters in this section concentrate on the commercially unsuccessful, critically denigrated, and academically neglected last films of Miriam Hopkins, Mae West, and Joan Crawford, which were made at a time when camp was increasingly recognized as an important cultural phenomenon, notably for subcultural critics and audiences. Each chapter concentrates on aspects of the aging star's performance while exploring how critics or audiences responded. Issues of good and bad taste surface here, along with a variety of ambiguous reactions generated by such things as seriousness and frivolity, mockery and self-mockery, parody and irony. In this section, Gabrielle Stecher, Kriszta Pozsonyi, and Martin Shingler salvage the reputation of a despised or generally denigrated film (one written off as "trash") while recognizing its value for film history and film studies, particularly star studies. While for Stecher and Pozsonyi this involves rethinking a film's significance in terms of both its artistic and social values, for Shingler this is more about acknowledging qualities that have ensured a film's longevity and ongoing appeal for cult film aficionados.

The discussion of camp raises important questions not only about how performers challenge the norms of sexual and gender behavior but also in terms of age-appropriateness. While there is evidence of how aging female performers like Mae West and Joan Crawford have continued to behave like their former selves in terms of both their earlier screen roles and star images, it also emerges from this section that performers have departed drastically from their previous incarnations with more sexualized versions of themselves, notably in the case of Miriam Hopkins. Yet these chapters also reveal that this situation is seldom clear cut, with aging stars often simultaneously evoking and departing from their earlier incarnations when performing in comeback films.

The three chapters that comprise the camp section of our book prove that comeback films typically forge a relationship between an aging star and her work from an earlier period of her career. This, however, becomes much more explicit in the chapters included in the "Connecting to the Younger Screen Self" section. The studies brought together under this heading are directly concerned with how an aging star's late career or comeback vehicle establishes links with their image and films from the peak of their career, sometimes with an early breakthrough role that once launched their stardom. Each of the chapters on Carroll Baker, Bette Davis, Woody Strode, and John Travolta discuss a number of films rather than one specific comeback vehicle when assessing how these stars' images and former screen roles have been evoked during later stages of their careers. For instance, although Lisa Duffy's chapter on Travolta is mostly focused on his drag performance as Edna Turnblad in *Hairspray* (Adam Shankman, 2007), the author also discusses the way his performance in *Pulp Fiction* (Quentin Tarantino, 1994) constitutes an initial comeback, with his dancing forging an important link with his younger star image.

While the third section, "Departing from the Younger Screen Self," raises similar issues to the previous one, the perspective shifts to focus on how stars have made a decisive break with their former screen roles and star image at a later stage of their career. One of the most decisive breaks in this respect features in one of the most commercially successful and critically acclaimed international coproductions of the late 1950s, *The Bridge on the River Kwai* (David Lean, 1957), costarring William Holden and Alec Guinness.[11] In his chapter in this section, Daisuke Miyao discusses this Anglo-American film set during World War II as a comeback vehicle for the Japanese actor and former star of Hollywood silent cinema Sessue Hayakawa, who was cast in a supporting role as Colonel Saito, the commander of a Japanese prisoner-of-war camp. Here, Miyao focuses on the way that a faded middle-aged Japanese film actor revived his film career in the late 1950s with a performance (and, subsequently, a published memoir) that capitalized on international interest in Zen Buddhism.

11. One of the biggest box-office hits of 1957, *The Bridge on the River Kwai* won seven Oscars—namely, Best Picture, Director, Actor in a Leading Role (Alec Guinness), Screenplay, Cinematography, Editing, and Music.

Hayakawa's characterization of Colonel Saito and the presentation of his life and career in his English-language autobiography marked a radical break from his earlier star persona during the silent era.[12] By conceiving of *The Bridge on the River Kwai* as a comeback film for Hayakawa rather than a David Lean film or a star vehicle for William Holden and Alec Guinness, Daisuke Miyao sheds new light on a well-known motion picture while acknowledging the Japanese actor's agency (through acting and autobiography), proving that, since the 1950s, post-peak stars haven't needed a starring role in order to make an impressive return to the big screen after a period of absence. When situated alongside case studies on Amitabh Bachchan (India), Jean-Pierre Léaud (France), Burt Reynolds (United States), and Alida Valli (Italy), Miyao's chapter on Hayakawa reveals how filmmakers across the world have produced a remarkably diverse set of aesthetic and narrative strategies for using faded or fading stars to generate powerful emotional reactions from cinemagoers around the world, including ones that are painfully poignant.[13]

Our book's fourth and final section, "Aging Star Bodies," provides several discussions of how disturbing and provocative the sight of mature performers can be. This section is devoted specifically to aging actors whose stardom was originally heavily invested in strong, youthful, or beautiful faces and physiques. It brings the book to a close with another diverse set of case studies, this time involving Swedish, Brazilian, and United States cinema. The comeback vehicles of Sônia Braga, Linda Hamilton, Viveca Lindfors, and Wesley Snipes illustrate how the tangible physical signs of age can provoke controversy, unsettling filmgoers and critics alike, while generating ambivalent reactions that result in negative reviews and unpredictable box-office returns. As Pedro Guimarães explains in his chapter on the Brazilian actor Sônia Braga, her leading role as a racially ambiguous, sexually active, and increasingly defiant sixty-year-old bourgeois woman in *Aquarius* (Kleber Mendonça, 2016) proved to be as controversial as it was impressive. This role also enabled the star to unite various aspects of

12. Hayakawa had originally achieved Hollywood stardom in the 1910s playing exotic romantic roles, including a sexy villain in *The Cheat* (Cecil B. De Mille, 1915).

13. See, in this volume, Stuart Bell's case study on Jean-Pierre Léaud in *The Death of Louis XIV* (Albert Serra, 2016) for a discussion of a painfully poignant evocation of an elderly faded film star.

her screen persona and public image when returning to prominence in her country of origin following her work in Hollywood, after initially achieving stardom in Brazil as a young actor in the 1970s. This film, along with the other examples of comeback films included in this section, suggests that aging remains a problematic or at least ambivalent factor in post–studio era cinema around the world. Yet it also indicates a willingness on the part of international filmmakers to gamble on mature and experienced performers even in the face of potential hostile criticism and derision.

Across the four sections of this book, we demonstrate that a diverse range of mature film actors have been confronted by different sets of challenges and opportunities when attempting to make a comeback after the peak years of their stardom. Each has navigated and emerged from these comebacks in their own unique way, sometimes in glory and triumph, at other times in shame and defeat. While male stars may well have generally been better able to sustain longer and more lucrative film careers than their female colleagues (certainly during the twentieth century), they haven't always done so, and many leading female stars have defied convention when rising to increasing levels of success and popularity after their fortieth birthday, including Joan Crawford, Bette Davis, Carroll Baker, Alida Valli, Sônia Braga, and Linda Hamilton. As several chapters of our book illustrate, such achievements are seldom gained without some form of transformation in star image and performance, which makes the job of charting the key stages of an enduring star's long career so fascinating and rewarding.

Across the Sections of This Book

Numerous common features exist between films discussed in different sections of this book, including the importance of the moment when an aging star enters a comeback film. Christa van Raalte describes the first sighting of a sixty-three-year-old Linda Hamilton in her boots and fatigues and a bulletproof vest in *Terminator: Dark Fate*, capturing the excitement of this star entrance. Similarly, Raj Sony Jalarajan and Adith K. Suresh describe how the camera advances slowly toward a fifty-eight-year-old Amitabh Bachchan at the start of *Mohabbatein* (Aditya Chopra, 2000) and how this momentarily denies audiences a clear close-up view of the veteran superstar of Hindi cinema, until he turns to face the lens and walks toward it to the dramatic accompaniment of drums on the soundtrack. This not only affords Bachchan a hero's introduction but also creates a tantalizing moment of anticipation for audiences when the famous star is revealed in stages.

As Gloria Monti notes in her chapter on Alida Valli, a star's entrance in a comeback film inevitably assumes greater importance than in other star vehicles, especially when they have been absent from the screen for a significant length of time and changed physically during the intervening period. In such cases, the narrative tends to be momentarily suspended, and, during that brief hiatus, the actor appears more as a star—as who they are now—rather than as the character they are playing. In subsequent scenes, the aging star's persona may be subsumed by their screen role or character. Having said that, given the degree to which they incorporate multiple references to the star's earlier films, comeback vehicles may continue to privilege the star's public identity and screen persona over characterization. When this happens, audiences will retain a strong impression that they are witnessing the star speaking, moving, and gesticulating for much of a comeback's narrative.

Some of our case studies suggest that aging stars remain visibly and audibly themselves throughout their comeback films, including *The Comeback*, *Sextette*, and *The Last Movie Star* (Adam Rifkin, 2017). These films contain many scenes in which the stars (respectively, Miriam Hopkins, Mae West, and Burt Reynolds) closely resemble their fictional characters. However, some case studies suggest otherwise: notably, *Hairspray* and *Terminator: Dark Fate*. Here, characters appear to have a more forceful presence than the star performing the role (John Travolta and Linda Hamilton). In such instances, it may only be in the very first seconds of the actor's appearance on the screen that their star image is palpable.

Although most major film stars have a distinctive and easily recognizable image and voice, their physical appearance is likely to have undergone significant changes when returning from a long absence from the screen. Some filmmakers have handled this with sensitivity, preserving both the dignity and the familiar identity of the aged actor. Stuart Bell, for example, observes a palpable sense of the tragedy of aging for male stars in his analysis of *The Death of Louis XIV* (Albert Serra, 2016). In his chapter, he describes the relentless and intense gaze of the camera upon the elderly Jean-Pierre Léaud as he portrays the French monarch on his deathbed. Visibly, he no longer resembles his iconic screen role as Antoine Doinel, the adolescent protagonist of François Truffaut's *The 400 Blows* (1959), and yet elements of his Truffaut films echo throughout *The Death of Louis XIV*, as Bell notes. These add immeasurably to the emotionality, sincerity, and poignancy of this very quiet, slow, and gentle—essentially contemplative—film. And, indeed, one of the things it not only allows but forces audiences to contemplate in close-up is the loose and aged skin of seventy-two-year-old Léaud's face. The effect is poignant but also painful, not dissimilar to shots of a stroke-damaged seventy-eight-year-old Bette Davis in *The Whales of August* (Lindsay Anderson, 1987).

Lucy Fischer describes the disturbing impact of beholding the real signs of age and infirmity upon Bette Davis's withered and semifrozen face, the legacy of a major stroke in 1983. Reminders of the actor's more youthful appearance are provided for the purpose of reminding audiences how she used to look like in her prime, with framed photographs incorporated into the sets as props, just as they are in Miriam Hopkins's *The Comeback*. It's worth noting here that a common trope among such diverse comeback vehicles as *Sunset Boulevard*, *What Ever Happened to Baby Jane?*, *The Comeback*, *The Whales of August*, and *The Last Movie Star* is the juxtaposition of the aged actor with photographs or film extracts of their younger, iconic selves.[14] This juxtaposition of young and old star images suggests that comeback films regularly juxtapose an aging star with their (more perfect) younger self as a way of understanding how physical decline is manifested beyond the prime of life, either simply as a way of comprehending the effects of aging or to confront the fears and anxieties of old age.

While *The Whales of August* and *The Death of Louis XIV* represent final flourishes at the end of the long careers of, respectively, Bette Davis and Jean-Pierre Léaud, others constitute a more gradual and uncertain return. For instance, Wesley Snipes, the star of the superhero *Blade* trilogy from 1998 to 2004, made his comeback in a supporting role after serving a three-year prison sentence in 2013. As Clem Bastow and Glen Donnar

14. As Jennifer Louise Field observes in her analysis of an aged Burt Reynolds in Adam Rifkin's affectionate fan-boy film *The Last Movie Star*, this film intercuts the elderly and infirm star with his virile characters in *Deliverance* (John Boorman, 1972) and *Smokey and the Bandit* (Hal Needham, 1977) in order to create conversations between his old and young selves.

note, when Snipes's character Doc was introduced in the third instalment of Sylvester Stallone's geriaction ensemble franchise *The Expendables* in 2014, the actor looked only slightly older than he had in *Blade* and his athleticism seemed undiminished. Nevertheless, despite the resilience of physical appearance and his action film skills, producers of big-budget Hollywood films remained reluctant to cast him in leading roles, forcing Snipes to take either supporting parts in multiprotagonist blockbusters or starring ones in low-budget productions. Of course, these compromises were nothing compared to those that one of Hollywood's most successful Black and Indigenous American (Blackfoot) stars of the early 1960s took when trying to sustain a film career in the 1980s and 1990s, Woody Strode.

Trading on his iconic roles in John Ford's *Sergeant Rutledge* and Stanley Kubrick's *Spartacus* of 1960, Strode ended his six-decade film career with a handful of bit parts between 1984 and 1995. With these small but racially significant projects, the actor made a profound mark. Will Dodson describes how Strode brought considerable symbolic weight to his roles as a doorman in *The Cotton Club* (Francis Ford Coppola, 1984), as a storyteller in *Posse* (Mario Van Peebles 1993), and as the undertaker Charlie Moonlight, a lurking presence in *The Quick and the Dead* (Sam Raimi, 1995). The historical racial resonances of his final screen roles—which are essentially cameos—make Woody Strode not, as he might seem, one of the least important aging stars in our anthology but rather one of the most significant. Strode emerges here less as a victim of Hollywood and the United States' racist and discriminatory past than as a survivor, one whose significance is to be found in the intricacies of his marginalized final performances.

Different Comebacks and Their Consequences

One of the things that will be seen repeatedly throughout this anthology is the fact that comeback films typically teem with references to their aged star's earlier work and persona, drawing attention to differences and similarities between then and now. Another very clear thing that emerges is that no two comebacks are the same. Even those that try to emulate the huge critical and commercial success of *What Ever Happened to Baby Jane?*, such as Carroll Baker's *Orgasmo* (*Paranoia*, Umberto Lenzi, 1969) and Miriam Hopkins's *The Comeback*, are different in tone, style, and plot.

Consequently, as this volume consistently proves, comebacks come in all forms. Sometimes they are exploitative, whether camp like Viveca Lindfors's *Taboo* or cruel like Joan Crawford's *Strait-Jacket* (William Castle, 1964). Many are more serious, notably those that treat their aging star with respect, such as Jean-Pierre Léaud's *The Death of Louis XIV* and Burt Reynold's *The Last Movie Star*.

Across a wide range of genres, aging actors have achieved career comebacks in starring roles (Sônia Braga and Linda Hamilton) and supporting ones (Sessue Hayakawa and Wesley Snipes). Occasionally, an actor transforms a cameo into a culturally significant comeback (Woody Strode). While some successful comeback films have lasting effects for star actors by opening up significant new chapters in their careers (as *Mohabbatein* did for Amitabh Bachchan and *The Spider's Stratagem* did for Alida Valli), others result in retirement (as *The Comeback* did for Miriam Hopkins and *Sextette* did for Mae West). In addition to providing examples of the various ways in which aging stars have succeeded and failed in comeback vehicles, the following chapters prove that there are not only numerous ways of making a cinematic comeback but also many different reasons for designating a film a "comeback."

Works Cited

Babuscio, Jack. [1977, 1978] 1999. "The Cinema of Camp (AKA Camp and the Gay Sensibility)." In *Camp: Queer Aesthetics and the Performing Subject: A Reader*, edited by Fabio Cleto, 117–35. Edinburgh University Press.

Bolton, Lucy, and Julia Lobalzo Wright, eds. 2016. *Lasting Screen Stars: Images That Fade and Personas That Endure*. Palgrave Macmillan.

Chapman, James, Mark Glancy, and Sue Harper, eds. 2007. *The New Film History: Sources, Methods, Approaches*. Palgrave Macmillan.

Desjardins, Mary R. 2015. *Recycled Stars: Female Film Stardom in the Age of Television and Video*. Duke University Press.

Dolan, Josephine. 2017. *Contemporary Cinema and "Old Age": Gender and the Silvering of Stardom*. Palgrave Macmillan.

Purse, Lisa. 2017. "Confronting the Impossibility of Impossible Bodies: Tom Cruise and the Ageing Male Action Hero Movie." In *Revisiting Star Studies: Cultures, Themes, and Methods*, edited by Sabrina Qiong Yu and Guy Austin, 162–84. Edinburgh University Press.

Jermyn, Deborah. 2012. "Get a Life, Ladies. Your Old One Is Not Coming Back": Ageing, Ageism, and the Lifespan of Female Celebrity. *Celebrity Studies* 3 (1): 1–12.

Jermyn, Deborah, and Su Holmes, eds. 2015. *Women, Celebrity, and Cultures of Ageing: Freeze Frame*. Palgrave Macmillan.

Jerslev, Anne, and Line Nybro Petersen, eds. 2018, "Introduction: Ageing Celebrities, Ageing Fans, and Ageing Narratives in Popular Media Culture." *Celebrity Studies* 9 (2): 157–65.

Harrington, C. Lee, Denise Bielby, and Anthony R. Bardo, eds. 2014. *Aging, Media, and Culture*. Lexington.

McKenna, Mark. 2019. "Sylvester Stallone and the Economics of the Ageing Film Actor." *Celebrity Studies* 10 (4): 489–503.

Morin, Edgar. [1957] 2005. *Les stars. The Stars*, translated by Richard Howard. University of Minnesota Press.

Purse, Lisa. 2017. "Confronting the Impossibility of Impossible Bodies: Tom Cruise and the Ageing Male Action Hero Movie." In *Revisiting Star Studies: Cultures, Themes, and Methods*, edited by Sabrina Qiong Yu and Guy Austin, 162–84. Edinburgh University Press.

Redmond, Sean, ed. 2021. *Starring Tom Cruise*. Wayne State University Press.

Richardson, Niall. 2019. *Ageing Femininity on Screen: The Older Woman in Contemporary Cinema*. I. B. Tauris.

Shelley, Peter. 2009. *Grande Dame Guignol Cinema: A History of Hag Horror from "Baby Jane" to "Mother."* McFarland.

PART I

CAMP AND THE VETERAN STAR

1

THE COMEBACK OF MIRIAM HOPKINS

Gabrielle Stecher

Miriam Hopkins's extensive Hollywood career began in 1930, and she quickly became one of Paramount Pictures' breakout stars. Described by Carey Parrish as "a slice of southern hell, cooked rare, and served up steaming hot" (2008, 34), Hopkins was an ambitious and passionate onscreen force, and her professional persona was often characterized by jealousy (especially toward her rival Bette Davis) and a kind of temperamental sensuality. She was one of many stars who was discovered on Broadway in the late 1920s and early 1930s and lured from the stage to help transition Hollywood into the sound era. As part of a five-year contract, Hopkins performed starring or supporting roles in thirteen Paramount features between 1930 and 1934; from there, she made films for RKO and signed a four-year contract with Samuel Goldwyn. While her Pre-Code films such as *Trouble in Paradise* (Ernst Lubitsch, 1932) and her major Academy Award–and Golden Globe–nominated performances in *Becky Sharp* (Rouben Mamoulian, 1935) and *The Heiress* (William Wyler, 1949) have remained popular with Hopkins fans and classic film enthusiasts alike, it is Hopkins's final film that has been massively overlooked. *The Comeback* (Donald Wolfe, 1970), alternatively titled *Hollywood Horror House* and *Savage Intruder*, was unpopular; the film was released on video rather than through a nationwide release in US theaters. A low-budget attempt at casting Hopkins as a Gloria Swanson or Bette Davis type in director, producer, and writer Donald Wolfe's attempt at *Sunset Boulevard* (Billy Wilder, 1950) or *What Ever Happened to Baby Jane?* (Robert Aldrich, 1962), *The Comeback* failed to experience similar mainstream success. The commercial failures of *The Comeback*, I argue, do not negate its important status as Hopkins's final feature film, which self-consciously centralizes a sixty-seven-year-old Hopkins's ability to perform the true-to-life role of an aged and reclusive actor.

Generically speaking, *The Comeback* is a film about the plight of a former starlet well past her prime and a ghost of her earlier glamorous glory, but it is also, importantly, a psychological thriller and protoslasher film. As a low-budget camp film, *The Comeback* is showy, excessive, and garishly psychedelic, and its horror derives from the usual bloody and outrageous (to the point of comical) violence. But even more important are the ways the film allows Hopkins to unapologetically perform the plight of the aging star in a nuanced way, with her body, personal experience, and an archive of mementos all at her disposal.

In *The Comeback*, Hopkins stars as Katharine Packard, an actor who has retired many years after the pinnacle of her film career to her crumbling estate, to be waited on hand and foot by a team of devoted servants. Packard suffers from loneliness and alcoholism, the extent of which is made abundantly clear when she breaks her leg after falling down the stairs. As a result, the nurse Vic Valance is hired to care for an out-of-commission Packard alongside her two older women servants, Leslie and Mildred, and the younger Greta, previously in the actor's employ. The issue is that Valance, following a traumatic childhood at the hands of his mother, has become a serial killer not just of women but especially of middle-aged and older women in Hollywood. All the women in this Hollywood horror house are murdered, including Katherine, who is imprisoned, psychologically and physically tortured, and unable to escape before being killed. If the plot of *The Comeback* is to be summarized in a single sentence, then the film is about the psychological torture and violent murder of women who have aged out of the Hollywood spotlight. Hopkins as Packard purposefully exits life and the film colony (or, better yet, is exited) as a former starlet. Rejecting Valance's seeming desire for a mother figure, Packard is no one's mother, nor is she the elderly and conservative aunt of the film's limited younger, fresher cast.

Notably, Hopkins's *Comeback* persona is not too far removed from her own, and this is important context for how the layers of self-referentiality embedded in her final film might be understood. Packard's becoming a hermit is not unlike Hopkins's own reclusivity in the late 1960s and early 1970s. As her most recent biographer, Allan R. Ellenberger, notes, Hopkins lost interest in parties and dating after suffering rejection in her advanced age, instead sleeping all day and staying up all night in her bedroom, where she would occasionally dine with friends (2018, 262–63). What Ellenberger does not mention, though, is how Packard's alcoholism in *The Comeback* mirrored Hopkins's own. Early in the film, Packard encourages herself to have just "one more glass of personality" before she goes to greet the partygoers that she believes await her downstairs. The "glass of personality" line riffs on one of Hopkins's own sayings, as one of her friends recalled her saying, barside, "Come over and let's have a glass of personality" (Ellenberger 2018, 259). Sadly, the party is a delusion; the home is empty, save for the servants, and Packard falls down the stairs as she performs her dramatic thanks to the imagined guests.

Alcohol, for the aging starlet, becomes a means of temporarily escaping the lived realities of isolation, however self-imposed, and the physical effects of aging. Yet the harsh truth is that her shattered tibia, the injury she suffers as a result of falling due to her heavy drinking, is what Packard ultimately succumbs to, as it demobilizes her and catalyzes bringing the killer nurse into her home. Hopkins's performance of alcoholism, then, can be read as what Anne Morey has called the "elegiac grotesque," or a role that centralizes the eccentricity, sickness, aging, or otherwise decline of the female star (2011, 105). This terminology is not intended to demean actors such as Hopkins who willingly played such characters. Rather, embodying the grotesque and testing the construction and limits of femininity should be understood as an opportunity to, on the one hand, "dramatize the problems of female celebrity" (Morey, 107) and, on the other, blur the line between "being and role playing" intrinsic to camp cinema (Babuscio 1999, 121). In his discussion of the theatricalization of camp, Jack Babuscio suggests that Hopkins was one of the stars who could always be herself on camera (125). While he makes no mention of *The Comeback*, I argue that her performance here is indicative of the kind of intensity that allowed Hopkins to, throughout her career, "project [her] hyperbolic persona" but, now, also draw on her authority, success, *and* suffering as a living, aging starlet (125).

Before Packard is murdered, however, she consciously works to seduce Valance, and this is one of the most intriguing aspects of Hopkins's final performance. From its inception, Hopkins's own film career was intimately tied to her obvious and vibrant sensuality, but even in her late sixties Hopkins had no reservations about using and revealing her body in the film as her character flirts with Valance. Not long at all into his tenure in the home, Valance becomes the object of Packard's pent-up desire. Packard's lust for the young man is even invigorating, inspiring her to return to the public eye and get the house into entertaining shape, as if he has made her feel blooming with youth once more. The older woman's attraction to the much younger man is incongruous (Babuscio 1999, 119), though her sexuality is ultimately not as deviant as Valance's turns out to be.

Importantly, Packard does not wait for the young man to make the first move, nor does she carefully harbor a silent, if not improper, crush. Instead, she directs him to flirt the exact way she wishes him to: "Now, put your arm around me. Now say something just lovely to me." Valance complies with the first task, but questions the second, to which Packard forcefully responds with a kiss as the scene ends. In her ultimate test or transgression of what is deemed age-appropriate behavior, especially onscreen, what begins as a back massage between patient and nurse turns into Hopkins partially flashing the camera as she, as Packard, jumps up when Valance's kneading of her flesh gets too intense. In this scene, her naked back and her turn to Valance as she covers herself recalls Hopkins's earlier seductive performance with Frederic March in the Pre-Code film *Dr. Jekyll and Mr. Hyde* (Rouben Mamoulian, 1931). At her most seductive, Hopkins's character, Ivy Pearson, passionately kisses the doctor, then swings her bare legs along the side of the bed as she begs him to come back for more, yet she keeps the rest of her undressed body carefully concealed. In *The Comeback*, the older Hopkins makes even less of an effort to conceal her breasts from the audience, much less from Valance, before she playfully asks her nurse for a kiss, throwing her arms around his neck.

In Packard's eyes, there need be no moral nor physical boundary between employer and employee. He is more than her eye candy, and she consciously works to seduce him. There is also no mistaking her sexual desire for Valance. Despite her mother-like chiding of Valance's manners before he is introduced to a group of real party guests, nothing about Packard's infatuation with the young man is maternal, to Valance's dismay. Eventually, she comes to her senses and recognizes that Valance only takes initiative (i.e., kissing or making any kind of affectionate physical contact with her) when she begins talking of spoiling him with clothes and cars. She blames her sexual desire, at her age and toward this young man, on her being lonely and, in her embarrassment and anger at Valance, attempts to throw him out of the house, but this only initiates her ultimate demise. Valance responds by secretly locking her in her room so that he can begin to torture and then slice open her body piece by piece.

Aside from her performance of sexual desire, what is perhaps most fascinating about Hopkins as Packard is that, throughout the film, the ghosts of Hopkins's body of work are materially embodied in props, from framed photographs and life-sized dolls to an embedded clip from one of her earlier films. These objects might appear frivolous or excessive at first glance, but they play a serious role in relaying how Packard's body and career have existed and transformed over time. As part of the aesthetics of camp, such artifacts can indicate self-fashioning, or, in this case, a conscious attempt to realize the vitality and validity of Packard's earlier stardom so that she cannot be or feel discredited (Babuscio 1999, 122). Even the film's opening sequence begins with the showcase of one of Hopkins's youthful headshots, though it is quickly replaced with a much older portrait. Packard's home is a museum to a younger version of herself for the explicit purpose of reminding, educating, and entertaining her guests. For Packard, these material relics cement her body and stardom at its highest peaks, and they personally play a large part in allowing her filming with English actor Ronald Colman, for instance, to remain "so vivid in my memory, as if it were yesterday." In this way, Packard's discussion of the mementos testifies to her strength of memory, while the objects on display become a means of attempting to convince Valance of what she once was, in her ploy to seduce the strapping young nurse. But she does not merely show him her old costumes and headshots as evidence of her youthful allure; the audience, alongside Valance, watches the bathtub scene from the romantic comedy *Wise Girl* (Leigh Jason, 1937) in which Hopkins starred as an heiress pretending to be a poor actor. Hopkins's performance in the clip brings together beauty, amusement, and power so that Valance can see and hear exactly what the talented starlet was like in her prime.

Despite Packard's intentional use and display of her mementos, it is ultimately Valance who conscripts her costumed dolls into his own service. The dolls, for instance, witness his murder of a pregnant Greta, his young lover, whose own fears and unhappiness threaten to disrupt his access to Packard and the estate, in the darkened gallery. Following Packard's murder, Valance is able to pretend she is alive to the rest of her household by replacing her with one of the dolls in her wheelchair—from a distance, this illusion is convincing enough. But the dolls perform other, perhaps more psychological than physical roles for Valance. They serve as a means of threatening whatever semblance of power Packard believes she holds in the moments her agency is completely stripped from her. When, terrified, she attempts to escape, she is backed into the room and onto the bed by an angry Valance as he shouts: "Did you think I was somebody you could buy with your little handouts? Was I to be another one of those mementos for your collection? You'd like me stuffed and put in a glass case for all your dinner guests to admire, wouldn't you?" This scene is Valance's ultimate rejection of the way she has sexually and physically objectified him, resulting in her violent murder. Once Packard is dead, one of the dolls becomes Valance's bedfellow. Deviating from what may be perceived as the "natural [heterosexual] order of things," Valance's use of the doll draws another "incongruous contrast" characteristic of the irony of camp cinema, here between animate/inanimate and young/old (Babuscio 1999, 119). The doll is seemingly a subversive source of sexual pleasure, and it becomes the object of Valance's own delusions as an inanimate composite and a surrogate of both his alcoholic, abusive, and promiscuous mother and Packard, a woman who similarly tried to abandon him by revoking what she could provide him with and throwing him out. In one of the film's more absurd moments, Valance's mother's laughing face is even superimposed over the dolls. Once all its inhabitants and any potential living witnesses have been murdered, Valance wheels the doll around the house in the wheelchair—his own mommie dearest cannot abandon him now.

Yet the film's emphasis on age and a bygone Hollywood era is not limited to Packard's identity and her treatment by Valance. The film's nostalgic, if not deteriorating and spectral, Old Hollywood mythos runs deep in both characterization and setting. Aside from the ways the film explicitly recalls Hopkins's earlier films, beauty, and glamour, its setting is also meant to evoke a similar nostalgia for Hollywood and its stars of the 1920s and 1930s. Like Hopkins's body, Old Hollywood's architectural remains must suffer the effects of time. The audience can only enter Hopkins's home after a sustained jaunt through and around a decrepit Hollywood sign, first constructed in 1923, with its previously white panels stained yellowish-brown and flapping in the wind. The camera eventually tilts down to the dirt, revealing an old woman's severed body and foreshadowing the violence to come. After brutally stalking and murdering a different innocent woman, Vic Valance arrives at Packard's home on a movieland homes bus tour in which the driver asserts that the home was "once the scene of lavish Hollywood parties" and cost over half a million dollars to build. The house itself is further explicitly associated with the earlier generation of stars who made Hollywood what it was beginning in the silent era. As legend has it, the soon-to-be house of horrors, a crumbling 1920s villa in which most of the film takes place, once belonged to Norma Talmadge, the silent star whose career peaked a decade before Hopkins's (and therefore Packard's) own. The film's credits explicitly support this theory with the statement that the film was, indeed, "filmed in Hollywood at the Norma Talmadge Estate," but there is no evidence to support its verity (Ellenberger 2018, 261). This setting is not entirely context-dependent—viewers in the 1970s could see its disintegrating facade during their own visit to Los Angeles.

Though Talmadge herself is not physically present in the film, a few of her contemporaries appear in supporting roles, further emphasizing *The Comeback* as a vehicle for these aging female actors who were once recognizable faces of Old Hollywood. In the dinner party scene, for instance, Minta Durfee, former wife of scandal-plagued Roscoe "Fatty" Arbuckle and silent film actor in dozens of shorts in the 1910s and 1920s, is cast alongside Riza Royce, actor and former wife of filmmaker Josef von Sternberg, as a dinner party guest. In more prominent roles than Durfee or Royce, veteran actors Gale Sondergaard and Florence Lake are cast as Packard's secretary and housekeeper, respectively. It is Mildred (Lake) who initially defends whatever may be left of Packard's youthfulness to Valance, who comments upon his arrival to the estate that he did not realize she was still around. "Around? She's very much around," Mildred says. "She's got a lot more youth . . . than all the young people you see in films and television nowadays. . . . They're all so callow . . . and disgusting." Valance's modern generation, she believes, are "self-centered animals," and it is clear she immediately distrusts the nurse, who has introduced himself comically as "Mr. Laurel N. Hardy." Together, Leslie and Mildred alike serve as living barriers between the old and young in the way they are quick to observe and judge the "noise" of Valance's generation, from music to lack of refinement and reserve. When Packard falters, Leslie is the one to remind her "you've been a great star, Katharine. You are an exceptional human being. But now don't destroy the past by making a fool of yourself over that Mr. Valance. . . . [He] is a vulgar opportunist."

Hopkins does not degrade or destroy her Hollywood past by making a fool of herself over *The Comeback*. Instead, she playfully makes an absurdist film about violence against older women a vehicle to assert her dramatic capabilities, sexuality, and that she, like her veteran costars Sondergaard and Lake, are (or, rather, were) still present and still willing and even powerful performers. The Hollywood surrounding them may be crumbling or, in the case of Hollywood Boulevard, unrecognizable, but its veteran stars remain capable. In this way, as a self-conscious camp film, to use Michael T. Schulyer's term, *The Comeback* is a more serious meditation on Hollywood's coexisting generations than might be given credit for. A film like this is exemplary of the ways "camp isn't just a homosexual domain but one inclusive of (at the very least) lesbian and heterowomen," and, in particular, older women and the veterans of Old Hollywood (Schuyler 2004, 18). Rather than being positioned as the film's solo camp or cult object, Hopkins is cast alongside her peers and keepsakes that work together to testify to the retention of her immense talent and beauty at all ages *and* to her earlier star status. Hopkins actively allows the mementos of her former stardom to be appropriated by the film, even, in the case of Valance's doll, as the killer's ostentatious fetish object. Such a film, through its interactions between human and material agents, can simultaneously be fun, absurd, and campy while taking seriously Hopkins's continued beauty, strength, and career well into her sixties. Hopkins's performance as Packard is at times excessive, bitchy, and hilarious, but it is always playful. Packard, like Hopkins herself, has her demons, but Hopkins does not hide behind her character; rather, she seems to embrace her ability to play this role because so much of it is true to her real lived experiences. Hopkins voluntarily accepted a role in a film that saw itself as a successor to retrospective camp films like *Sunset Boulevard*. As such, *The Comeback*'s overlooked status is worth salvaging because, above all the poorly rendered gore, it deliberately embraces Hopkins's age and makes it clear that she, at the very least in mind and attitude, was still steaming hot.

Works Cited

Babuscio, Jack. [1978] 1999. "The Cinema of Camp (AKA Camp and the Gay Sensibility)." Reprinted in *Camp: Queer Aesthetics and the Performing Subject: A Reader*, edited by Fabio Cleto, 117–35. University of Michigan Press.

Ellenberger, Allan R. 2018. *Miriam Hopkins: Life and Films of a Hollywood Rebel*. University Press of Kentucky.

Mamoulian, Rouben, dir. 1931. *Dr. Jekyll and Mr. Hyde*. Burbank, CA: Warner Archive Collection, 2018. DVD.

Morey, Anne. 2011. "Grotesquerie as Marker of Success in Aging Female Stars." In *In the Limelight and Under the Microscope: Forms and Functions of Female Celebrity*, edited by Su Holmes and Diane Negra, 103–24. Bloomsbury Academic.

Parrish, Carey. 2008. "Southern Hell: A Portrait of Miriam Hopkins." *ReFRESH Magazine* 52:32–34.

Schuyler, Michael T. 2004. "Camp for Camp's Sake: Absolutely Fabulous, Self-Consciousness, and the Mae West Debate." *Journal of Film and Video* 56 (4): 3–20.

Wolfe, Donald, dir. 1970. *The Comeback* (*Hollywood Horror House* or *Savage Intruder*). Congdon Productions. YouTube video, 1:30:27. Posted October 28, 2019. https://www.youtube.com/watch?v=4t6xnINZSEg.

2

AGING CAMP/CAMPING AGE

Mae West in *Myra Breckinridge* and *Sextette*

KRISZTA POZSONYI

After almost thirty years, Mae West returned to the silver screen twice in the 1970s. In her comeback, the comedy *Myra Breckinridge* (Michael Sarne, 1970), she took on a supporting role, sometimes labeled erroneously as a cameo. The second time, nearer the end of the decade, she returned in the feature role of *Sextette* (Ken Hughes, 1978), an adaptation of her own play. Ever since their premieres, *Myra Breckinridge* and *Sextette* (and West's performance) have been largely panned by film scholars and critics. The films have also been met with criticism from queer and feminist film scholars, although both scripts touch on subjects that should pique their interest: the first centers on a trans woman character set on destroying patriarchy starting with Hollywood, while the latter focuses on the unapologetic sexual escapades of an aging woman.

Challenging this reception, in this chapter I offer a reading of West's performance in these two comeback films as aging camp/camping age. Here, the aging performer does not simply reference her young star text and the camp appeal thereof, but rather critically subverts the nostalgic impulse characteristic of such referencing, with its inherent privileging of youth. I suggest that West's characters in these late films experience the past as a source of joy and pleasure that fuel their present, rather than expressing a wishful yearning for a long-gone past celebrity status.

West's (Early) Camp Appeal

Mae West's work is undoubtedly camp. Yet, whether and how this canonical camp status holds up specifically for her last two films—as opposed to the films that established her cinematic persona and star text in the 1930s—is a different question. In order to address the latter question and push back against the way these films have been positioned within West's body of work, I begin by briefly surveying West's canonical status from early theorizations of camp, especially that of Susan Sontag (1966), to the analysis that most fully fleshed out West's feminist camp appeal, by Pamela Robertson (1996).

West's performance of her signature character, established in ten films from the early 1930s to the early 1940s, served as a primary example in early theorizations of camp and has remained an intriguing case study to theorists since then. Sontag named West as a primary example of "successful Camp" in her seminal "Notes on 'Camp'" ([1964] 1966, 282–83). Three decades later, West served as one of the main subjects for Robertson's book-length study of feminist camp, *Guilty Pleasures: Feminist Camp from Mae West to Madonna.* It is no coincidence that West is referenced in practically every other chapter in Fabio Cleto's reader, *Camp: Queer Aesthetics and the Performing Subject* (1999), which compiles some of the most influential writings on the subject, from authors like Christopher Isherwood and Sontag to more specifically cinema-focused scholars such as Jack Babuscio, Richard Dyer, Matthew Tinkcom, and Robertson. Thus, one could say that West has enjoyed an impressive longevity as a point of interest for scholars of camp, not unlike the longevity of her cinematic work.

Beyond the mere fact of West's camp status, it is notable that her campness appears so often within this literature alongside concepts of changing and aging. Sontag mentions West in the section of her "Notes" where she (somewhat infamously) discusses the difference between what she calls "naïve" (or pure, unintentional) and "deliberate" camp, placing West firmly in the latter category ([1964] 1966, 282–83). The naïve-deliberate binary has, of course, often come under fire in later responses to Sontag's text (Cleto 1999, 23–26). For my purposes here, it is important that Sontag need not be understood as expressing a general preference for the former category over the latter. Although Sontag begins this section with stating that deliberate camp, which "knows itself to be Camp ('camping') . . . is usually less satisfying" than "pure" camp ([1964] 1966, 282), she notably concludes this same section by pointing out that Oscar Wilde, to whom the whole essay is dedicated and whose epigrams fuel and structure the notes, is also assigned to the supposedly "less satisfying" category of deliberate camp. She states, "An example of [wholly conscious Camp, one that plays at being campy]: Wilde's epigrams themselves" (283). Similarly to Wilde, Mae West is enlisted among the examples of intentionally "camping" artists (283). The question of creative intentionality, West's (and Wilde's) knowing wink to their audience, is crucial both to how Sontag positions West in terms of change and aging, and to how West's later, aging performance is received by camp literature.

Sontag argues that West's deliberate "camping" in her early films is (already) tied to a change in her artistic intentionality and, more specifically, to her engagement with her own reception. In making this argument, Sontag contrasts objects with artists: "Objects, being objects, don't change when they are singled out by the Camp vision. Persons, however, respond to their audience. Persons begin 'camping': Mae West, Bea Lillie, La Lupe" ([1964] 1966, 283). Importantly, the concepts of change and aging are entangled while also in conflict with each other throughout Sontag's text. Although she points out in the quotation above that objects themselves cannot change, she highlights that their cultural status and fashionability can, and this change is crucial to their becoming camp objects: "So many of the objects prized by Camp taste are old-fashioned, out-of-date, démodé. It's not a love of the old as such. It's simply that the process of aging or deterioration provides the necessary detachment—or arouses a necessary sympathy" (285). Similarly, Robertson claims that at the heart of the early Mae West character lies this precise "out-of-fashion" self-styling, calling West "a deliberate anachronism already in the 1930s" (1996, 27). Changing and aging are thus related and crucial for camp's effectiveness in the case of objects, which stay the same even though they age and while their reception or perception change.

Sontag extends the logic of this unchanging aging to characters and personae. Here, too, a certain resistance to change becomes essential to the success of camp. She writes:

> Camp is the glorification of "character." . . . What the Camp eye appreciates is the *unity*, the force of the person. In every move the aging

> Martha Graham makes she's being Martha Graham, etc. . . . What Camp taste responds to is "instant character" . . . and, conversely, what it is not stirred by is the sense of the *development* of character. Character is understood as a state of *continual* incandescence. ([1964] 1966, 286, emphasis mine)

Camp's ideal is a character that remains relentlessly unchanging. West's signature character, Robertson points out, fits this notion perfectly, as West performed versions of the same character again and again, onstage and onscreen, from before the 1930s until the 1970s. In Robertson's words, "Neither West nor her audience seemed able to differentiate between the Mae West personae of the 1940s theatrical comeback, the 1950s Vegas rock-and-roll musclemen act, the 1970s caricatures of *Myra Breckinridge* and *Sextette*, and the initial 1930s film career, let alone her earlier vaudeville and theatrical career" (1996, 27). In this sense, *Myra Breckinridge* and *Sextette* continue the performance traditions established in West's early films.

While Sontag's piece was written in 1964, in the decade preceding West's return to film production, the above quotation about Martha Graham could be adapted to West's comeback films as well. If, in Sontag's words, "in every move the aging Martha Graham makes she's being Martha Graham," in every mov(i)e the aging Mae West makes, she's being Mae West. West's last films can be understood as the perfect continuation of her camping character. Yet these films have enjoyed a drastically different treatment than West's early work. Sontag's "jottings" (as she at one point calls them) were, of course, written before *Myra Breckinridge* and *Sextette* even premiered. However, scholarly accounts that attend to West's camp work with more specificity and detail, especially that of Robertson and, to a lesser degree, that of Caryl Flinn (1995), bracket off these last two films from the work and effect produced at the "pinnacle" of West's cinematic work in the 1930s.

In her last two films, West's performance registers in both Robertson's and Flinn's accounts as a grotesque caricature of West's early figure that no longer harbors the feminist political ambitions and potentials of the early performances. Robertson sees the essence of West's early camp appeal as follows: "West's early camp effect allowed her to parody herself while still functioning as both an object and subject of desire with whom female spectators could identify" (1996, 53). In so doing, according to Robertson, "West not only parodies female stereotypes and images but, at the same time, embodies and identifies with those images" (34). Like Robertson, Flinn, who focuses on camp's "preoccupation with decay and death . . . as it has been applied to human bodies in particular–and to feminized ones more particularly still" (1995, 54), brackets off the last two films from the rest of West's career. While camp, masquerade, and parody have been central to scholarly accounts of West's early embodied performance on film, these late films have thus mostly been treated as either simply not worthy of close analysis or, worse, as failing to live up to the feminist potentials of West's star text. Contesting this understanding, here I offer a brief close reading of the two films.

Myra Breckinridge

After decades of working on stage and appearing briefly on television, West finally returned to filmmaking in 1970, taking on a supporting role in *Myra Breckinridge*. As is the case for West's own appearance within it, the film's general camp appeal is unquestionable, but its precise politics and virtues have been debated. The film was, on the one hand, a commercial flop that critics and most viewers alike declared obscenely bad, sometimes with campy delight (Watts 2003, 297–98; Diffrient 2013). On the other hand, *Myra Breckinridge* immediately gained and has since maintained a queer cult following due to its sexual outrageousness, as well as for its function as a comeback vehicle for West. As Jill Watts notes, when West arrived in person at the film's New York City premiere at the Criterion Theater, "pandemonium broke lose [*sic*]" (2003, 297) among the audience gathered on-site. West was thus clearly one of the primary selling points for the film, and her appearance proved especially important among queer audiences.

Just as in her screen debut in *Night After Night* (Archie Mayo, 1932), West only had authorial agency over her own role within *Myra Breckinridge*. Despite that limitation, she made powerful changes. The film was adapted from Gore Vidal's 1968 epistolary novel of the same title. Granted the right to have "complete control over her dialogue" (Watts 2003, 293), West accepted the role of the man-eating talent agent Leticia Van Allen, who crosses paths with the titular character (Raquel Welch).

West completely transformed Van Allen into an updated iteration of the classic Mae West figure and added a twist on the character's age. West's work in the film thus serves as a case study of creative self-fashioning in terms of sexuality and aging, which she would more fully develop in her next film, *Sextette*.

West had no issue with playing Van Allen as a character who lusts after, sexually objectifies, and acts sexually inappropriately with her potential and actual clients—specifically, "studs." However, she expunged the increasingly extreme sadomasochistic relationship that develops between Van Allen and her main talent, Rusty, in the book. She categorically declined to play a character who is masochistic, claiming it is more likely that "[she] might send *him* to the hospital" (Watts 2003, 293, emphasis mine). The West character of the 1930s had a sexually assertive quality that she did not see as compatible with the book's version of Van Allen; West chose to stay loyal to the former rather than the latter. Just as importantly, by omitting this character development, West kept the character flatter, more superficial—in other words, more in line with classic camp character aesthetics.

West, in her seventies at the time, had to make decisions about how to treat the age difference between her and the book's character. In the book, Van Allen is a forty-year-old who voices her fear of being abandoned by Rusty as soon as the two start a romance, saying the following to Myra: "I want him all to myself as long as possible which won't be very long, since once he starts making a living he'll be off with the cute young chicks, leaving poor old Letitia to her Scotch and casting couch" (Vidal 2019, 194). When West molded the character to her style, she omitted the character's complaints and insecurities about feeling old in an industry filled with young actors. Instead, the final scene of her and Rusty shows the young man passed out on the bed in exhaustion, while West expresses that she is ready for "another round." Thus, West did not just change the character's age but also how the character related to her age, removing the self-deprecating notes on aging and appeal. West has often been charged in reviews and scholarship for "disregarding" her own age (Robertson, 26). Instead, I read West's work—her writing and performance—in her last two films as expanding her camping tactics into the field of aging. West chooses to take pleasure in her aging self against societal expectations and limitations regarding aging women's sexuality and sex appeal.

Sextette

While in *Myra Breckinridge* West transformed her character into a new version of her classic persona, her final film, *Sextette*, evinced her full return to form. West once again took center stage, both as a writer and as a performer. The film is an adaptation of a play West herself wrote and staged beforehand, as had been the case with some of her early films, including *She Done Him Wrong* (Lowell Sherman, 1933), adapted from her play *Diamond Lil*. With *Sextette*, West had authorial agency over the entire film again. The premise and main character also share similarities with early films. Akin to *I'm No Angel* (Wesley Ruggles, 1933), *She Done Him Wrong*, and *My Little Chickadee* (Edward F. Cline, 1940), *Sextette* focuses on a performer, Marlo Manners (played by West), whose romantic entanglements accelerate the plot. Crucially, in *Sextette*, these entanglements are rooted in and reinvigorate the past. The film's title, a nod to West's (in)famous early play *Sex*, primarily refers to Manners's quest to consummate her marriage to her sixth husband, while all of Manners's previous husbands, including the one previously thought dead, appear. The return of the past is thus the main theme of the film, both in its narrative and its style, as it invokes and restages West's early cinematic authorial vision.

Persistently citing West's previous films, *Sextette* attaches visual cues of the past to a sense of pleasure. For instance, costuming functions as an important gesture to West's past, both on the level of production and within the film's diegesis. Edith Head, who had previously worked with West on *She Done Him Wrong* and in *Myra Breckinridge*, is the costume designer for this film. During a fitting scene, Manners admires herself in lavish dresses while murmuring her signature one-liners. This and similar scenes become crucial moments of Manners not simply invoking the past with pathos, but rather fully indulging in herself. Beyond reuniting with Head, West also enlisted familiar faces of her cinematic past. One of the many cameos of the film is by actor George Raft, who had played the feature role in *Night After Night* (Archie Mayo, 1932), West's screen debut. References and reminders of the past, then, populate the entire world of

Sextette.[1] In essence, the film is a comedy about the past becoming excessively present as to facilitate Manners's unapologetic self-love.

Film critics, however, did not share in the main character's joyousness. As was the case with *Myra Breckinridge*, reviewers panned the film, but in an even crueler way this time. Some criticism pertained to the film's formal qualities, such as its generous use of soft focus to the point of having a "milky" quality. However, this kind of commentary was far outweighed by reviews that ridiculed West. *Variety*, for instance, called the film "a cruel, unnecessary and mostly unfunny musical comedy," specifically criticizing West for "[being] on screen for most of the film, mostly attempting Mae West imitations and lip-syncing a series of undistinguished musical numbers" (1978). In a similar vein, *The New York Times* summarized the film as a "disorienting freak show," in which West "does a frail imitation of the personality that wasn't all that interesting 45 years ago" (Canby 1979). In these reviews, the word "imitation" serves to differentiate between the "original," West's young performance, and a "failed" and fake copy, the aging performance. This differentiation, however, disregards both the importance of repetition at the very heart of West's young performances, and the fact that this repetition, precisely despite aging, is what Sontag identifies as the key to camping. The reviews pinpoint the very feature of the performance, unchanging aging, that should qualify it as camp and use that feature to dismiss the overall value of her performance.

Sextette fared no better in film journals, either. *Film Comment* concluded in a piece titled "Go West, Old Mae" that the film is so bad that "its badness is not campy" (Adair 1980).[2] Thus, Adair, like the reviewers above, criticizes the film for failing in camping, attributing the failure to West's aging. According to him, West's error was her still "daring" to perform her signature act despite being in her eighties. Twisting Cocteau's aphorism about Victor Hugo, Adair states, "Mae West is a madwoman who thinks she is Mae West" (1980). Instead of showing a genuine interest in

1. Examples beyond casting, staffing, script, and plot discussed here include costumes from earlier West (stage and film) productions reused throughout the film, or Manners's "swan bed," one of the most outstanding visual elements of the film, being a direct reference to her famous swan bed in *Diamond Lil* and its adaptation *She Done Him Wrong*.
2. A reference to West's film *Go West, Young Man* (Henry Hathaway, 1936).

the film's engagement with aging and sexuality, these contemporaneous reviews seem to follow a similar line of argumentation, reducing the film reviewer's intellectual work to pondering about what is appropriate behavior for an aging woman performer.

What these reviews miss or misunderstand about West's performance is that she is simply demonstrating in the film what Sontag calls a "state of continual incandescence" ([1964] 1966, 286) of the camping performer. At the very core of West's early performance, and representative of camp in general, Sontag sees unapologetic self-love: "even when it reveals self-parody, [it] *reeks* of self-love" (20, emphasis mine). This unapologetic self-love is what West's aging performance inflects: Through the invocations of the past, West and her character experiences, demonstrates, and demands unflinching adoration of herself.

Whether on the level of transforming her character in *Myra Breckinridge* or constructing the whole world of a film in *Sextette*, West's late films provide a rich example of self-fashioning in terms of sexuality and aging. Continuing to play the "Mae West character" with such longevity, West faced increasing criticism rooted in ageism and sexism. Such criticism appeared in contemporaneous reviews and has unfortunately creeped into recent film scholarship as well.[3] In these two films, West's aging camp/camping age tactic creates a new version of her signature character. The new version, I argue, is one who is consistently aware of her aging—thus her constant citation of the past—but who rejects the narrative of character development often demanded of older subjects: a narrative that would position the past, and therefore youth, as the most valuable.

3. Diffrient, for instance, describes West as a "geriatric actor." Of her performance in *Myra Breckinridge*, he writes: "There is something decidedly necromantic about the camera's fixation on the actress's death mask of a face, momentarily unfrozen by the occasional blink and virtually blank as a screen on which the audience's own memories of a much younger Mae West can be projected." Diffrient confronts this reading with his analysis of the other "geriatric actor," John Huston, of whom "the same thing cannot be said," as he instead is a "charismatic actor-director . . . who hams it up as Buck [Loner]" (2013, 54).

Works Cited

Adair, Gilbert. 1980. "Go West, Old Mae." *Film Comment*, June 1980.

Canby, Vincent. 1979. "Screen: Mae West, 87, Does an Encore: Trying for 6th Marriage." *New York Times*, June 8, 1979. https://www.nytimes.com/1979/06/08/archives/screen-mae-west-87-does-an-encoretrying-for-6th-marriage.html.

Cleto, Fabio, ed. 1999. *Camp: Queer Aesthetics and the Performing Subject: A Reader*. University of Michigan Press.

Diffrient, David Scott. 2013. "'Hard to Handle': Camp Criticism, Trash-Film Reception, and the Transgressive Pleasures of *Myra Breckinridge*." *Cinema Journal* 52 (2): 46–70.

Flinn, Caryl. 1995. "The Deaths of Camp." *Camera Obscura: Feminism, Culture, and Media Studies* 12 (2): 52–84.

Robertson, Pamela. 1996. *Guilty Pleasures: Feminist Camp from Mae West to Madonna*. Duke University Press.

Sontag, Susan. (1964) 1966. "Notes on 'Camp.'" In *Against Interpretation and Other Essays*, 275–92. Farrar, Straus & Giroux.

Variety. 1978. "Sextette," January 1, 1978. https://variety.com/1977/film/reviews/sextette-1200424180/.

Vidal, Gore. 2019. *Myra Breckinridge*. Vintage International.

Watts, Jill. 2003. *Mae West: An Icon in Black and White*. Oxford University Press.

3

JOAN CRAWFORD

From Comeback Queen to Camp Goddess

MARTIN SHINGLER

The author, critic, philosopher, and political activist Susan Sontag began her published list of fifty-eight notes on camp in a 1964 issue of the left-leaning, New York–based *Partisan Review* by stating that this essentially gay sensibility is "a certain mode of aestheticism" ([1964] 2018, 4). She insisted that it was a way of seeing the world not only aesthetically but also in terms of artifice and stylization. "Notes on Camp" was one of the earliest attempts to define this cultural phenomenon that was making its way steadily from the cultural margins into mainstream culture in the 1960s, largely via cinema and film criticism. At the same time, as Sontag noted, film criticism was instrumental in popularizing camp (7). Yet it was Sontag who did more than anyone to establish a coherent understanding of camp, as well as to recognize its social importance and subversive potential. In the process, she made it possible for many more people to identify and appreciate it, while lending it academic credibility as a concept. As her notes made an indelible impression on popular, critical and academic understandings of camp, Sontag's way of seeing camp as a way of seeing the world in terms of artifice and stylization became *the* way of seeing camp.

Had Joan Crawford read "Notes on Camp," she might have been proud of her final four films rather than spurned them. It's on record that the star "virtually disowned" the low-budget exploitation films she made for William Castle in the United States and Herman Cohen in Britain (Spoto 2012, 269). After stating that she refused to discuss *Strait-Jacket* (William Castle, 1964), *I Saw What You Did* (William Castle, 1965), *Berserk!* (Jim

O'Connelly, 1967), and *Trog* (Freddie Francis, 1970) with interviewers in the 1970s, Crawford's biographer Donald Spoto claims that "her contempt for them was widely shared by audiences" (2012, 269). If that's true, it didn't prevent large numbers of people from enjoying them or, indeed, paying money to see them when first released into cinemas, the films earning decent profits at the box office. Profitable or not, Spoto concluded that *Trog* was "a regrettable coda to a distinguished motion picture career of forty-five years" (274). Reviews by leading British film critics in 1971 support this notion when describing it variously as a "very shabby piece of sci-fi" (Robinson), a "monstrously comic affair" (Thirkell), a "gormless horror weepie" (Hibbin), and a "farrago of nonsense" (Taylor).

However shabby, monstrous, idiotic, or nonsensical these low-budget shockers seemed to mainstream film critics when released, young adult cinemagoers enjoyed them, despite Spoto's claim to the contrary (2012, 269). They appealed especially to viewers with a love of black comedy, suspense, excess, gore, and camp. Moreover, Crawford's final four films represent a consistent body of work characterized not only by ludicrous plots and clichéd dialogue but also by the aging star's straight-faced and deadpan performances. Crawford maintained a remarkable degree of conviction regardless of her films' ridiculous and unbelievable storylines. In fact, the more unlikely the plots became, the more she compensated with an intensely serious performance.

In this chapter, I shall explore how the star's determination to play it straight in her exploitation films rather than to camp it up paradoxically made Crawford one of cinema's most successful exponents of camp. Additionally, I will consider what her example reveals more generally about the treatment of Hollywood's aging female stars in low-budget thrillers. Finally, I will challenge the idea that *Strait-Jacket*, *I Saw What You Did*, *Berserk!*, and *Trog* constitute an embarrassing or regrettable end to an illustrious film career.

Crawford's Comebacks

From the age of thirty-nine, Joan Crawford made a series of comebacks when written off as a has-been, first in *Mildred Pierce* (Michael Curtiz, 1945), for which she won an Academy Award for Best Actress, again in *Sudden Fear* (David Miller, 1952), and again ten years later in *What Ever*

Happened to Baby Jane? (Robert Aldrich, 1962). These were all major commercial and critical successes, achieved long after the start of her career in 1925. There's no doubt that one of her great achievements as a film star was to survive in an industry where attractive and glamorous female performers were expected to retire gracefully from the screen in middle age. After turning forty in 1946, Crawford worked hard to maintain both her glamorous image and her bankability as a film star well into her fifties and sixties.

Originally hired by Metro-Goldwyn-Mayer on the strength of her dancing skills, Crawford rose swiftly through the ranks, her elevation to stardom being aided by impressive performances in dramas such as *Grand Hotel* (Edmund Goulding, 1932) and comedies such as *Susan and God* (George Cukor, 1940).[1] She also became one of America's best-known celebrities due to relentless self-promotion and skillful image management.[2] Nevertheless, Crawford's career faltered during World War II, particularly after the commercial failure of *Above Suspicion* (Richard Thorpe, 1943). Sensing a need for change, she bought herself out of her MGM contract and signed a new deal with Warner Bros. in 1943 (Spoto 2012, 170–71). After winning an Oscar for *Mildred Pierce*, she displaced Bette Davis as the studio's top female. A string of hits followed, along with an Oscar nomination for *Possessed* (Curtis Bernhardt, 1947). Films such as *Humoresque* (Jean Negulesco, 1946), and *The Damned Don't Cry* (Vincent Sherman, 1950) exploited the forty-something star's hallmark qualities of intensity and glamour. However, Crawford's career stalled again in 1951, prompting her exit from Warner Bros. shortly after making *This Woman Is Dangerous* (Felix E. Feist, 1952).

Crawford soon shrugged off the suggestion that she was a has-been with a thrilling performance in *Sudden Fear*, made by Joseph Kaufman Productions but largely produced by the star herself and distributed by

1. Other Crawford hits at MGM included *Our Dancing Daughters* (Harry Beaumont, 1928) and *Letty Lynton* (Clarence Brown, 1932). Even the fact that she was labeled "box office poison" in 1938 by the Independent Theatre Owners Association of America (along with Marlene Dietrich, Katharine Hepburn, and others) didn't hamper her success, since she achieved major hits with *The Women* (1939) and *A Woman's Face* (1941), both directed by George Cukor (Spoto 2012, 133–34).
2. See Lugowski 2011, 129.

RKO (Spoto 2012, 217). To maintain her public profile and marquee value, she worked as a freelance artist for a wide range of companies thereafter, including Republic, Universal, and Columbia.[3] Her image now combined glamour and grit, suggesting a steely personality beneath an elegant façade. Yet she struggled to secure leading film roles at the end of the 1950s, working mostly in television until Robert Aldrich cast her as a wheelchair-bound faded film star in *What Ever Happened to Baby Jane?* This top-grossing sensational shocker became Crawford's third major comeback, one that irrevocably propelled her into exploitation cinema and B movies.

Baby Jane's success was predicated on the combination of elements that appealed equally to young adult and cult audiences. According to Cynthia Baron and Mark Bernard, its outlandish plot, corny dialogue, Baroque mise-en-scène, and outrageous performances were all part of a strategic attempt to create something quintessentially camp (2013, 266). These authors observe that major Hollywood studios like Warner Bros. released such "bad" films in the 1960s as a way of courting "oppositional" audiences with material intended for "camp enjoyment" (266). The "deliberately campy" films of Robert Aldrich and others often featured the aging woman "as an object of derision," constituting a form of revenge on "once powerful female stars" (266). However, as Anne Morey has argued, such grotesque portrayals of aging women by critically acclaimed and highly competent studio-era stars also displayed "an actress's artistic effort and ability to perform at the margins of conventional femininity" (2011, 104). These divergent readings by Baron and Barnard, on the one hand, and Morey, on the other, stem partly from the ambivalent treatment of aging female stars in exploitation comeback vehicles. They also expose an ambiguous set of audience reactions.

Has-Been Stars in Comeback Vehicles

Although essentially a derogatory term denoting that an actor is beyond the peak of their stardom or even no longer at their best as a performer,

3. At Republic, Crawford starred in *Johnny Guitar* (Nicolas Ray, 1954). At Universal, she headlined in *Female on the Beach* (Joseph Pevney, 1955), while receiving top billing for her role in *Queen Bee* (Ranald MacDougall, 1955) at Columbia.

"has-been" at least acknowledges an individual's previous high-level achievement. While granting an aging actor a degree of (albeit ambivalent) respect, it also suggests the possibility of a comeback, one that might even be an actor's greatest accomplishment. Notable examples include Gloria Swanson's performance as the delusional aging silent film diva Norma Desmond in *Sunset Boulevard* (Billy Wilder, 1950) and Bette Davis's portrayal of Margo Channing, the feisty and frustrated forty-year-old Broadway prima donna tired of playing twenty-something heroines, in *All About Eve* (Joseph L. Mankiewicz, 1950). These were meticulously crafted prestige pictures produced by Paramount Pictures and 20th Century Fox, respectively. By contrast, many of the comeback vehicles of aging female stars in the 1960s were low-budget B movies made by small independent studios. Many exploited the formula pioneered by Robert Aldrich in *Baby Jane*, featuring an outlandish and gruesome plot that thrust an aging movie queen into a challenging, confusing, and highly emotional situation.[4] Typically, these films revel in the degrading spectacle of the star grappling not only with a monster or serial killer but also with distinctly shoddy material. The wonder is that highly esteemed actors would take on such roles, given the potential for reputational damage, leading to the inevitable assumption that most were faced with the prospect of either doing this sort of film or nothing at all.

Baron and Bernard state that the expansion of roles for male stars that led to an increasing roster of buddy films and road movies during the 1960s came at the cost of fewer roles for women, who were mostly cast as either sex kittens and sex workers or spinsters, psychotics, and zombies (2013, 263). The increasing replacement of romantic genres with violent and more sexually explicit ones as the Production Code dissolved after 1965 (finally relaxing the censorship rules that had existed since 1934), displaced strong females with those whose claim to fame rested largely on their sex appeal for young adult males, such as Ursula Andress and Raquel Welch. Yet an older generation of female stars was able to use intentionally "bad" material to showcase their emotional range and courage while

4. Examples include *The Night Walker* (William Castle, 1964) starring Barbara Stanwyck, *What Ever Happened to Aunt Alice?* (Lee H. Katzin, 1969) with Geraldine Page and Ruth Gordon, *The Mad Room* (Bernard Girard, 1969) with Shelley Winters, and *The Comeback* (Donald Wolfe, 1970) starring Miriam Hopkins.

confounding expectations that age had diminished their acting skills. Despite being an exploitation film, *Baby Jane* enabled Bette Davis and Joan Crawford to astonish critics and audiences with the sheer power of their acting prowess. So, even if this film originated from a desire to mock an earlier generation of Hollywood female stars, it resulted in a renewed appreciation of their resilience and dedication, virtuosity and versatility.

Yet Crawford's performances in William Castle's psychodrama *Strait-Jacket* and prank-call comedy-thriller *I Saw What You Did* in 1964 and 1965, respectively, risked being regarded as uncontrolled rather than virtuosic. Capitalizing on the star's newfound reputation as the doyenne of low-budget psychothrillers, these films sacrificed credibility in favor of sensationalism, suspense, and a succession of laughably shocking events. They also required the star to perform an erratic series of emotions, reactions, and attitudes. For instance, in *Strait-Jacket*, Crawford played an axe-wielding murderer who is released into the care of her adult daughter after spending many years in a psychiatric hospital. Her rehabilitation is jeopardized, however, by her daughter's elaborate and insane attempt to frame her for the murder of her fiancé's wealthy parents. Meanwhile, in *I Saw What You Did*, Crawford had a smaller role as a wealthy widow enamored with a paranoid psychotic killer who stabs her to death after killing his wife in the shower.

In the first two of these B movies, Crawford was required to segue directly from subdued to explosive, instantly turning frailty into fury, as well as transforming from a shy and retiring woman into a predatory sexual cougar within a single scene. She was also called upon to evoke madness and sanity from one moment to the next to keep the audience guessing about the identity of the psychotic axe-wielding serial killer. Consequently, although *Strait-Jacket* showcased Crawford's range as an actor, the sudden transition from one state to another combined with the weak motivation for her character's seemingly unpredictable behavior produced the impression that the veteran star had lost her capacity to maintain consistent and credible characterization in the mid-1960s.

Becoming Camp by Not Going Berserk

The exclamatory title of *Berserk!* may well have suggested someone or something going spectacularly out of control. Nevertheless, Crawford was not required to go crazy on this occasion, nor veer wildly from one emotion to another. The plot was certainly as ludicrous as anything concocted by producer-director William Castle, featuring a series of gruesome murders at a touring circus, a tightrope walker's attempt to acquire a share in the circus by inveigling his way into the affections of his boss, along with a spoiled daughter's vain effort to destroy her mother's business so that they could spend more time together. Throughout all the bizarre twists and turns of this incredible story, Crawford's character retains her composure. At the same time, the star exercised a great deal of creative control, especially in terms of her performance and appearance.[5]

As can be seen in the screenshot (figure 3.1), Crawford adopted a glamorous image for her role as the circus owner and ringmaster Monica Rivers, one that showcased her slim physique, as well as a characterization that emphasized the steely persona of a hard-nosed businesswoman with strong maternal and romantic feelings. *Berserk!* gave her the chance to combine aspects of her highly acclaimed character Mildred Pierce with the grit and glamour of her 1950s star image. Consequently, Crawford was able to present Monica as an ambiguous person, someone who could either be the serial killer slaughtering a succession of circus performers to boost box-office takings or a potential victim of other suspects, including the short-tempered but seductive tightrope walker Frank Hawkins (Ty Hardin). When the true culprit is revealed to be Monica's daughter Angela (Judy Geeson), this comes as a major surprise, even though it recalls similar storylines in *Mildred Pierce* and *Strait-Jacket*. It constitutes *Berserk!*'s cataclysmic climax, which reaches truly astonishing proportions when Angela flees the scene of her final crime, trips over a cable, and electrocutes herself during a thunderstorm and torrential downpour. According to John Russell Taylor, film critic of *The Times*, this was the last in a series of farcical events that rendered *Berserk!* "grotesque, if unforgettable" (1967). "Presumably the film's makers know this, and bank on it to sell the film," he added, implying that its comically twisted and outrageously exaggerated plot was both intentional and potentially profitable.

5. One of Crawford's earliest biographers described how the star wore her own clothes in *Berserk!*, while personally commissioning and paying for Hollywood costume designer Edith Head to create her ringmaster's outfit (Thomas 1978, 229).

FIGURE 3.1. Joan Crawford as Monica Rivers, the glamorous circus and ringmaster in *Berserk!* (Jim O'Connelly, 1967), flanked by her tightrope-walking lover Frank and serial-killing daughter Angela. Screenshot.

When Cecil Wilson informed *Daily Mail* readers that *Berserk!* was a "British-made heap of blood-stained corn," some people might have regarded this as exciting entertainment while others dismissed it on the grounds that it sounded like tasteless sensationalism and trite sentimentality (1967). Wilson was less ambiguous when describing Crawford as looking "very dashing in her red tail coat and black tights" (1967). Others also praised the star for her looks, with Dilys Powell noting her "lovely legs" in *The Sunday Times*, and Richard Roud insisting in *The Guardian* that, while "Joan is getting on a bit . . . she still manages to turn out well as a circus manageress in tights" (1967). Yet it was Wilson who highlighted Crawford's straight performance when stating that she "acts, with head erect and eyes ablaze, as if she really believes all this bosh" (1967). This confirms that, at the time of the film's release in Britain, at least one major reviewer observed that Crawford was performing idiotic material (i.e., bosh) with a surprising or unwarranted amount of pride and seriousness (i.e., her erect head).

Crawford's performance is decidedly deadpan in *Berserk!*, even during the hysterical final scenes. Rather than being hammy or ironic, she abides by the advice given to her by the director of one of her earliest films, *Sally, Irene, and Mary* (Edmund Goulding, 1925), which was to avoid exhausting the audience by overacting (quoted in Spoto 2012, 33). Crawford retained Goulding's advice as a guiding principle thereafter, producing muted performances that substituted internalized thoughts and feelings for outward displays of emotion and gestural expression. In the 1930s, as David M. Lugowski observes, she was "most effective doing less rather than more, allowing the planes of her face and her expressive eyes to carry emotional weight" (2011, 136). By the mid-1940s, she had attained "an extraordinary degree of engagement and concentration" (Raeburn and Shingler 2013, 394). Consequently, her Oscar-winning performance in *Mildred Pierce* resulted from an ability to identify closely with her character in combination with an understanding of when to hold back and hold in her emotions (395).

Crawford's ability to empathize with her character and internalize strong emotions is as evident in *Berserk!* as it is in *Mildred Pierce*. She can be seen mixing stillness and restraint with sudden bursts of more energized physical and vocal actions in both films, constantly adjusting the scale and tone of her reactions to harmonize with her coactors. Her work in *Berserk!* indicates that she was still adept at creating intensely felt but essentially contained performances in her final years as a screen actor. Meanwhile, her ability to act with total conviction seemed stronger than ever at this time, notably when performing alongside Billy Smart's elephants, a pack of acrobatic pooches and a bearded lady. Yet the audience's ability to suspend disbelief was challenged when the sixty-year-old star attempted to maintain her glamorous image in a succession of designer outfits that have more to do with Crawford's star persona than her character's job as the manager of a traveling circus.

Audience credibility is strained during Monica's romantic candlelit supper with her younger lover, Frank. Although Crawford looks feminine here in a diaphanous nightgown and with her long auburn hair falling loosely to her shoulders, the soft-focus lenses cannot disguise the telltale signs of age, including the hardness of her skin and the wrinkles around her eyes and mouth. The attempt to make the star look much younger than her sixty years in this scene fails—and it is this failure that renders Crawford's performance in this scene camp. Elsewhere in *Berserk!*, the combination of the star's almost age-defying and glamorous appearance with her defiantly serious and subdued acting style makes her seem camp. In part, this is due to the fact that the attempt to make her look younger can be discerned, along with the fact that she doesn't appear as young as her character is supposed to be. That failure, along with Crawford's insistence on making her character seem more glamorous than one might expect of a circus manager, creates a palpable sense of camp, and not just any old form of camp but, rather, what Susan Sontag insisted was camp's most successful form—that is, "naïve" or "pure" camp ([1964] 2018, 13).

When first publishing her "Notes on Camp," Sontag argued that camp's ultimate form was not parodic but one that emerged from a failed seriousness ([1964] 2018, 16). She stated that, "Camp which knows itself to be Camp ('camping') is usually less satisfying" (13). The deliberate act of "camping" inevitably resulted in a less successful form of camp than when a performer took their work seriously and played it straight, hence her comment that "pure examples of Camp are unintentional; they are dead serious" (13). She even suggested that the intention to be "campy" is probably always harmful and undermined such "famous would-be Camp films of the fifties as *All About Eve*" (14).

It's the unwarranted nature of Crawford's serious performance in *Berserk!* that makes it seem so camp—in other words, treating the film like it's the equivalent of a quality or prestige production, such as *Mildred Pierce*, when it has a weak script, ludicrous plot, and low-budget production values. In contrast, Diana Dors, Crawford's costar in *Berserk!*, plays her role as the magician's assistant with a twinkle in her eye and a tongue in her cheek to let the audience know that it's all rather silly—that is, she camps it up, as I describe in *Diana Dors: Film Star and Actor* (Shingler 2022, 117). While Dors metaphorically nods and winks at the audience, Crawford remains deadly serious when performing in the same film, giving no hint that she thinks it's beneath her or a waste of her talent as a dramatic actor. Yet, because her costars seem to be in on the joke that the plot of *Berserk!* is nonsensical, Crawford's serious approach fails to persuade audiences to take the film seriously, so this sense of failed seriousness renders her more camp than Dors. At the same time, it establishes Crawford's performance in *Berserk!* as the one that conforms the most to Sontag's notion of "naïve" or "pure" camp.

Sontag argued not only that real camp (that is, pure or naïve) has an innocent quality but also that it "is art that proposes itself seriously, but cannot be taken altogether seriously because it is 'too much'" ([1964] 2018, 17). For her, camp wasn't simply a matter of extravagance or stylishness, even though style was a crucial ingredient (18). "Style is everything," she declared (25). Yet Sontag recognized that the real significance of style for camp was its potential to "dethrone the serious" by being "playful" and "anti-serious" (26). Acknowledging that camp's tendency to treat serious issues frivolously, while taking seemingly frivolous things seriously, she hit upon the power of this quintessentially gay sensibility to not only invert normative hierarchies but also to diffuse some very real threats for sexual minorities in the 1960s. In other words, camp offered members of subjugated and subcultural groups a means to transform serious and potentially threatening things into something to be laughed at.

At the same time that it ignores and defuses anxieties about seemingly immutable aspects of life, camp celebrates and promotes passionate attachments to what are seemingly inconsequential things, such as fashion and film stars. One example of camp, therefore, is an intense interest in the outfits worn by a female star like Crawford in a film such as *Berserk!* Another is an appreciation of Monica River's red and black ringmaster's outfit, which can even be regarded as epitomizing camp taste due to its gaudy and spectacular qualities, as well as what some might consider to be an unseemly or inappropriate display of the sixty-year-old star's legs. To the camp cognoscenti, these are important factors rather than minor details, which make a film like *Berserk!* worth watching. Such things, moreover, cater to camp taste, which—so far as Sontag was concerned—consists of a generous enjoyment and appreciation of something even when it fails.

For Sontag, camp taste finds "success in certain passionate failures" ([1964] 2018, 32). True camp even possesses what she called a "*tender* feeling" (italics in the original), along with a genuine enjoyment that comes from laughing with rather than at the camp person or thing (33). This suggests that when audience members laugh at a camp performer or character in a film, they are experiencing a pleasurable form of empathy with that actor or fictional person. This further suggests that responses to aging female stars in 1960s exploitation films consisted of much more than derision and hostility. For when such performances are "purely" or "naïvely" camp, according to Sontag's definition, they become worthy of respect and are even capable of inspiring an intense identification. Moreover, in being recognizably camp, such performances acquire a more subversive power, including a propensity to disrupt normative hierarchies that, in addition to rendering style subservient to substance, typically privilege youth over age, male over female, and straight over gay.

Given the extent to which Crawford appears to conform to so many of Sontag's definitions of camp—as well as qualify as an almost perfect object for camp appreciation—it seems odd that the author made no mention of the star or any of her films in "Notes on Camp." Perhaps Crawford would have been included as an example of pure or naïve camp if the author had written her essay a few years later, for it was in the same year that "Notes on Camp" was published that the veteran star entered the fabulous realm where style triumphs over substance, where trivia is taken seriously and the serious is treated frivolously, as well as where artifice becomes the ultimate ideal. She did so, moreover, playing a recovering psychiatric patient whose apparently sane but deeply traumatized daughter has inherited the ability to wield an axe with devastating consequences in *Strait-Jacket*. Subsequently, Crawford consolidated her status as a doyenne of camp in *I Saw What You Did* and *Berserk!* And there was no doubting the fact that the star was operating within the realms of "pure" camp—according to Sontag's definition—when making *Trog*.

In the early 1970s, *The Times*'s film critic John Russell Taylor stated that "no one could hand-on-heart say that her latest film, *Trog*, is in any normal sense good. It is camp." After acknowledging that "there is a fearful joy in observing what outfits she considers proper for pot-holing," the critic observed that, "throughout this farrago of nonsense, Joan Crawford walks erect," concluding that she "appears to take it all seriously" (1971). Here, "fearful joy" and "farrago of nonsense" economically convey the critic's mixed reactions to Crawford's final film. Meanwhile, the attention drawn to Crawford's proud posture and her apparently serious attitude establishes that the star's portrayal of a stylish and unflappable anthropologist was nothing if not camp of the purest kind. If Taylor recognized this as camp in 1971, surely Susan Sontag and readers of "Notes on Camp" would have done so, too?

Crawford's Camp Conclusion to a Long Career

The claim that Crawford became one of the most successful exponents of cinematic camp after 1964 rests largely on her determination not to camp it up or be "campy." The artificial aspects that abound throughout *Strait-Jacket*, *I Saw What You Did*, *Berserk!*, and *Trog* may have thwarted the star's ambition to perform serious drama, yet they inadvertently resulted in what America's foremost spokesperson on camp conceived of as its most successful form. For the cognoscenti, Crawford's straight and serious performances in her final four films were recognizable as instances of pure camp at a time when this formerly marginal sensibility was making its way indelibly into mainstream public consciousness via cult movies and film criticism (Sontag [1964] 2018, 7).

If it's true that Crawford disowned *Strait-Jacket*, *I Saw What You Did*, *Berserk!*, and *Trog* and refused to speak about them to interviewers in the 1970s, then clearly these exploitation films were a source of revulsion and shame for the aging star. This also indicates that she regarded them as aesthetic failures, which suggests that Crawford lacked an understanding and appreciation of camp. It's very likely that the star had little comprehension of either the joys of camp or its more subversive qualities, including its power to dismantle orthodoxies of taste and judgment. "Notes on Camp" might have given the star a better idea of how her late-career performances could be seen to invert the established ideologies of age, gender, and sexuality that typically constrained not only older women but also—and most especially—accomplished, successful, and powerful older women like herself. Sontag's notes might well have changed Crawford's opinion of the films she made for William Castle and Herman Cohen to the point of making them seem more astonishing than unmentionable and more impressive than forgettable.

Works Cited

Aldrich, Robert, dir. 1962. *What Ever Happened to Baby Jane?* Featuring Bette Davis and Joan Crawford. Los Angeles, CA: Warner Bros. Entertainment. DVD.

Baron, Cynthia, and Mark Bernard. "Cult Connoisseurship and American Female Stars in the Sixties: Valuing a Few Withered Tits in the Midst of a Mammary Renaissance." In *Cult Film Stardom: Offbeat Attractions and Processes of Cultification*, edited by Kate Egan and Sarah Thomas, 259–75. Palgrave Macmillan, 2013.

Castle, William, dir. 1964. *Strait-Jacket*. Featuring Joan Crawford. N.p.: Sinister Film, 2019. DVD.

Castle, William, dir. 1965. *I Saw What You Did*. Featuring Joan Crawford. Los Angeles, CA: Universal Studios, 2018. DVD.

Curtiz, Michael, dir. 1945. *Mildred Pierce*. Featuring Joan Crawford. Atlanta: Turner. Entertainment Company, 2005. DVD.

Francis, Freddie, dir. 1970. *Trog*. Featuring Joan Crawford. Burbank: Warner Bros. Entertainment.

Hibbin, Nina. 1971. Review of *Trog*. *Morning Star*, June 18, 1971.

Lugowski, David M. 2011. "Norma Shearer and Joan Crawford: Rivals at the Glamour Factory." In *Glamour in a Golden Age: Movie Stars of the 1930s*, edited by Adrienne L. McLean, 129–52. Rutgers University Press.

Morey, Anne. 2011. "Grotesquerie as Marker of Success in Aging Female Stars." In *In the Limelight and Under the Microscope: Forms and Functions of Female Celebrity*, edited by Su Holmes and Diane Negra, 103–24. Continuum.

O'Connelly, Jim, dir. 1967. *Berserk!—Circus of Death*. Featuring Joan Crawford. Sony Pictures Home Entertainment, 2011. DVD.

Powell, Dilys. 1971. Review of *Berserk!*. *Sunday Times*, November 19, 1971.

Raeburn, Anna, and Martin Shingler. 2013. "Joan Crawford and Star Acting in *Mildred Pierce*." *Screen* 54 (3): 388–96.

Robinson, David. 1971. Review of *Trog*. *Financial Times*, June 18, 1971.

Roud, Richard. 1967. Review of *Berserk! Guardian*, November 17, 1967.

Shingler, Martin. 2022. *Diana Dors: Film Star and Actor*. Edinburgh University Press.

Sontag, Susan. [1964] 2018. *Notes on "Camp."* Penguin.

Spoto, Donald. 2012. *Possessed: The Life of Joan Crawford*. Arrow.

Thirkell, Arthur. 1971. Review of *Trog*. *Daily Mirror*, June 18, 1971.

Taylor, John Russell. 1967. "Berserk with a Star." *Times*, November 18, 1967.

Taylor, John Russell. 1971. "Joan Crawford, Super Star: A Fearful Joy." *Times*, June 18, 1971.

Thomas, Bob. 1978. *Joan Crawford: A Biography*. Bantam.

Wilson, Cecil. 1967. Review of *Berserk!*. *Daily Mail*, November 17, 1967.

PART II

CONNECTING TO THE YOUNGER SCREEN SELF

4

"YOU CAN'T STOP THE BEAT"

John Travolta as Aging Dancer

LISA DUFFY

In 1994, nearly twenty years after his instant star-making feature film role debut, John Travolta reemerged into the zeitgeist in the most fitting way possible: twisting his hips to collect a dance trophy in *Pulp Fiction* (Quentin Tarantino). While gangster Vincent Vega was certainly different from any character he had portrayed before, the familiarity of Travolta's body in motion draws an instant parallel with the fresh-faced twenty-three-year-old strutting down the street in *Saturday Night Fever* (John Badham, 1977). In a career that spans six decades and several comebacks, dance remains the primary signifier of Travolta's star image. As he ages, the use of dance keeps his body consciously and deliberately on display, centering his corporeal form in motion as the essential apparatus in his films. The figure of the dancing man in Hollywood has traditionally been seen as one of duality, occupying feminine and masculine interpretations simultaneously, a trait that readily lends itself to camp readings. These camp connotations become most pronounced in his role of zaftig doo-wop housewife Edna Turnblad in *Hairspray* (Adam Shankman, 2009). However, the excessiveness of this part seems to have invited too much scrutiny, with Travolta excising all dance moments from his subsequent films, a decision that has coincided with a precipitous downfall in his career. Dance is the central component of the Travolta persona, a constant that serves as a link to his younger superstar self, and without it his familiarity fades in the public consciousness.

Young Travolta as Dancing Man

From the beginning, critics made note of Travolta's body, either connecting it overtly with dance or citing it as an important element on the screen. Richard Sonnenshein observed, "The most talked about Hollywood talent of recent vintage is John Travolta, who has risen to stardom primarily because of his supple and dynamic dancing style" (1978, 500). In her review of *Saturday Night Fever*, Pauline Kael noted, "One can read Travolta's face and body, he has the gift of transparency" (1977, 60), privileging his body as an essential component to be read on the screen. Jesse Green of *The New York Times*, in reflecting back on Travolta's early film roles, wrote, "He became a movie star on the basis of a physicality so intense—and so specific to each role—that it almost seemed choreographed . . . his ability to create character in the shape of his spine, the tilt of his pelvis, the isolation of various parts of his body was a revelation in films, whether musical or not" (2007). Travolta's body is read as a dancing body even when it is not engaged in terpsichorean feats and stands as the site of central importance in his overall star persona.

Travolta as a dancing man onscreen naturally conjures up comparisons to his classical Hollywood forbearers and their negotiation of masculinity while engaging in something typically seen as the domain of women. In his work examining Fred Astaire as an example of the "feminized" song-and-dance man, Steven Cohan notes that his "'feminization' arises from a highly self-conscious and theatrical performance that constructs his masculinity out of the show-business values of spectatorship and spectacle" (1993, 47). Similarly, Travolta is often framed as possessing a "feminized" masculinity in his early roles. David Kehr pinpoints the "fetishizing" of Travolta's body throughout *Saturday Night Fever*, arguing that this drew Travolta "into the narrow romantic roles once exclusively reserved for female stars" (1979, 12). In his essay on masculinity as spectacle, Steve Neale cites Travolta in the same film as an example of the "feminization" of the male body when it is knowingly and unashamedly displayed as spectacle, rather than hiding its eroticization, as is proper of masculinity (1983, 15). It is perhaps Gene Kelly with whom Travolta shares the most with as a dancing man. Cohan observes that Kelly exerts "the eroticized spectacle of a male performer whose dancing 'with balls' exceeded heterosexual regulation yet without his ceasing to appear manly" (2005, 151). This dancing "with balls"—shaping dance to be a masculine art form by actively participating in his eroticization—was something Kelly was obsessed with, and Travolta seems to pick up that erotic mantle in his own dancing. In a 1983 interview with *Playgirl*, he stated, "I know that, physically, I move in a very sexual way, especially in dance," acknowledging the narcissistic focus he brings to his movements to craft a desirous image (Schipper, 97). Travolta's onscreen movement tends to be pelvis-led, best exemplified in the specific way he struts down the street in the beginning of *Saturday Night Fever*, cocky in every sense of the word. This knowing sexuality would become the trademark of Travolta's body in motion throughout his career, consciously inviting the audiences' gaze.

Travolta's image as a "feminized" dancing man creates a masculinity that is constantly shifting between "hard" and "soft" constructions, a duality that carries forward throughout his career (Garvey 2021, 82). His body is centralized in these early films as an object of desire, openly displayed as a form to aspire to or lust after, with Travolta, in his promotional interviews, positioning himself as an active participant in shaping this fantasy. However, this brand of masculinity fell out of favor in the 1980s, and Travolta's career faltered in an era devoted to "hard bodies," where peak physiques stood in symbolically for the aggressive Reaganomics and rise in nationalism that swept America (Jeffords 1994, 6). Travolta made every attempt to conform his body to match this muscular style, bulking up for his role in *Staying Alive* (Sylvester Stallone, 1983), something *Rolling Stone*'s Nancy Collins referred to as "the Stallonization of John Travolta" (1983, 46). As always, Travolta's body was centered in the press surrounding the film—a *Playgirl* feature on the star described his body as "perfectly toned, muscular and graceful—a body to stop sculptors, among others, dead in their tracks" (Schipper 1983, 29)—but it did not pass as an authentic encapsulation of 1980s standards, and his popularity plummeted. Jeff Yanc pointed out that because *Staying Alive* "fetishizes the male body in a nonviolent (and feminized) context" (1996, 46), unlike the war displays in the films from the likes of Sylvester Stallone, Arnold Schwarzenegger, and Jean-Claude Van Damme, Travolta's dancing body, even when covered in rippling muscles, runs counter to the decade's idealized male physique. The key characteristics of the Travolta persona, the "'pin-up' passivity, gender ambiguity, and fluid sexuality" created from his inherent duality, relegate him to the sidelines for the whole of the 1980s (Zigelstein 1997, 2).

A Comeback with Dance

Travolta's big comeback in *Pulp Fiction*, and his reentry into superstardom, comes more than a decade after *Staying Alive*, and the changes in his body are pronounced. But, while his hard body had gone soft, the primacy of dance in his overall star persona remains and is arguably the reason his comeback was so successful. The iconic image that emerges from *Pulp Fiction* is that of Travolta and Uma Thurman doing the Twist on the makeshift stage in the retro restaurant Jack Rabbit Slim's. The sight of the older Travolta continuing to move like young Travolta throws into relief the dichotomies inherent to his persona, both masculine and feminine, serious and silly, charming and off-putting. Jesse Zigelstein read the Twist scene as one of "deterioration," stating that the audience "cannot help but recall the lost mastery of the dance floor king" (1997, 3). I would argue against this interpretation, as Travolta's dancing in the film creates a direct bridge to his former, younger image. While the character of Vincent Vega is certainly a departure from Travolta's previous roles, when he dances he is suddenly light on his feet, moving with a grace that eludes the character at other points. His dancing is essential to the nostalgia of the film not because it feels different from his younger persona, but because it acts as a natural continuation of this star image.

Throughout the decade that followed *Pulp Fiction*, Travolta's body remained central to the press narrative surrounding his stardom. He became a physically malleable figure, famously gaining and losing weight throughout his various roles, and publicity surrounding his films in this comeback era nearly always inserted observations about his body, which Travolta happily participated in, reinforcing a narrative of complete control over the aesthetics of his body. The interest in his body was so ubiquitous in the press that headlines became simpler and simpler, with one headline in the *Chicago Tribune* on the film *Basic* (John McTiernan, 2003) just reading: "John's Six-Pack" (Armour 2003), something he was only too happy to show off in public whenever he could. It is interesting, then, that this career-long obsession with Travolta's body ultimately leads to him obscuring it completely under the fat suit he dons to play Edna Turnblad in *Hairspray*.

Camp Spectacle

As Edna, Travolta drags up to perform an exaggeration of femininity, giving in to the aesthetic of overblown camp toward which his status as dancing man seemed inevitably mutating. Camp as a topic is notoriously difficult to define with any consensus, but Travolta's Edna certainly conforms to Susan Sontag's ideas of the centrality of artifice and exaggeration to the subject ([1964] 1999, 53). Indeed, his comeback image itself can be enveloped in a theory of camp, turning to Andrew Ross's argument that when stars of an earlier, bygone era reemerge in the present, the overall product of their star image becomes redefined and distorted through contemporary codes of taste (1999, 312). Looking at camp specifically within the classical Hollywood musical, Cohan defines camp as "the ensemble of strategies used to enact a queer recognition of the incongruities arising from the cultural regulation of gender and sexuality" (2005, 1). It is this inherent queerness that is so interesting when looking at Travolta, as that is something that had been existing just under the surface of his star image since the very beginning, an inescapable whisper for a dancing man. By accepting the role of Edna, Travolta also opened himself up to the loudest speculation about his sexuality at any time in his career.

Hairspray is a film adaptation of the 2002 Broadway musical, which is itself an adaptation of John Waters's 1988 camp classic. The original film had drag queen Divine in the role of Edna, and the divide between this Edna and Travolta's—or even Harvey Fierstein's stage version—is noticeable. Rather than replicating the "filth" and "trash" Waters is lovingly known for, the film musical smooths out any roughness from the original film, something Suzanne Woodward calls the "antithesis" of the 1988 version: "a family-friendly drag queen to soothe the nerves of heteronormative film spectators" (2012, 116). I would argue that the result is not as settled as this claim suggests. There is an ease that Travolta seems to have in this role, a palpable joy exuded throughout, but this is married with an unease in the spectator at seeing Travolta blatantly feminized in an exaggerated body. These ideas of femininity and of the centrality of his body that are essential to his star image are writ large in Edna in ways that, to return to Cohan, "exceed heterosexual regulation" (2005, 151).

Travolta's sexuality has been a topic of speculation from the very beginning of his career, though, in the early days of his stardom, articles usually alluded to these rumors as the typical gossip that come to any man who experiences success. By the 1980s, the whispers were less subtle, with *Rolling Stone* asking Travolta, point blank, "Are you gay?," to which he succinctly replied, "No" (Collins 1983, 20). Part of the publicity cycle that swirled around the opening of *Hairspray* centered on Travolta's insistent comment on the role: "There is nothing gay in this movie. I'm not playing a gay man" (Walls 2007). It is tempting to read Travolta as the Player Queen from *Hamlet*, protesting too much to cover up the truth, but, as I have been tracing throughout this chapter, when it comes to Travolta there are never absolutes in one direction or the other. His sexuality exists, much like his overall persona, as a duality never to be fully resolved.

This insistence from Travolta that he is not playing a gay man reads true at least in his personal approach to the role. He has stated, "Playing a woman attracted me, playing a drag queen did not. . . . I didn't want any winking or camping" (Green 2007). While there is no escaping the campness inherent to the role, the sincerity of Travolta here fits his persona, his desire to give himself fully to a role in service of entertainment and his fixation on the overall look of the part. *The New York Times* profile of Travolta released to publicize the film noted that his Edna "has cleavage and a waist and a kind of geologic sex appeal" (Green 2007), with the desirous image that Travolta had cultivated in his youth still peeking through the prosthetics. Travolta cites Sophia Loren and Anna Magnani as the main inspirations he drew upon to craft his version of Edna, two actors that certainly would have been impactful growing up in his Italian American household in the 1950s and 1960s (Green 2007). There is a specific form of glamour and femininity interlaced in these inspirations, and, as exaggerated as Travolta ends up looking, his Edna exudes a kinder expression of womanliness than Divine or Fierstein. Travolta's focus on these older ideas of feminine beauty connects him in a wistful way to that younger pin-up version of himself, looking for totems of an exoticized European allure as the base from which to construct Edna.

While his body is fully obscured by his fat suit, he still has the opportunity to dance across the screen, reminding the audience what lies beneath the pounds of rubber. Edna is an agoraphobic housewife who is transformed into a confident woman through music and dance. In stage productions of *Hairspray*, Edna's sudden shift into performing choreography is often played for laughs, with the nondancer actors portraying her creating the believable movements of a housebound woman who thinks dancing is immoral. But, with Travolta in the role, her movements are given a lightness, and her embrace of dance feels inevitable rather than incongruous. While Travolta's range of movement is slightly restricted by the prosthetics, most noticeably when trying to kick up his legs, the assuredness of his body in motion is never curtailed. The trademark knowing sexuality of his dancing is still on display, though in this feminine mode the center of his movements shifts from his pelvis to his derriere. Rather than strut with his hips jutted out, he bends his frame forward to wiggle his padded backside as a method of seduction, moving with the same intent he has always had in inviting the audience's gaze. Though the sight of Travolta's exaggerated form at the beginning of the film might bring about shock for how different he looks compared to his other roles, once he begins to dance his youthful persona overtakes the extra years and layers of latex put on his body, becoming a familiar presence onscreen.

The choreographed numbers act in a similar way as the Twist did in *Pulp Fiction* a decade prior, suddenly spotlighting a former version of the star who still exists in the audience's collective memory, creating not a rupture with this former image, but a nostalgic bridge to it. This is particularly seen in the number "You're Timeless to Me," a love duet sung and danced alongside Travolta's onscreen husband, Christopher Walken, himself a song-and-dance man before cinema decided he was something different. Watching these two older hoofers move first tenderly, then with exuberance, showcases the importance of movement in creating connective ties throughout the lifespan of a star image. The familiarity of Travolta's body in motion cannot be separated from his superstar beginnings decades earlier, and the simultaneous existence of Young Travolta and Old Travolta in the same body, now ensconced in overtly feminine trappings, amplifies the camp connotations that his star persona was always hurtling toward.

Distance from Dance

While *Hairspray* provides this ultimate form of Travolta as dancer onscreen, one that moves to the forefront the duality that has always existed in his star image, there is a finality that the film brings. He has shifted to making dour films that almost all revolve around some kind of action plot. Throughout his career, Travolta always found ways to insert brief moments of dance into his films, even if there was nothing to suggest the need for a dance break. In *Look Who's Talking* (Amy Heckerling, 1989), he even performs a dream ballet, something that had been out of vogue in film for decades, and yet the desire to continue to view Travolta as a dancer has outweighed the need for narrative believability. These moments of dance occur regardless of genre, but they completely disappear in his post-*Hairspray* work. His career has taken a precipitous downfall, with the majority of Travolta's projects in the past decade released direct-to-video. It seems like the ultimate excess brought to his moving body when portraying Edna Turnblad and the camp associations that came from that role proved to be too much. Rather than embrace the campness that had always lurked in his image, Travolta has decided to attempt to shut down any associations with femininity and homosexuality. By removing dance from his roles, Travolta has effectively severed the link to his younger self in his professional life, fading once again in Hollywood popularity.

However, the essence of Travolta is not completely gone—his public appearances outside of his film roles continue very much in the mold of the charismatic, slightly narcissistic dancer first established in the 1970s. In 2021, he appeared in a commercial alongside his daughter, Ella, filming a TikTok video of the "Born to Hand Jive" choreography from *Grease* (Randal Kleiser, 1978). At the Academy Awards in 2022, he reunited with his *Pulp Fiction* costars Thurman and Samuel L. Jackson, immediately bursting into the iconic twist on stage. And, if he makes any talk show appearance at all, you can bet that he will dance. Richard Dyer notes that "star images have histories" (1998, 63), and aging celebrities engage with these past personas in all manner of ways, from clinging to the way they were to reinventing themselves whole cloth. While the aged Travolta resists conforming to his established star persona in his acting roles, the desire to remain connected to his youthful image still persists.

Works Cited

Armour, Terry. 2003. "John's Six-Pack." *Chicago Tribune*, March 2, 2003.

Badham, John, dir. 1977. *Saturday Night Fever*. Hollywood, CA: Paramount Pictures.

Cohan, Steven. 1993. "'Feminizing' the Song-and-Dance Man: Fred Astaire and the Spectacle of Masculinity in the Hollywood Musical." In *Screening the Male: Exploring Masculinities in Hollywood Cinema*, edited by Steven Cohen and Ina Rae Hark, 46–69. Routledge.

Cohan, Steven. 2005. *Incongruous Entertainment: Camp, Cultural Value, and the MGM Musical*. Duke University Press.

Collins, Nancy. 1983. "Sex and the Single Star: John Travolta." *Rolling Stone*, August 8, 1983, 14–20, 62.

Green, Jesse. 2007. "John Travolta in *Hairspray*: Keeping His Rhythm, Even in Drag." *New York Times*, July 18, 2007.

Garvey, Adrian. 2021. "Travolta Fever." In *Grease Is the Word: Exploring a Cultural Phenomenon*, edited by Oliver Gruner and Peter Kramer, 81–96. Anthem.

Jeffords, Susan. 1994. *Hard Bodies: Hollywood Masculinity in the Reagan Era*. Rutgers University Press.

Kael, Pauline. 1977. "Nirvana." *New Yorker*, December 26, 1977, 59–60.

Kehr, David. 1979. "A Star Is Made." *Film Comment* 15 (1): 7–12.

Neale, Steve. 1983. "Masculinity as Spectacle." *Screen* 24 (6): 2–17.

Ross, Andrew. 1999. "Uses of Camp." In *Camp: Queer Aesthetics and the Performing Subject: A Reader*, edited by Fabio Cleto, 307–29. University of Michigan Press.

Schipper, Henry. 1983. "John Travolta." *Playgirl*, September 1983, 28–32, 96–97, 109–10.

Shankman, Adam, dir. 2007. *Hairspray*. Hollywood, CA: New Line Cinema.

Sonnenshein, Richard. 1978. "Dance: Its Past and Its Promise on Film." *Journal of Popular Culture* 12 (3): 500–506.

Sontag, Susan. [1964] 1999. "Notes on Camp." In *Camp: Queer Aesthetics and the Performing Subject: A Reader*, edited by Fabio Cleto, 53–65. University of Michigan Press.

Tarantino, Quentin, dir. 1994. *Pulp Fiction*. Hollywood, CA: Miramax.

Walls, Jeannette. 2007. "Travolta Says *Hairspray* Isn't a Gay Film." *Today*, July 3, 2007. https://www.today.com/popculture/travolta-says-hairspray-isnt-gay-film-wbna19512551.

Woodward, Suzanne. 2012. "Taming Transgression: Gender-Bending in *Hairspray* (John Waters, 1988) and Its Remake." *New Cinemas* 10 (2–3): 115–26.

Yanc, Jeff. 1996. "'More Than a Woman': Music, Masculinity, and Male Spectacle in *Saturday Night Fever* and *Staying Alive*." *The Velvet Light Trap* 38:39–50.

Zigelstein, Jesse. 1997. "Staying Alive in the 90s: (John) Travolta as Star and the Performance of Masculinity." *CineAction* 44:2–11.

5

THE BAD SISTER

Bette Davis, Aging, and Sisterhood

Lucy Fischer

Nobody's as good as Bette Davis when she's bad.

—Warner Bros. advertisement

In 1987, seventy-nine-year-old Bette Davis starred in *The Whales of August* (Lindsay Anderson). In it, she plays one of two elderly sisters (the other role going to Lillian Gish), a role she had played in five other works. Especially noteworthy, however, is that in four of them—all but the one titled, ironically, *The Bad Sister* (Hobart Henley, 1931)—the woman she incarnates is disagreeable or dangerous and counterposed to a more benevolent sibling: *In This Our Life* (John Huston, 1942), *A Stolen Life* (Curtis Bernhardt, 1946), *What Ever Happened to Baby Jane?* (Robert Aldrich, 1962), and *Dead Ringer* (Paul Henreid, 1964).

In this chapter, I will examine Davis's onscreen persona, her acting style, and the way age affected her over a period of some four decades—all while performing the consistent part of a sister. It is important to note that, in all these movies, she had starring or costarring roles, rather than cameo appearances (the fate of many other entertainers), maintaining her stature as a Hollywood luminary even into old age.

Old Folks at Home

The Whales of August portrays two elderly siblings residing in one of their Maine summer homes. Sarah (Gish) is the gentle and caring one who attends to the blind, selfish, and petulant Libby (Davis). At the time, Gish was in her nineties and Davis nearly eighty, and, without much makeup, both actors appear to be precisely their ages. It would be Gish's final film and Davis's penultimate (Archer 1964). The two sisters tend to conform to their broader historic screen identities. Gish often plays a compassionate female character, and so she does here, as she assists Libby in activities of daily life: preparing her meals or helping her take walks. Similarly, Davis is the harsh, unkind individual from such earlier works as *Of Human Bondage* (John Cromwell, 1934) or *The Letter* (William Wyler, 1940).

Libby's churlishness is apparent when she mocks Sarah for serving cold tea. Similarly, when Sarah is hesitant once in responding to Libby, the latter shouts, "You didn't answer me!" Although Libby depends on Sarah for keeping the house in order, she derides her sister for always being "busy, busy, busy." When Sarah talks of time passing, Libby morbidly interjects: "Everything dies sooner or later." People who call on the sisters use terms like "difficult," "cantankerous," and "wicked" to describe Libby behind her back. Even Sarah calls her "bitter" and "cruel." Libby is jealous of all guests to the house. In particular, she is suspicious of Mr. Maranov (Vincent Price), an elderly island visitor. So she is distressed when Sarah invites him to dinner and warns, "He'll be here for the rest of your life if you let him." Moreover, she insults him during the meal, declaring, "Do not expect to find refuge here."

Clearly, Libby is an impossible woman (a familiar type for Davis), and Sarah tells a friend that she doubts that she can continue to deal with her. Suspecting this, Libby confronts Sarah, asking, "You're thinking of leaving me, aren't you?," to which Sarah confesses, "Maybe it would be for the best." Uncharacteristically, Libby finally admits that Sarah has been a "good sister," and there is a note of optimism at the film's end, when the two of them clasp hands and walk to the beach. The other hopeful sign is that throughout the drama there have been discussions of whether to add a picture window to the cottage to provide a view of the sea. Of course, Sarah has been opposed to it, saying, "It's too expensive," and "We're too old for new things." In the final scene, she hints at approving the project and cheerfully declares it "a beautiful morning." Unfortunately, her transformation has been too abrupt and the happy denouement too predictable.

Davis's acting style in the film is highly exaggerated and sometimes borders on camp. As can be seen in the screenshot (figure 5.1), to emphasize Libby's haughtiness, her head is always held high and her diction is loud, overly deliberate, and elevated. Of course, Davis has been "mannered" throughout her career, but in this film she seems to take it to another level. This leads to a final point, spurred by a (regrettably sexist and ageist) quote by Rick Groen, who finds "the waxen close-ups [of the two leading ladies] . . . distractingly *ghoulish*" (1988, emphasis mine). While Davis starred in several quite terrifying grand dame guignol films, looking at real aging in *The Whales of August*, though poignant, is disturbing enough without recourse to horrific special effects and makeup as Davis's stroke-drawn face departs from her younger screen self—her youthful visage in countless earlier screen performances emblazoned on the viewers' minds.

Mistaken Identities and Switched Places

A much younger Davis embodies the twins, Kate and Pat Bosworth, in *A Stolen Life*, set on a New England island. In the film's early scenes, as she develops a romance with Bill Emerson (Glenn Ford), nothing is revealed of her sister. But whenever Bill suggests walking her home, she declines. One

FIGURE 5.1. Bette Davis as a haughty Libby Strong in her penultimate film, *The Whales of August* (Lindsay Anderson, 1987). Screenshot.

night when Kate returns to Craven Cottage, the camera happens upon her identical twin sister, Pat (also played by Davis), who inquires whether she has been out with a man. Kate discloses nothing, suggesting that she is hiding Bill's existence from Pat and Pat's from Bill. The next day Kate has a lunch date with Bill, but as he approaches the restaurant Pat passes by, and he mistakes her for her twin. Realizing that he is Kate's secret beau, Pat pretends to be her sister. Over lunch, Bill remarks on how "Kate" seems different. While before she was a "cake without frosting," now she is "well frosted." Suddenly, the real Kate appears, and Bill recognizes his error. When the next day Bill takes a train to Boston, Pat contrives to sit behind him. Back on the island, Kate and Bill attend a square dance that Pat also attends, despite her disdain for such folksy get-togethers. She whisks Bill off, and they spend the rest of the night together, leaving Kate distraught and alone.

Pat and Bill wed, and Kate sees little of them. An aspiring artist, Kate pursues her craft and has a gallery show in New York City. Eventually, however, she abandons her artistic quest and returns to the island, where she is surprised to find Pat, as she was supposed to travel to Chile with Bill. The sisters go sailing with Pat at the helm. The weather suddenly turns stormy, and the boat collides with the rocks. Pat falls into the sea, and Kate tries to save her by gripping her hand, but manages only to grasp her wedding band before falling unconscious. When she awakens, she is in bed wearing Pat's ring, with others calling her "Mrs. Emerson." She decides to go along with the ruse, realizing it is the one way that she can finally have Bill. When the couple are reunited in New York, Kate is shocked to learn that they are on the verge of divorce since Pat has been involved with Jack Talbot (Bruce Bennett) a wealthy island resident. "Pat" tells Bill that she wants to reconcile, but he insists that she must first leave her lover. When "Pat" meets Talbot to break up, he angrily taunts her with all the other affairs that she has had, making Bill the "laughingstock of the island." Hearing how malicious Pat has been, Kate can no longer pretend to be her. She flees Bill and New York and returns to the island. As she walks on the fog-bound cliffs that she once roamed with Bill, he suddenly appears calling out for "Kate," revealing that he knows her true identity and loves her despite her subterfuge.

Obviously, a film about identical twins is not like one about other types of sisters. Here the women's uniformity tunes into notions of the doppelgänger. Theories concerning this trope have stressed stark oppositions between the two beings (Webber 1996). So how should the "sororal" double figures be read in *A Stolen Life*? Clearly, one sister (Kate) is represented as benevolent and the other (Pat) as malevolent. So, here, the more youthful Davis is not relegated entirely to the bad sister role as she is in certain films as she ages. Stylistically, Pat's perverse nature becomes immediately clear when she first appears in Kate's cottage room, bathed completely in shadows. But where lie the fault lines between the two sisters? In general, Kate is identified with attributes deemed desirable in female behavior, while Pat is not.

The first fault line has to do with eroticism. Pat is "frosted," and Kate is not, meaning that the former is sexy, and the latter isn't. Pat's allure is registered in her flirtatious eyes, girlish giggles, coy way of speaking, forward gestures, and chic fashion. When Bill first mistakes Pat for Kate, he remarks, "You're all dolled up!," having noticed an appealing change. While Kate is feminine enough, she is restrained and a bit shy. At one point, she tells Pat, "I know my limitations and I'm satisfied to stay within them." A male artist friend, Karnock (Dane Clark), calls her "stiff," and "all closed up," a quality that can be readily discerned in figure 5.2.

FIGURE 5.2. Bette Davis as the stiff, restrained, and shy Kate Bosworth (on the left), as well as her alluring, flirtatious, and chic twin sister, Pat (on the right), in *A Stolen Life* (Curtis Bernhardt, 1946). Screenshot.

When both twins appear at the square dance, Kate wears a high-buttoned blouse and a long, tailored skirt while Pat wears a low-cut, flouncy dress with ruffles. When Bill asks Kate to help him choose a birthday present for Pat, she selects a diaphanous negligee and seems uncomfortable when he asks her to hold it up against her body. Moreover, Kate has a go at being an artist, while Pat seeks only diversions with men. The macho Karnock opines that Kate's professional goals are merely a substitute for having a man. When he surmises that she has lost the love of her life to her sister, he chides her for being passive. In this sense, Kate has been typically "feminine." On the other hand, Pat (a male nickname) has been typically "masculine" (sexually and interpersonally aggressive).

The second fault line is that of earnestness versus duplicity. As the "good" woman, Kate seems fundamentally honest—valuing Bill's work, way of life, and company and openly expressing her deep fondness for him. Of course, she is temporarily deceitful after her sister dies. Pat, on the other hand, is an essentially deceptive person. The moment she meets Bill, she pretends to be Kate. Then she pretends to like square-dancing to find another occasion to be with him. Finally, she arranges to take the same train as he to Boston. Furthermore, after marrying Bill, she feigns to like island life, has secret affairs, and lies to her sister about why she has not gone to Chile (claiming a cold vs. impending divorce).

The third fault line involves kindness versus cruelty. Kate is compassionate, even to the man who has jilted her and the sister who has taken her lover. Pat, on the other hand, is unkind to Kate, stealing the man she adores. She is brutish to her spouse, cheating on and humiliating him before others. Certainly, *A Stolen Life* conforms well to psychologists Nathan Wolfenstein and Martha Leites's view: that, in cinema, "sisters tend to be love rivals. . . . When a twin is thrown by chance into her sister's place, she is not apt to feel . . . that this is an embarrassing situation, from which she would be happy to escape. She is likely to have desired this position for a long time" (1950, 15).

Interestingly, four years before *A Stolen Life*, Davis made another film about sisters entailing a similar "theft" of lovers. In *In This Our Life*, she plays Stanley, sibling to Roy (Olivia de Havilland) (Olivia de Havilland). As the drama opens, Roy is married to physician Peter (Dennis Morgan), and Stanley is engaged to lawyer Craig (George Brent). Almost immediately, however, chaos ascends when it is discovered that Stanley has run off with her sister's husband. As the story develops, the inevitable collapse of the new couple's relationship ensues: Stanley becomes impatient at being left alone while Peter spends hours at the hospital, annoyed at his criticism of her spendthrift ways. Meanwhile, Roy's romance with Craig burgeons. Thus, the sisters' partners have been exchanged. Like the twins, the sisters are radically opposed.[1] Roy is sedate and wears monotone outfits, whereas Stanley occasionally sports loud prints. Roy is kind and altruistic, whereas Stanley is cruel and selfish. Roy is restrained, whereas Stanley is flirtatious and manipulative. She is also more carnal, as emblematized by her love of dancing and music. She not only destroys her family but, after running over a woman and child while driving, blames the accident on a Black household worker. Like most "bad sisters," she dies at the end in a second car crash of her own making.

Grand Dame Guignol

Like *The Whales of August*, *What Ever Happened to Baby Jane?* features Davis appearing with another star who plays her sister, Joan Crawford. Davis was then fifty-four, which in that era was seen as "over the hill" for a lead screen performer. When Joan Crawford read and became interested in Henry Farrell's 1960 novel of the same name, she suggested Davis as her costar, and Davis agreed. This is somewhat surprising, since there had been a long-standing rivalry between the two women (Gomez 2017). Such offscreen bitterness well suited the narrative, which concerns two elderly sisters (both former entertainers) who profoundly dislike each other. Jane (Davis) was once a vaudeville child star whose stage name was Baby Jane Hudson, known for performing sentimental song and dance routines. Her later attempt at a film career failed. Conversely, Blanche (Crawford) had found success as a movie star, but at the height of her fame was paralyzed in a car crash as she returned to her house one night. The tabloids blamed Jane for the accident, since she was an alcoholic, disappeared for days after the catastrophe, and was assumed to have driven her sister home that evening. Now, decades later, the two reside in their old abode (once owned by Valentino). Blanche is a paraplegic, confined to her bed or wheelchair, overseen by Jane, who alternately tends to and torments her. In some ways, the film had overtones of an earlier one,

1. It is curious that in the film both sisters are given masculine names.

Sunset Boulevard (Billy Wilder, 1950), about a pitiful, aging movie star also played by a real one (Gloria Swanson), holed up in a timeworn Hollywood estate. Both films show clips of movies in which the stars had appeared. Thus, in *What Ever Happened*, the viewers see excerpts of the Crawford film *Sadie McKee* (Clarence Brown, 1934), shown on television to the rave comments of a moderator, and the 1933 Davis films *Parachute Jumper* (Alfred E. Green) and *Ex-Lady* (Robert Florey), shown in a flashback to the disparaging remarks of producers who call her a "no-talent broad."

The reason *What Ever Happened* falls within the grand dame guignol genre is that it involves two prominent female entertainers placed in a horrific and violent context. It is also deemed a psycho-biddy film (a misogynistic/ageist term) because it deals with an older deranged woman (Jane). In playing her, Davis has clearly moved entirely into the "bad sister" category. In part, Jane's viciousness stems from having learned that Blanche intends to sell their house, putting her future at risk. Beyond this, Jane's hatred of her sister has long involved jealousy over the rise of Blanche's career as her own declined, and her sister's greater appeal to men.

Jane abuses Blanche in myriad ways (e.g., hitting her, spying on her, hiding her fan mail, forging her checks, and ripping the phone line from the wall), but her most onerous acts involve the meals she serves her. After cleaning Blanche's birdcage, Jane announces that the pet has flown away. Later that day, when Blanche lifts the silver cover from her dinner plate, she finds the dead bird underneath it. Similarly, after Jane tells her that there are rats in the cellar, one such rodent is served for Blanche's next meal. This cruelty makes Blanche afraid to eat and leads to her gradual starvation. In some ways the contrast between the bad and good sisters falls again within a conventionally gendered paradigm. In her harsh, antagonistic manner and with her vicious streak, Jane can be seen as more "masculine" than Blanche, who, in her immobility, is necessarily passive (a trait traditionally linked to the female). Also, Blanche seems fairly courteous to Jane, despite the latter's nasty behavior toward her. Finally, she seems to have a good relationship with Elvira, the maid (Maidie Norman), while Jane can relate to no one except the musician she eventually hires to help her make a comeback.

Shot in black and white, the film has the right tone for its macabre subject. It also allows for stark contrasts between light and shadow that lends the film a noir-ish look. While color was once considered for the movie, Davis thought that it would make a "sad story look too pretty."[2] Ernest Haller's cinematography also contributes to the film's unsettling aura—in the overhead shot of Blanche spinning around in her wheelchair after finding a rat on her dinner plate, in the zoom shots of the downstairs phone out of her reach, and in the high-angle shots down the staircase that she cannot traverse.

Wanting to isolate Blanche, Jane soon fires Elvira. But, fearing for Blanche's safety, Elvira lets herself into the house while Jane is away and finds Blanche bound and gagged in her bedroom. When Jane suddenly returns home, she kills Elvira. In addition to being an abuser and a sadist, Jane is now a murderer. Another sign of Jane's insanity is her regression to childhood. She puts an ad in the newspaper for a pianist to accompany her in her imagined return to the stage (a parody of the aging star's comeback). A sorry musician, Edwin (Victor Buono), answers the ad and comes to the Hudson house to find Jane dressed up in a version of the white frilly dress that she wore as Baby Jane, with her hair adorned in ringlets. She performs for him her trademark (maudlin) song "I've Written a Letter to Daddy" (which imagines her parent in heaven).

While Crawford, as the rather sympathetic Blanche, has a very restrained role and looks quite natural, Davis is all superfluity. As can be seen in figure 5.3, when Jane dresses to go out in her antique automobile, she is exaggeratedly adorned with dated rhinestone jewelry. With Davis taking charge of her makeup process, Jane is fashioned in a deadly pale Kabuki-like white-face, supplemented by penciled eyebrows, dark lipstick, kohled eyes, and a false beauty mark—creating an unsettling visage that contributes to her perverse characterization. As Davis is reputed to have said, "What I had in mind no professional makeup man would have dared to put on me."[3] Certainly, Davis's acting style augments this portrayal of Jane. In speaking to Blanche (with a hoarse, raspy voice), she yells, spits out barbed mocking jibes, cackles, and curses whenever her sister's buzzer rings ("Oh, shut up!"). Furthermore, she continually rolls her eyes at Blanche in visible annoyance. When Edwin is around, however,

2. IMDB, "*What Ever Happened to Baby Jane?*," https://www.imdb.com/title/tt0056687/trivia/ (accessed January 21, 2025).

3. IMDB, "*What Ever Happened to Baby Jane?*," https://www.imdb.com/title/tt0056687/trivia/ (accessed January 21, 2025).

FIGURE 5.3. An overly adorned Bette Davis as Jane Hudson in *What Ever Happened to Baby Jane?* (Robert Aldrich, 1962), in an excess of dated rhinestone jewelry and a Kabuki-like painted mask, which add significantly to her perverse characterization. Screenshot.

her demeanor changes: she bats her eyes and speaks more sweetly. This behavior seems entirely inappropriate, given her bizarre appearance and clear psychological imbalance.

At the time of the film's release (fittingly, on Halloween), its critical reception was not very positive. Bosley Crowther of *The New York Times*, for instance, found that it did "not afford [Davis or Crawford] opportunity to do more than wear grotesque costumes, make up to look like witches, or chew the scenery to shreds" (1962). Nonetheless, the film received five Oscar nominations, including Davis for Best Actress. With horror studies burgeoning in later decades, as well as an appreciation of camp sensibility, *What Ever Happened* was looked on more favorably. From a feminist perspective, however, the vision of Jane as an elderly and mentally ill woman was, of course, seen as regrettable. Mindy Buchanan-King, for instance, calls her a "monster" (2020, 409). Despite any drawbacks to the film, one has to admire the boldness and complete lack of vanity shown by Davis in taking the part of Jane at this point in her storied Hollywood career (even allowing her actual films to be bad-mouthed by producers in the movie). Interestingly, Baby Jane, tells Edwin that Daddy once told her that "you can never lose your talent." In the case of Davis, Daddy was right.

Double Trouble

In *Dead Ringer*, Davis plays identical twins for the second time. Once more they are alienated from one another, but here the source of tension lies in the past and again concerns their love of the same man. Edith was the first to have a romantic relationship with the wealthy Frank De Lorca. Then, Maggie stole his affections and, claiming pregnancy, forced him to marry her. This led to an eighteen-year rift between the women, finally interrupted by Edith's attendance at Frank's funeral. Edith soon realizes, however, that the heartless Maggie never loved Frank and feels no grief at his passing ("I don't look good in black," she intones). Beyond that, Edith learns that Maggie only feigned pregnancy to ensnare Frank. Soon, her hatred and vengeance toward her sister boils over, and she decides to kill Maggie and take her place, leaving a suicide note signed by "herself" (Edith)—shades of *A Stolen Life*. Instead of being a dowdy bar owner, hopelessly in debt, Edith (as "Maggie") becomes a rich, pampered society lady. She quickly comprehends that Maggie was having an affair with Tony (Peter Lawford). When he resumes their liaison, however, he realizes that she is an imposter and is actually Edith. He blackmails her, and, when his scheme is detected by the police, she allows her dog to attack and kill him so her secret will not be disclosed. In searching Tony's apartment, though, the police find arsenic and conclude that he and Maggie poisoned Frank (whose death had earlier been ascribed to a heart attack). Now, in her new identity as "Maggie," Edith is a murderer again, a fate that she had hoped to evade through her ruse. She is ultimately tried and sentenced to death. Before switching identities, Edith had been dating a police officer (Karl Malden), and, at one point, when he speaks to "Maggie" after her crime is known, she tries to tell him that she is really Edith. He refuses to believe her, saying that Edith was kind and would never hurt a fly.

In this film, at age fifty-six, Davis essentially plays two bad sisters. Goodness is nowhere to be seen (despite the policeman's naïve view of Edith). The black-and-white film stock, suspenseful and dramatic score, and chiaroscuro lighting emphasize its malevolent atmosphere. Edith, while always a tough cookie, initially seems to be the better sibling, earning her own way in life and having a good heart (e.g., employing jazz musicians who need the gig, helping poor neighbors). Of course, this all changes when she murders her sister and constructs a web of lies. Maggie's negative qualities are always apparent, but at first they seem limited to having stolen Edith's lover and living a frivolous life of entitled wealth. Then her wrong-doings worsen: including the feigned pregnancy to entrap Frank, the cheating on him, and, finally, the murder. Interestingly, there is no need of Grand Guignol excess in this film for Davis's malevolent characterizations to emerge—it is all there in her actions. As can be seen in figure 5.4, two years after her appearance as Baby Jane she looks quite stunning as Edith/Maggie, especially in the latter more fashionable role. Here, she elicits no pity for an aging star supposedly compelled to play demeaning versions of her former self. Rather, though the characters she inhabits are evil, she presents them in a dignified manner consonant with traditional aspects of her screen persona and acting style. As the epigraph to this chapter proclaims, "Nobody's as good as Bette Davis when she's bad."

The most visually arresting moments of *Dead Ringer* occur when Maggie wears a black mourning hat with an attached long black veil that fully covers her face—almost giving her the look of a nun (an irony). In part, this costume works to keep her visage hidden for a while, withholding the fact that Edith has a twin. But it also has symbolic significance. In listing Davis's twenty top roles, the British Film Institute (BFI) includes *Dead Ringer* as number eight (and *What Ever Happened* as number three). But, more importantly,

FIGURE 5.4. Bette Davis playing two bad sisters in *Dead Ringer* (Paul Henreid, 1964): the dowdy and impoverished Edith (on the left), and the rich and glamorous Maggie (on the right). Screenshot.

the cutoff year for these films—for any in which Davis has a starring role—is 1964 (that of *Dead Ringer*'s release). Therefore, the mourning veil becomes a metaphoric emblem of bereavement for the greatest part of Davis's career, although she takes on film and television roles for years to come.

In her films between 1942 and 1987, when Davis ages from thirty-four to seventy-nine, she often played a woman's sister, and twice that of identical twins (tour de force performances involving stark dramatic oppositions). Moreover, as she grew older, she sometimes portrayed two pernicious siblings (Maggie and Edith) or the more difficult of the pair (Libby and Jane).

Although *What Ever Happened to Baby Jane?*, with its chilling, overblown vision of the older woman, might incur more wrath from feminist theorists (Buchanan-King 2020) than the naturalistic *Whales of August*, it is a vastly superior film and Davis's performance in it far better. Furthermore, the sight of a seventy-nine-year-old Davis photographed realistically may be more unsettling to the audience than that of a fifty-four year-old Davis plastered in weird face paint. Interestingly, within the logic of the film's narrative, Libby cannot see herself, because she is blind. However, the audience is familiar with Davis's appearance as a young woman from her catalog of prior films, since it is the nature of each frame of cinema to fix a single moment in time forever unchanged. The frozen celluloid image of Davis's past youthful self is perhaps eerily symbolized in the creepy Baby Jane doll that haunts the 1962 film.

Considering these films, there are two ways to read this temporal and thematic evolution. First, in terms of ageist and sexist stereotypes of the senior female, Davis's roles might be viewed as hormonal, postmenopausal "bitches," unable to control their adverse, raging emotions or their rejection by male society—drawing on more ancient tropes, they might also be viewed as "hags" or "witches," old, ugly, women linked to noxious spells and frightening misdeeds. But a second perspective would place Davis's later roles within the broader context of her overall body of work. First, even as a young actor, she often took on unappealing parts, as in *Mr. Skeffington* (Vincent Sherman, 1944). Second, she was never regarded as a classic Hollywood beauty, so her lack of vanity in aging was not a sign of abjection. As Davis notes in her 1962 autobiography, "According to all existing Hollywood standards, my face was not photogenic. Embarrassment always made me have a one-sided smile. . . . My hair, my clothes, my God!" (112). Third, there was always a severity to her performative affect and delivery, so finding her in harsh, unsentimental parts in later years was aligned with her screen persona and history. Finally, it seems no accident that two of the films discussed here made it to the BFI list of her top twenty performances—making it clear that the film roles she inhabited in her fifties were not woeful parts thrust upon a "has been" star forced to demean herself before the public. Rather, despite their bearing certain unfortunate clichéd elements, they were mature, venerable performances worthy of the rest of the Bette Davis canon.

In four of the films discussed, there are moments when Davis as the bad sister looks into a mirror, a familiar stance for the onscreen woman, given that females are conventionally seen as vain. In *What Ever Happened* this gesture occurs after Jane sings a childhood song, then screams at the sight of herself. In both *A Stolen Life* and *Dead Ringer*, the mirror scenes happen after the good sister has switched places with the bad and is pondering her new identity, and, in *In This Our Life*, when Stanley trades her mourning clothes for a colorful dress. Though the character who peers back at the actor from the looking glass changes from part to part, it is really always Bette Davis that she sees—confident of her ability to inject each role with skill, talent, and vitality, no matter its ideological valence.

Works Cited

Archer, Eugene. 1964. "*Dead Ringer*." *New York Times*, February 20, 1964.

Buchanan-King, Mindy. 2020. "Joan Crawford: Problematizing the (Aging) Female Image and Sexuality in *What Ever Happened to Baby Jane?*" *Quarterly Review of Film and Video* 37 (5): 408–30.

Crowther, Bosley. 1962. "Screen: Bette Davis and Joan Crawford—They Portray Sisters in Melodrama." *New York Times*, November 7, 1962.

Davis, Bette. 1962. *The Lonely Life: An Autobiography*. Putnam.

Gomez, Patrick. 2017. "Feud: Why Joan Crawford and Bette Davis' Rivalry Began Long Before *Whatever Happened to Baby Jane?* [*sic*]." *People*, March 6, 2017.

Groen, Rick. 1988. "*The Whales of August*, a Cinematic Shrine Devoid of Life." *Globe and Mail*, April 1, 1988.

Webber, Andrew J. [1996]. 2011. *The Doppelgänger: Double Visions in German Literature*. Oxford University Press.

Wolfenstein, Nathan, and Martha Leites. 1950. *Movies: A Psychological Study*. Free Press.

6

WHATEVER HAPPENED TO *BABY DOLL*?

Carroll Baker's Italian Thrillers

LEON HUNT

Carroll Baker achieved initial fame, and some notoriety, as the child bride in Elia Kazan's *Baby Doll* (1956), a film condemned by the Catholic League of Decency. The most frequently reproduced stills from the film show her sucking her thumb and sleeping in a crib while driving husband (Karl Malden) mad with desire. She also appeared in *Giant* (George Stevens, 1956) the same year, alongside James Dean and Elizabeth Taylor, but few people are likely to remember *Giant* for Carroll Baker, and probably even fewer remember Carroll Baker for *Giant*. It was *Baby Doll* that remained a reference point throughout her career, including the title of her autobiography. The 1962 pressbook for *Station Six-Sahara* (Seth Holt, 1962) referred to Baker trying to escape "the tyranny of a hit performance." While she was Method trained, *Baby Doll*'s place in Baker's career would often pull her toward sex symbol roles. In films such as *The Carpetbaggers* (Edward Dmytryk, 1964), *Sylvia* (Gordon Douglas, 1964), and *Harlow* (Gordon Douglas, 1965) (all three produced by Joseph E. Levine), David Thomson has characterized her as a "splendidly vulgar creature, capable of a specially daft sexiness" (1980, 27), which seems to be the version of Baker that Levine was keen to promote. In 1967, after a series of contract disputes and conflicts with Levine and her husband, Jack Garfein, who had directed her in the independent film *Something Wild* (1961), she followed a tradition of Hollywood stars moving to Italy to relaunch her career.

Most characteristic of her European work was a series of eight suspense thrillers that led to her being dubbed "la regina del giallo" (the queen of the murder mystery) in the Italian press (Ceretto 1971, 13): *Il dolce corpo di Deborah* (*The Sweet Body of Deborah*, Romolo Guerrieri, 1968); *Orgasmo* (*Paranoia*, Umberto Lenzi, 1969); *Così dolce . . . così perversa* (*So Sweet . . . So Perverse*, Umberto Lenzi, 1969); *Paranoia* (*A Quiet Place to Kill*, Umberto Lenzi, 1970); *La última Señora Anderson* / *In fondo alla piscina* (*The Fourth Victim*, Eugenio Martin, 1971); *Il coltello di ghiaccio* (*Knife of Ice*, Umberto Lenzi, 1971); *Il diavolo a sette facce* (*The Devil Has Seven Faces*, Osvaldo Civirani, 1971); and *Il fiore dai petali d'acciaio* (*The Flower with the Deadly Sting*, Gianfranco Piccioli, 1973).[1] While Baker made other kinds of films in Italy, too, I focus here on her thrillers as a means of examining how the Italian cinema of the 1960s and 1970s functioned as a space for extending or relaunching careers that had run aground, failed to ignite, or seemingly passed their sell-by date in Hollywood. In Baker's case, this is inextricable from her status as a sex symbol as she approached middle age. An increasingly permissive Italian cinema allowed her to extend her "sexy" image further than before, but often framed it within narratives that also reminded the viewer of her status as an older woman. I will focus mainly on the first four films named above, which capitalized particularly on Baker's sexy image and pushed it further by having her appear nude, something that had only been teased in the films she made with Levine in Hollywood.[2] They established what became known as the *giallo-erotico*, a forerunner of the erotic thriller, a genre defined by Linda Ruth Williams as "*noir*ish stories of sexual intrigue incorporating some form of criminality or duplicity" (2005, ix–x).[3]

While the films capitalized on Baker's willingness to appear naked, they also adapted her image to playing older characters than portrayed in

1. Rather confusingly, two different films are known as *Paranoia* in different markets. The first was released as *Orgasmo* in Italy and *Paranoia* in English-speaking markets. The second was called *Paranoia* in Italy and *A Quiet Place to Kill* in its English-language version. They will subsequently be referred to as *Paranoia* and *A Quiet Place to Kill*.
2. Baker's willingness to appear nude is the most consistent element of her European career, by the end of which she was in her mid-forties.
3. *Giallo-erotico* is a term that was being used as early as the review of *Paranoia* in *Corriere della sera* (Grazzini 1969, 13).

her Hollywood films. Stephen Thrower cautiously refers to her characters as being "*slightly* older women" (2020), wealthy widows and divorcees, still beautiful women whom men nevertheless find attractive primarily for their money. The narratives play out *Diabolique*-like marital intrigues, dangerous attractions, and attempts to gain inheritances prematurely. Baker was in her mid-to-late thirties when she began working in Italy and early forties when she made her final *giallo*. Thus, these films mark a point in between her initial career as Hollywood sex symbol and her return to the United States as a character actor in the late 1970s.

Faded Stardom/Relocated Stardom: Baker in Italy

In what way could Baker at this point be seen as an aging or older star, considering that she was still fairly young by modern standards and clearly regarded as sexually desirable? Aging is "a highly ambiguous and subjective process" (Shary and McVittie 2016, xi), and also a gendered one. In her essay "The Double Standard of Aging," Susan Sontag argues that women "become sexually ineligible much earlier than men do . . . even good-looking women," going on to suggest that they are regarded as "old as soon as they are no longer very young" (1972, 31, 32). The key phrase here is "no longer very young." Baker was still being presented as a sex symbol, but her sexual eligibility sometimes seemed to be in question both in the films themselves and in their critical reception. A couple of reviewers seemed embarrassed or disturbed by Baker's nude scenes in *The Sweet Body of Deborah*, seen by one to offer "an embarrassing measure of alleged titillation" (Murf 1969, 30). "In this feverish effort to project sexual excitement, she becomes only frightening," added another (Murphy 1968, 46).

Baker was also vulnerable to being seen as a faded star—worse, a faded sex symbol. "Carroll Baker's appeal as a much plotted-over heroine has rather faded over the years," claimed a review of *A Quiet Place to Kill* (Combs 1973, 105). Hollywood stars moving to Italy to resume or rescue their careers was rarely seen as a positive sign—Clint Eastwood was unique in achieving major stardom through this route.[4] A particularly

4. While gender is probably a factor here—Eastwood flourished initially in the most masculine of genres, the Western—it should be acknowledged that no other male star repeated his level of success by working in Italy.

mean-spirited article published in *Corriere della sera* in 1969 characterized Baker's Italian career as a sign of decline: "È tramontata una stella" (A star has set/declined) was the headline. "In Milan a few evenings ago, I saw Carroll Baker. She was blonde, very blonde, as always, but there weren't hordes of admirers" (Falvo 1969, 11). No longer recognizable as "Baby Doll," she was now "only a beautiful lady, not even overwhelming, who passes through the crowd unobserved" (11). Alongside the obvious misogyny there was also the view that "Hollywood on the Tiber" was a step down for her—"Would Carroll Baker have come to Rome if she wasn't practically unemployed?" (11).

The sense of Baker's "real" career being over once she left Hollywood is partly reinforced by her autobiography, published in 1983. The filmography, probably not written by Baker herself but presumably approved by her, barely mentions her Italian work, although she is quite candid about the main reasons for relocating to Rome: she was virtually broke after her Hollywood problems and now able to work regularly in Europe. There was an additional bonus: contrary to Falvo's insinuations about her diminished sex appeal, she was enjoying the attention of an assortment of eligible Italian men, something on which she places great emphasis in her autobiography.

Three years after her autobiography, in 1986, Baker published a Jackie Collins–style novel called *A Roman Tale*, a heavily fictionalized and remarkably explicit account of her time in Rome. Her fictional stand-in, Madeline Mandell, is described as "a world-renowned sex symbol" with a "famous body" (10, 9) eager to escape Hollywood. "For twelve years she had been a slave to the studio and its system, to the studio bosses and most (worst) of all to her sex-symbol image. The image had taken shape after her first film, *Venus Awakening*. . . . Ever since, when she had been talked or written about, it was as Venus, not Madeline" (10). *Venus Awakening* could be seen as a substitute for *Baby Doll*. Madeline even makes a film called *Paranoia*, directed by "a man whose tastes gave prurience a bad name" (160).[5] This director is named Alfonso Razzi in the novel and might be a fictionalized version of Umberto Lenzi or possibly an amalgam of the various Serie B directors with whom she worked in Italy. There is very little

5. While this fictional *Paranoia* doesn't sound exactly like any of her actual *gialli*, it does have some similarities to her first film with Lenzi.

doubt about Baker's own feelings toward these thrillers: "*Paranoia* was supposed to be a mystery, but the only mystery was why it was being made" (1986, 160). But Madeline, like Baker, needs to work and must grind her way through the tawdry *giallo*. Approaching thirty-five, a couple of years younger than Baker would have been, she is "heading for her sexual prime, if the books and doctors were to be believed . . . she was a perfect candidate for the rampant *la dolce vita*" (12). According to Sontag, the double standard of aging "cheats" women of these years, "likely to be the best of their sexual life" (1972, 33), and, while Baker's steamy novel largely presents a sex-positive narrative, the thrillers she made during this period are more ambivalent: she still possesses *il dolce corpo* but is at an age that makes her vulnerable to dangerous attractions.

Baker appears to have placed little value on her Italian thrillers, or her European career more generally, and they are usually passed over quickly in accounts of her career. Thomson, for example, gives no impression of having seen them when he dismisses *The Sweet Body of Deborah* and *Paranoia* (under its *Orgasmo* title) as "lurid concoctions" based on their titles alone (1980, 28). However, in more recent years, they might be some of her most watched films because of the cult surrounding Italian genre cinema: they are often accorded seminal status in books about the Italian *giallo*-thriller (e.g., Bruschini and Tentori 2013; Bartolini 2017; Curti 2022). Prior to Dario Argento, the most famous Italian director of thrillers and horror films, arguably no one was more important in establishing the *giallo* as a cinematic genre than Baker. Despite the odd jibe about having "faded," she retained more of her Hollywood star aura than most American stars who landed at Cinecittà. Moreover, this was arguably the first time in her career that she inhabited a stable persona over a series of films—as *la regina del giallo*.

While Baker's *gialli* are either coproductions or sole Italian productions, they downplay their "Italianness" and aspire to a more broadly European identity, as Baschiera and Di Chiara argue: "a borderless Europe inhabited by cosmopolitan characters belonging to the high bourgeoisie," an "exotic and vicious Europe also familiar to the American market through the 'licentious' and 'subversive' European art films" (2010, 35). They take place in luxurious tourist locations (Geneva, Nice, Paris, Mallorca), hotels and villas where a swimming pool is never far away. Marjorie Bilbow characterized *A Quiet Place to Kill* as being "as effortless to swallow as a sweet martini" (1973, 20), and the image of a glamorous, if murderous, jet set is a large part of their appeal. The word "camp" occasionally appeared in reviews of the films, an impression that time has probably amplified. But while they traded on thrills and flashes of bare flesh, they also looked to more respectable cinema, full of borrowings from French thrillers in particular: *Les diaboliques* (*Diabolique*, Henri-Georges Clouzot, 1955) most frequently; *Plein soleil* (*Purple Noon*, René Clément, 1960); and *La piscine* (*The Swimming Pool*, Jacques Deray, 1969). Sometimes, they also drew inspiration from Hollywood thrillers. At one point in *Paranoia*, the young couple trying to drive Baker mad and ultimately kill her serve her a meal that includes a live toad on a silver platter. More than one critic at the time noticed the likely influence of *What Ever Happened to Baby Jane?* (Robert Aldrich, 1962), in which Bette Davis serves Joan Crawford a dead rat. *Paranoia*'s narrative of home invasion by stealth also has some similarities with Olivia de Havilland being trapped and tormented in her private elevator in *Lady in a Cage* (Walter Grauman, 1964). Like Baker's character, de Havilland is playing a wealthy widow, albeit an older one, tormented by younger antagonists. Davis, Crawford, and de Havilland were part of a trend for casting older female stars in grotesque thrillers and horror films, sometimes referred to, tellingly, as "hag horror" or "hagsploitation." Baker was considerably younger than these stars, but *Paranoia* operates in a not dissimilar territory.

So Sweet . . . So Perverse: Baker and the *Giallo-Erotico*

According to Williams, "Some erotic thrillers are primarily thrillers, some erotic thrillers are primarily sex films. All contain sex and must use sex as a motivating narrative device" (2005, 1). Baker's thrillers fall into the first category—they are full of twists and turns, but they also provide opportunities for her to take steamy showers, perform a tightly framed love scene, or lie naked across a bed, as in a scene when she phones her mother from a hotel in Nice in *The Sweet Body of Deborah* (figure 6.1). Bilbow summed up this mix by calling *The Sweet Body of Deborah* "two films for the price of one": both a "nudie rudie" and "your traditionally involved, cheerfully unbelievable thriller diller with its double twist ending" (1968, 4). While exploitation cinema risks being a one-size-fits-all category for sensational genre movies, these were certainly titillating films, as the titles

FIGURE 6.1. Carroll Baker as Deborah with Jean Sorel as Marcel in *The Sweet Body of Deborah* (Romolo Guerrieri, 1968). Screenshot.

promised, with their references to sweet bodies and perverse desires. One Italian review likened them to "magazines in closed wrappers" (Grazzini 1969, 13), and these were the sorts of films featured as erotic diversions in *fotoromanzi* (photo comic strips) aimed at adult male readers (*So Sweet . . . So Perverse* appeared as a photo-strip in the magazine *Cinestop*). Sex and money are generally the two motivating forces in these films, which were simultaneously derivative (film noir, French thrillers) and pioneering ("erotic thriller" was a term not widely used until the 1980s).

In *The Sweet Body of Deborah*, Marcel (Jean Sorel) is plotting to kill his new wife Deborah (Baker) for her inheritance. When this plan instead leads to his death, it is Deborah who becomes richer because of his insurance policy. "You can never be rich enough," she observes in the final line of dialogue. Throughout much of the film, Deborah is terrorized by mysterious phone calls, Tchaikovsky's Symphony No. 6 constantly appearing without explanation on record players or a piano with no visible player, and people who seem to come back from the dead. Dressed in mourning at the end, she betrays little regret over either Marcel's plan to kill her or his death, observing with amusement the irony of having become richer because of it. The scene is staged and performed as if it were a twist, rather than the logical conclusion to events, and as if she and her new partner Robert (Marcel's killer) were the real villains who were always going to outplay Marcel. There is a similar scene at the end of *So Sweet . . . So Perverse* (by the same writer, Ernesto Gastaldi) where Baker's character, Nicole (a clear villain this time), sits on a plane to Rio Janeiro with her accomplice, seemingly having got away with their murderous schemes but spotting the suspicious police inspector a few rows back. This partly arises out of the films' need to produce the maximum number of twists and character turns, but it also speaks of a misanthropic cynicism that pervades the whole cycle.

At the end of *Paranoia*, in a slightly awkward coda designed to see justice done, the film reveals that Baker's character, Kathryn—seemingly blameless up to that point—probably murdered her husband. In *So Sweet . . . So Perverse*, Nicole initially seems to be an unwilling participant in a sadomasochistic relationship, attracting the chivalrous and romantic attention of Jean (Jean-Louis Trintignant), a womanizer unhappily married to the frustrated Danielle (Erika Blanc). But Nicole is not what she seems, duplicitous and bisexual, plotting with Danielle to kill Jean and then eliminating her for her money with the aid of her accomplice. Baker had refused to play the role intended for her (Bartolini 2017, 92), the older wife terrorized by sinister phone calls and nocturnal revenants and therefore closer to Baker's other characters in the *giallo-erotico*, insisting on playing the role of the femme fatale intended for Blanc, eleven years younger than Baker. Roberto Curti (2022, 130) calls this "a fatal casting flaw," and Lenzi seems to have agreed, but it is indicative of Baker pushing back against being deployed as a "faded" sex symbol and possessing sufficient clout to get her way.

In *A Quiet Place to Kill*, Baker's character, Helene, is reunited with ex-husband Maurice (Jean Sorel). Divorcing Helene after having spent all her money, Maurice is now married to Constance (Anna Proclemer), an older woman who is painfully aware that the same scenario is about to be played out again. The two women agree that Maurice is too attractive, too good in bed, too irresistible to just leave, so their only way of freeing themselves of him is to kill him. "He's a vice, a sort of drug," observes Constance, "We have no defense against Maurice—against his cynicism, his way of making love, his overbearing manner." When it comes to it, however, Helene cannot bring herself to kill this unreliable lothario, and it is Constance who ends up in the sea. While Baker had played a sexually provocative and disruptive figure in several films in her original period of stardom—"She Made a Man's World Explode!" was the poster tagline for *Station Six-Sahara*—in her Italian thrillers it is often male lotharios who are dangerously attractive, and, as if to prove Sontag's point, they need not necessarily always be younger. Maurice is visibly younger than Constance, but Sorel and Baker have similar ages. Nevertheless, Helene is, in her own words, "the overly romantic American," while Maurice deploys his sex appeal with cynical precision. By the end of the film, he is revealed to be in league (and a sexual partnership) with Constance's daughter, Susan, barely out of her teens; she lost her virginity to him when she was either fifteen (Italian version) or fourteen (English version). According to Susan, Helene's jealousy toward her is understandable: "She's old," she says bluntly.[6] The faithless male partner (Sorel again) also plots with a younger woman (another Susan) in *The Sweet Body of Deborah*. Susan is Marcel's supposedly dead former lover who has been alive and in on it all along; the film makes no mention of her age, but she is played by Ida Galli (billed as Evelyn Stewart), who is substantially younger than Baker.[7] During a scene in which Marcel and Deborah make love, their voices continue on the soundtrack, but what is shown onscreen is Marcel's memory of having sex with Susan, Galli's body substituted for Baker's. "I feel like you're with me, but you still have your arms around her," says Deborah, and, even before the twist is revealed, the film confirms this to be true.

At the start of *Paranoia*, Baker's character, Kathryn, newly widowed, is dressed in mourning as she arrives at Fiumicino airport in Rome. She is greeted like a film star by a swarm of paparazzi, as if restaging Baker's own arrival (figure 6.2). The question of age and aging, as relative terms, is addressed much more explicitly in this film. In a discussion of women in Douglas Sirk's 1950s melodramas, Karen Stoddard refers to the films' reliance on a "still-attractive-but-past-her-box-office-prime actress to portray the difficulties and anxieties of women who are being shifted out of their previously central social roles and starting down the road to senescence" (1983, 71). Kathryn is presented as a character who has lost track of what constitutes "age-appropriate" behavior for someone who is "still young," according to people older than she is, but aware that she is "no longer very young" (as Sontag puts it) and therefore not young at all. She looks to a young couple, who may or may not be brother and sister, to "teach me

6. The dialogue is different in the Italian version; this line only appears in the English version.

7. There is some disagreement over Galli's year of birth, sometimes given as 1939 and sometimes 1942. Baker was born in 1931.

FIGURE 6.2. Carroll Baker as Kathryn, arriving like a movie star at Fiumicino airport in *Paranoia* (Umberto Lenzi, 1969). Screenshot.

to be young again." Her late husband was considerably older than she was, and the impression that she has been aged before her time by a middle-aged lifestyle now feels like a trap. More so than in the other *gialli-erotici*, her dangerous liaison in the film will be with somebody substantially younger than her—the working title of the film was *Una pazza voglia d'amare* (a crazy desire to love). Lou Castel's character, Peter, who is considerably younger than the male leads in Baker's other *gialli*, turns up at Kathryn's villa on the outskirts of Rome supposedly because his car needs repairing.[8] But he is soon inviting himself inside, admiring a nude self-portrait she painted, and then joining her in one of Baker's obligatory shower scenes. Both irritated by and attracted to his youthful arrogance, she is quickly besotted: "Dirty me, dirty me!" she cries as he paws her bare breasts with oily hands. When she visits him in the Piazza Navona apartment from which he is about to be evicted, she tries to give him money to settle his debts, which only makes him angry. She apologizes, offering the excuse that "it's just my repressed maternal instinct," and he calls her his "mammina mancante" (absent mommy). Some of Baker's later Italian films in other genres will return to this age-gap scenario, sometimes casting her as

8. Castel also brings a different set of associations to the role because of his participation in a more countercultural cinema and his political activities in Italy. Claudio Bartolini calls him a "counterculture actor-symbol" (2017, 209).

the sexual educator of a younger man, but Kathryn is the one who seeks an education of sorts in *Paranoia*.

Kathryn's desire for Peter is also shown to be a desire to recapture a youth that has passed prematurely during her marriage. Baker is made to look slightly older than in her other *gialli* in order to stage both this attempt to rejuvenate and her physical and mental decline as her torment progresses. When they are joined by Eva, supposedly Peter's sister or step-sister (his revised claim when Kathryn finds the two of them in bed), she becomes Kathryn's model for an ideal youthful femininity. Eva is young and slim, with fashionably short hair. Kathryn dances with them while wearing a green minidress and in one scene puts on a wig that approximates Eva's pixie cut. Having settled into a married life older than her years, Kathryn's attempt to recapture her youth is presented as going too far the other way, to the amusement of her soon-to-be tormentors, and leads to an unraveling bolstered by drink and sleeping pills (on which she is already dependent) and being secretly drugged by Peter and Eva. In one scene, she wakes up between the two of them (figure 6.3), unable to remember how she got there. They subsequently blackmail her with photos of her in bed with Eva, and the psychological torture is ramped up for the remainder of the film.

There is an extraordinary cruelty in the film's main resolution, before the guilty parties get their comeuppance in a rather tacked-on coda.

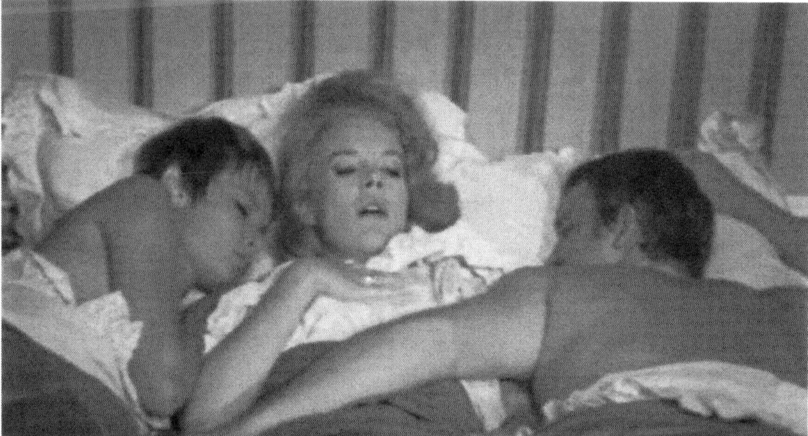

FIGURE 6.3. Carroll Baker as Kathryn, waking up between Eva (Colette Descombes) and Peter (Lou Castel) in *Paranoia* (Umberto Lenzi, 1969). Screenshot.

Kathryn's lawyer and friend Brian is her one hope and remaining emotional connection. Brian is an older man, very likely the same age as her husband; at one point he seems about to propose to her. But she is finally driven to attempt suicide by a fake telegram announcing his death. As she teeters on the bay window roof, she sees Brian arrive but loses her balance and falls to the balcony below, badly injured. Brian rushes to her, lifts her up in his arms, pauses, and then drops her from the balcony to the ground below, killing her. The *giallo-erotico* constantly aims for a last nasty twist, and Brian is in league with Peter and Eva, fabricating adoption papers that will enable them to claim her inheritance after her death. As in *A Quiet Place to Kill*, Baker is vulnerable to the alliance of men of all ages with younger women. But, here, there is also the sense of a sadistic dismantling of the Hollywood diva, from her arriving at Fiumicino like a film star to her unravelling and humiliating fate.

The *gialli* made by Baker after *A Quiet Place to Kill* largely move away from the erotic aspects of the first four and cast her in more diverse roles. Only *The Flower with the Deadly Sting* features some brief nude scenes. In *Knife of Ice*, her character is mute for most of the film because of a trauma in her past. Seemingly one of the targets of a serial killer, she turns out to be the killer herself, only speaking when she is caught at the end of the film. The finale effectively regresses her, reciting a passage from *Alice in Wonderland* that she last delivered as a child. In *The Devil Has Seven Faces*, she plays one of a pair of identical twins, seemingly mistaken for the other one by gangsters hunting a stolen diamond, the "devil" of the title. *The Fourth Victim* initially seems to give her another treacherous husband, but his remarkable capacity for being widowed (three times already) proves to have been merely unfortunate. In *The Flower with the Deadly Sting*, her final thriller, she is cast in more of a supporting role, despite sharing top billing.

In the early 1970s the Italian *giallo* was establishing a different kind of female lead through the likes of Edwige Fenech, Barbara Bouchet, and Dagmar Lassander. They were younger, European rather than American, and also physically different—voluptuous where Baker was slim. Fenech married producer Luciano Martino, who had produced two of Baker's initial *gialli*, as if to confirm that she was her replacement. Even more tellingly, Baker would play Fenech's mother in the comedy *La moglie vergine* (*At Last, at Last*, Marino Girolami, 1975). Secondly, Baker continued to play sexually active older women, now in her early-to-mid-forties, in other films. In *Lezioni private* (*The Private Lesson*, Vittorio De Sisti, 1975), she plays the piano teacher desired by one of her pupils, while in her final Italian film, *La moglie di mio padre* (*My Father's Wife*, Andrea Bianchi, 1976), she is married to an older man who has lost sexual interest in her and reignites his aging libido with much younger women. Baker's character, Laura, retaliates with an affair with her stepson from her husband's first marriage. In one scene, she visits a sex worker and pays her for advice on how to keep her husband interested in the bedroom, a cruder version of Kathryn's search for her lost youth in *Paranoia*. The film veers into *giallo* territory for its conclusion as Laura is murdered by her now jealous husband. Unusually for Baker, she did not dub her own voice in the English version of the film—a sign that her Italian career had drawn to a close.

Baker's Return to Hollywood

When Baker resumed her Hollywood career, she shed every vestige of her sex symbol status in *Andy Warhol's Bad* (Jed Johnson, 1977). Mrs. Aitken is a markedly deglamorized role, one character calling her "a dried-up piece of stale white bread" before drowning her in a sink filled with water. For much of the remainder of her career, she worked as a character actor, although *The World Is Full of Married Men* (Robert Young, 1979), adapted from a Jackie Collins novel, cast her again as a sexualized older woman, along with some brief nudity.[9] This phase of her career is probably easier to frame as a comeback, a homecoming, and a return, for the most part, to "respectability" and "proper" acting. But a Hollywood-centric account of her career risks being misleading, irrespective of how little regard she had for her European output. Moreover, the cultification of the Italian suspense thriller has brought one of the most interesting stages of her career back into close attention: her four films with Lenzi were packaged as a Blu-ray box set in 2020, promoted as "landmark films that changed the erotic thriller and *giallo* genres forever." Italy did not make her a bigger star necessarily, but nor did it simply add her as a faded name in secondary roles.

9. Another Collins adaptation, *The Stud* (Quentin Masters, 1978) had extended the sex symbol status of another middle-aged female star into more permissive territory—namely, her sister Joan.

From the imperiled bride or widow with *il dolce corpo* to the "frustrated housewife" of *My Father's Wife*, it allowed Baker to play out the middle years of her star career in a provocative and sometimes unexpected way.[10] After Clint Eastwood, who was a similar age but at a rather different stage in his career, one might suggest that Baker was the Hollywood star who enjoyed the most fruitful relaunching of her career in Italy outside of art cinema.[11] She remained a top-billed star, helped popularize a genre that has since been reevaluated, and—as seen in the case of *So Sweet . . . So Perverse*—clearly exercised more power than she had in Hollywood, at least some of the time, able to get her way in being cast in her preferred role. More than simply acting the diva, Baker might have not unreasonably felt that if her body was still a commercial draw in the *giallo-erotico* then what was so implausible about her playing the woman who leads a younger man to infidelity? The films themselves, and their reception, are sometimes marked by misogyny or ageism—both, in the case of *Paranoia*—but, in others, the combination of glamour and experience make her the winner at the end, even if only temporarily. Maybe the same can be said for Baker herself.

Works Cited

Baker, Carroll. 1983. *Baby Doll: An Autobiography*. Arbor House.

Baker, Carroll. 1986. *A Roman Tale*. Headline.

Bartolini, Claudio. 2017. *Il cinema giallo-thriller italiano*. Gremese.

Baschiera, Stefano, and Francesco Di Chiara. 2010. "Once upon a Time in Italy: Transnational Features of Genre Production 1960s–1970s." *Film International* 8 (6): 30–39.

Bianchi, Andrea, dir. 1976. *La moglie di mio padre / My Father's Wife*. N.p.: Televista Inc., 2009. DVD.

Bilbow, Marjorie. 1968. "The Sweet Body of Deborah." *Daily Cinema*, October 7, 1968.

Bilbow, Marjorie. 1973. "A Quiet Place to Kill." *CinemaTV Today*, April 7, 1973.

10. The film is also known as *Confessions of a Frustrated Housewife*.

11. British actor Anne Heywood, the same age as Baker, had a similar sojourn in Italy—including thrillers and erotic films—but with less success. She walked away from the role subsequently played by Baker in *Baba Yaga* (Corrado Farina, 1973), an erotic horror film.

Bruschini, Antonio, and Antonio Tentori. 2013. *Italian Giallo Movies*. Profondo Rosso.

Ceretto, Alberto. 1970. "Baby Doll puritana." *Corriere d'informazione*, July 5–6, 1970.

Ceretto, Alberto. 1971. "Regina del 'giallo.'" *Corriere della sera*, March 24, 1971.

Combs, Richard. 1973. "*Paranoia (A Quiet Place to Kill)*." *Monthly Film Bulletin* 40 (472): 105.

Curti, Roberto. 2022. *Italian Giallo in Film and Television: A Critical History*. McFarland.

Falvo, Angelo. 1969. "È tramontata una stella." *Corriere della sera*, September 26, 1969.

Grazzini, Giovanni. 1969. "Orgasmo." *Corriere della sera*, March 29, 1969.

Guerrieri, Romolo, dir. 1968. *Il dolce corpo di Deborah / The Sweet Body of Deborah*. Firenze: CG/CineKult, 2012. DVD.

Lenzi, Umberto, dir. 1969. *Orgasmo / Paranoia*. Los Angeles, CA: Severin Films, 2020. Blu-ray.

Lenzi, Umberto, dir. 1969. *Così dolce . . . così perversa / So Sweet . . . So Perverse*. Los Angeles, CA: Severin Films, 2020. Blu-ray.

Lenzi, Umberto, dir. 1970. *Paranoia / A Quiet Place to Kill*. Los Angeles, CA: Severin Films, 2020. Blu-ray.

Murf. 1969. "The Sweet Body of Deborah." *Variety*, February 26, 1969, 30.

Murphy, Brian. 1968. "The Sweet Body of Deborah." *Films and Filming* 15 (7): 46.

Shary, Timothy, and McVittie, Nancy. 2016. *Fade to Grey: Aging in American Cinema*. University of Texas Press.

Sontag, Susan. 1972. "The Double Standard of Aging." *Saturday Review*, September 23, 1972, 29–38.

Stoddard, Karen M. 1983. *Saints and Shrews: Women and Aging in American Popular Film*. Greenwood.

Thomson, David. 1980. *A Biographical Dictionary of the Cinema*. Secker & Warburg.

Thrower, Stephen. "Carroll and Umberto's Final Stab." Interview. *The Complete Lenzi-Baker Giallo* Collection. Los Angeles, CA: Severin Films, 2020. Blu-ray.

Williams, Linda Ruth. 2005. *The Erotic Thriller in Contemporary Cinema*. Edinburgh University Press.

7

"ONE THING ABOUT TIME"

Woody Strode's Late Films

WILL DODSON

"Thank God We Thought We Were Equal": The Athlete and the Actor

Woody Strode was among the small number of Black athletes who integrated football, first at UCLA in 1937, and then professional leagues in the 1940s.[1] Groundbreaking as his athletic career was, Strode is perhaps best known for his equally pioneering career in Hollywood. Dubbed in *JET* magazine the "Jackie Robinson of cinema," Strode was among the first professional athletes to transition into an acting career, carving a path for many to follow (Manchel and Strode 1995, 37).[2] After a string of nonspeaking background parts, Strode earned acclaim as a supporting actor as the gladiator Draba in *Spartacus* (Stanley Kubrick, 1960)—for which he was nominated for a Golden Globe—and as Braxton Rutledge in *Sergeant Rutledge* (John Ford, 1960). Yet, even after success in these high-profile films, racial barriers limited Strode's options in Hollywood,

1. For a complete history of the integration of UCLA football, see James W. Johnson, *The Black Bruins: The Remarkable Lives of UCLA's Jackie Robinson, Woody Strode, Tom Bradley, Kenny Washington, and Ray Bartlett* (University of Nebraska Press, 2017). Strode played for the Bears from 1940 to 1942, before serving in World War II. He returned to football at age thirty-two with the Rams in 1946.
2. Strode also played football with Jackie Robinson, who joined the UCLA Bruins in 1939 after transferring from a junior college.

and from the late 1960s onward he mostly worked in Europe as a star in Italian genre films.

Three of Strode's late film appearances both pay him homage and comment on the historical significance of his career. In *The Cotton Club* (Francis Ford Coppola, 1984), he was cast as Holmes, the doorman of the eponymous club, which features Black performers but bars Black patrons in Depression-era Harlem. He is the Storyteller who gives framing narration in the revisionist Western *Posse* (Mario Van Peebles, 1993). In his final film appearance, he is the undertaker Charlie Moonlight in the Spaghetti Western tribute *The Quick and the Dead* (Sam Raimi, 1995). Strode died just before its release, and the film is dedicated to him. Strode's brief appearances in these films link them to their B-movie roots in gangster films, race films, and Westerns and, when considered in context of his professional life, gesture to the racist history of Hollywood, and the United States.

Coppola and Van Peebles deliberately position Strode to comment on race, film genre, and American history. In *The Cotton Club*, Strode's role emphasizes the violence of segregation and the suppression of Black talent. This emphasis is even more explicit in Coppola's reedited version of the film (*The Cotton Club Encore*, 2019), which restores and foregrounds several sequences featuring Black actors, who were, ironically and pointedly, suppressed by the producers in the theatrical cut. Strode delivers a monologue in *Posse* about the number of Black cowboys in America's historical West in contrast to their representation in Western films. Strode's appearance in *The Quick and the Dead* evokes the several Spaghetti Westerns in which he appeared—his brief but memorable role in *Once upon a Time in the West* (Sergio Leone, 1968) in particular—and encourages genre fans to identify intertextual elements throughout the film and to recall several key moments of Strode's biography. As a group, these late films feature Strode as a catalyst by which viewers may reflect on his metatextual symbolism.

Strode's appearances in these films point to histories often rendered invisible by dominant film discourse. His presence offers viewers opportunities to reflect on Strode's significance in the twilight of his career and life. Strode was a pioneer, though the term "pioneer" is somewhat ironic given its resonance in America's colonial and postcolonial history and Strode's identity as both Black and Indigenous (Strode and Young 1990, 1–4,

177–78).[3] All the men endured racist exclusion, and often racist haranguing from fans. But, as Strode put it, they "had no fear of them. . . . I used to tell Kenny when we were playing for the Rams, 'Thank God we thought we were equal'" (64). In 1948, Strode played football professionally in Canada for the Calgary Stampeders and later became one of the first Black professional wrestlers. As a wrestler touring the South and Southwest throughout the 1940s and early 1950s, he learned to win over even the most outwardly racist crowds. "I dressed all in white: white trunks, white shoes," he wrote. "I was the clean colored boy. . . . I've wrestled in the most prejudiced states in the country beating the shit out of a white man because I knew the psychology" (122). Strode's athleticism, showmanship, and careful, stoic navigation of racism and prejudice eventually led him to success on the wrestling circuit, and to the notice of an agent, who saw Strode's matches on television and began signing him up to "some half-assed acting jobs" (179). He became an actor full-time, one of the first Black athletes, and certainly the first Indigenous athlete, to break into Hollywood. His late films therefore carry with them not only the history of integrating sports and entertainment, but also an extraordinary individual life.

"The Ofays Pays, Man": *The Cotton Club* and *The Cotton Club Encore*

Francis Ford Coppola intended *The Cotton Club* as an homage to gangster films and Black musical talent in the Jazz Age. The film's narrative concerns two sets of brothers trying to make their way in the intertwined industries of entertainment and the underworld, which coalesce at the famed Cotton Club of Harlem. A white jazzman, evocatively named Dixie Dwyer (Richard Gere), flits between white and Black worlds and finds himself slowly pulled into the orbit of gangster Dutch Schulz (James Remar). Dixie's wannabe gangster brother, Vincent (Nicholas Cage), actively auditions to become one of Dutch's men, but his increasingly erratic behavior spells his doom. The second pair of brothers, Sandman (Gregory Hines) and Clay Williams (Maurice Hines), are up-and-coming dancers, but Sandman's grand ambitions and impatient frustrations with racist segregation

3. Strode claimed Creek, Blackfoot, and Cherokee ancestry on both sides of his family, but did not often call attention to it.

threaten their partnership. While the pairs of brothers mirror one another, the theatrical release cut devotes the majority of its time to Dixie's story. Set in Harlem between 1928 and 1932, the cast includes a bevy of Black singers and dancers, including Mario Van Peebles as a background dancer and performer in a duet with the character Lila Rose (Lonette McKee). Strode first appears about fifteen minutes into the film in a slight low-angle shot from his back as he sweeps the sidewalk and street at the entrance of the Cotton Club. Sandman and Clay exit the club and have a brief exchange with him.

HOLMES: How did your dancing audition go?

SANDMAN: They loved us.

HOLMES: [*laughing*] You think the Cotton Club's gonna put you to work? Hey, man, on your way to the big time!

CLAY: Man, we'll see. He's showing off again!

HOLMES: Yeah, but he's got a lot to show off!

SANDMAN: [*preening*] Showing off is how you become a star!

HOLMES: [*as the two walk away*] Good luck, boys!

This bit of small talk follows a scene in a tenement building in which the family matriarch, Tish Dwyer (Gwen Verdon), finishes a dance lesson with a little white boy. The boy does a rudimentary step as he leaves the apartment, and the film transitions via a diagonal wipe to a shot of the club, where Holmes sweeps (figure 7.1). The small talk about the brothers' audition deepens in context with the boy, linked to the Dwyer family and to Dixie, whose whiteness gives him access to both white and Black performance spaces. The movement of the diagonal wipe edit matches Holmes's sweeping action, as if to suggest with that rhythmic move that the barrier between ambition and opportunity is a color line. Holmes speaks to the Williams brothers easily, optimistically, yet they both know the barriers they face, and the narrow limits to which they can aspire.

Sandman chafes at restrictions that keep him from white spaces. Clay is more cautious. That combination of frustration and caution speaks to Strode's own experience. He knew well the careful path he had to tread, as

FIGURE 7.1. Strode as Holmes sweeping in front of the titular Cotton Club (Francis Ford Coppola, 1984). Screenshot.

an athlete and as an actor. As a football player, Strode was always paired with Kenny Washington when the team traveled so that they would each have a roommate when they had to find lodgings separate from the rest of the team, and they carefully avoided dancing with or speaking to white women. Strode recalled, having read about lynchings in Black newspapers, "If I saw Kenny looking at a white girl, I'd yell out, 'TO THE TREES!'" (Strode and Young 1990, 21). They played on a team with white players, cheered on by white crowds, but had to temper their ambitions and check themselves constantly if they socialized in white spaces. Every step carried danger with it. Strode's most famous starring role dramatized the worst-case scenario. In *Sergeant Rutledge*, Braxton Rutledge had to sit silently at the mercy of an all-white court martial, dependent on a white lawyer to prove him innocent of raping and murdering a young white woman. Innocence was almost incidental to the affront of taking a Black man's word over that of a white man. *The Cotton Club* is suffused with that menacing specter of history, codified by segregation, in which crossing an invisible line can lead to humiliation or worse.

One of *The Cotton Club*'s structuring motifs involves opening doors, having doors opened, crossing thresholds, ascending and descending stairs, and being denied entry. Holmes's job is to open the door, specifically for white people. Nearly halfway into the film, a second scene frames

Holmes from a high angle, looking down on the entrance to the club, as a line of fancy cars waits. Holmes is again shot from his back, opening car doors and ushering patrons into the club. In a third scene, another low-angle shot of Holmes sweeping the sidewalk reveals Strode's face for the first time. Dixie walks up, greets Holmes, and asks if the club owner, Owney Madden (Bob Hoskins), is upstairs. "Yeah, he's in," replies Holmes, a wooden smile on his face. He is friendly with Dixie, but not at ease in the way he is with the Williams brothers. Dixie bounds up the very stairs from which, a few scenes earlier, Sandman was barred, threatened, and sent to the alleyway service entrance by the racist club manager.

In Strode's final scene, late in the film, Dutch is forcibly dragged down the stairs and thrown out of the club, and Holmes can be seen at the edge of the frame, trying to stay out of the way. There is a knowing irony in the film's motif of access and obstruction, positioning Strode as a gatekeeper who caters to whites, given that, by virtue of his career, Strode opened doors for so many Black athletes and actors who followed him. Can we think of Jim Brown, Fred Williamson, Rosey Grier, Bubba Smith, Kareem Abdul-Jabbar, even Dwayne Johnson, without also thinking of Strode?

The Cotton Club was panned upon its initial release in 1984 and failed at the box office, and Coppola was vocal about his frustrations with producers who altered his cut of the film.[4] *The Cotton Club Encore* restores musical numbers and much of the storyline of the film's Black characters (though Dixie remains the primary character). The new edit also includes more dialogue scenes for Holmes, who is elevated to a full-fledged supporting character.

In *Encore*, Holmes has a central role in the opening scene. The film begins with the camera at a high angle, looking down on Holmes, who is opening a car door for a couple. The camera begins descending to street level in front of the Cotton Club as Holmes stops the couple and says, "This lady looks like a colored lady to me." The man protests that she is from Barcelona as Dixie enters the shot. The camera begins to track behind Dixie and stops as he pauses to watch the exchange between Holmes and the couple. Holmes replies to the man, "Well, don't they have colored folks in

4. In an interview on the 2019 *Encore* Blu-ray release, Coppola confirmed that the producers were uncomfortable with the number of scenes focused on the Black characters, fearing it would alienate their primarily white target audience.

Barcelona? I'm sorry." Offended, the couple walk off in a huff. Rather than shooting Strode from behind, as in the theatrical edit, the film cuts to a two-shot of Dixie and Holmes together. Dixie says, "Tell me something, Holmes. What're you doing hustlin' for the ofays here?" He replies, "The ofays pays, man. Who you workin' for?" He pats Dixie on the chest as he speaks. Sandman enters the shot and talks with them about placing bets on the numbers. This opening scene establishes a long-standing relationship between Dixie and Sandman, and a much closer bond between Holmes and Dixie. Significantly, in this version of the film, not only does Holmes open doors for white patrons but also actively bars Black people from the club. There is irony here, as later in life Strode was characterized as somewhat reactionary in terms of his own views on race. As Frank Manchel writes, Strode "had tremendous pride in his ethnic heritage and in his personal achievements, but he had great difficulty in reconciling his deeply held assimilationist views with those of current black [*sic*] activists" (Manchel and Strode 1995, 39). The fact that Strode as Holmes takes "ofays" money to bar Black patrons from the club may be an oblique reference.[5]

The *Encore* edit deepens and complicates the relationships among Holmes, Dixie, and the Williams brothers and puts Holmes and the Williamses in contrast. As in the theatrical edit, *Encore* includes the scene of Holmes sweeping in front of the club and asking the Williams brothers about their audition. After they talk, the brothers start to leave, but Sandman sees Lila Rose walking toward the entrance and turns to come back to the club. She rebuffs his advances and goes through the front door and up the stairs—again, the motif of ascending and descending stairs. Sandman impulsively opens the door and starts to follow, Holmes calls out, "That Cotton Club lady pushed you over the cliff." "Yeah," replies Sandman. "I'm gonna climb back up." Holmes calls out off camera, bemusedly, "I'll see you later, man." Sandman runs up the stairs and into the rehearsal space, where the club manager expels him and bars him from entering through the front entrance. Though the sequence is the same as the theatrical edit, it takes on deeper resonance in context with Holmes's additional opening scene. Holmes navigates segregated America, working in menial

5. One of Strode's interview responses used to illustrate his supposed reactionary view was, "I'm tired of this black, black, black business. . . . Me, I don't care. If the money is right, I'll play Mickey Mouse" (quoted in Manchel and Strode 1995, 39).

jobs while maintaining his dignity as best he can. "The ofays pays, man." Whatever anger or cynicism he may feel, he does not express it to Dixie. The younger Sandman, on the other hand, impatient with racist barriers, is willing to take risks to bypass them. Holmes does what he has to do, at times regretfully, but he eschews outward displays of frustration and risk-taking. There is greater irony in this, Coppola's more nuanced depiction of Strode-as-Holmes.[6] Driving home the ambivalence of Holmes's role as a gatekeeper, another shot shows him letting patrons into the Cotton Club just before Lila Rose (Lonette McKee) sings "Stormy Weather."

"People Forget Their Past. They Forget the Truth. But Pictures Don't Lie": *Posse* and *The Quick and the Dead*

Posse bookends Strode as the Storyteller speaking over the opening credits and in an epilogue, along with footage of Western race films which are incorporated in a montage during the end credits. In linking him to these films, specifically made with Black casts for Black audiences, Van Peebles crystallizes an extratextual persona for Strode. He is a gateway to—indeed an icon of—hidden histories. Strode's first uncredited film appearance was in the World War II film *Sundown* (Henry Hathaway, 1941). It was the first of many such uncredited appearances. As he put it, "Because of my mixed background I could play anyone from the third world. I played natives in the old jungle pictures; I fought Tarzan to the death. They stuck a pigtail on me for *Genghis Khan*, and slanted my eyes and made me Chinese in *Seven Women*, and I could play all the Indians" (Strode and Young 1990, 5–6). He got a small break when Cecil B. DeMille elevated him from a nameless slave character to the King of Ethiopia in *The Ten Commandments* (1956).[7] This led to larger supporting roles and a big break with *Pork Chop Hill* (Lewis Milestone, 1959). Strode plays Franklin, an infantry

6. Strode recounts visiting several clubs in Los Angeles as a young man, in particular Club Alabam, which he describes as the West Coast equivalent to New York City's Cotton Club (Strode and Young 1990, 22).
7. Strode later wrote that he was reluctant to take the role, because the background slave guaranteed five weeks pay, while the King of Ethiopia only guaranteed one. Happily, Strode was able to keep the slave role and get paid for both, because DeMille could not tell that Strode in the different makeup and costumes was the same actor (Strode and Young 1990, 185–88).

private serving in the last days of the Korean War who wants to desert his company rather than die in a suicide mission. John Ford was impressed with his performance and cast him in *Sergeant Rutledge* (1960).[8] Warner Bros. pressured Ford to cast better known Black actors Sidney Poitier or Harry Belafonte, but he refused, saying, "They aren't tough enough!" (McBride 2001, 607). From then on, Strode mostly appeared in Westerns, and became indelibly associated with the genre and with Ford, who cast him in *Two Rode Together* (1961), *The Man Who Shot Liberty Valance* (1962), and *Seven Women* (1966). Seeing Strode in the opening scene of *Posse* brings all his Westerns into the moment; as he muses on the Old West, cinematic memories of Strode as a Buffalo Soldier, an Indian warrior, a gunman, and a scout swirl around him.

The film's opening credits play on the left side of a long shot while Strode sits in profile at a desk on the right and hefts a pistol. Light beams around his head and then drapes him in shadow. The Storyteller begins to speak, and the camera tilts from a close-up of his face down to the gun. Shots of Strode then alternate with a montage sequence of photos of Black and Indigenous people in the Old West: "Colt .45, single shot. You had to cock it every time you shot. It's called a peacemaker, but I haven't seen much peace that it brought. . . . History's a funny thing. They got us believing Columbus discovered America, and the Indians were already here." The racist portrayal of Indigenous characters in Hollywood cinema is well documented, their characters generally ranging from bloodthirsty, shrieking hordes, as in *Stagecoach* (John Ford, 1939), to reductive "noble savages"—for example, in *Broken Arrow* (Delbert Daves, 1950). Strode's place in cinema history is complicated in part due to his Black and Indigenous heritage. When Strode wrestled in Canada, a promoter asked him why he did not tout this aspect of his identity. Strode replied, "If I advertise I'm an Indian, the Black people will figure I'm putting them down. The Indians already know. Let's just leave it at that." He went on, "That's what being a breed does to you" (Strode and Young 1990, 177). He felt the weight of representing Black people, while at the same time he chafed at

8. Strode had met Ford several times while he played college football. Ford supported two Hawaiian players at UCLA whose family he had gotten to know while vacationing in Hawaii. Later, when Strode married the Hawaiian Princess Luukialuana (Luana) Kalaeloa, by coincidence Ford had also known her family (Strode and Young 1990, 76, 198).

some of the insularity in his own Black community, where many disapproved of his marriage to a Hawaiian (114–17). Certainly, most white film reviewers at the time—and even contemporary film scholars—have elided Strode's specific racial heritage. Ken Nolley, for example, approvingly cites Richard Maltby's analysis of what Nolley called racist content in John Ford's work, particularly non-Indigenous actors portraying Indigenous characters: "[Maltby] goes on to point out that things get more complex when the non-Indian actor is black, as in Woody Strode's impersonation of Stone Calf in *Two Rode Together*" ([1961] 1998, 79). Strode's heritage certainly impacted some casting decisions. Strode recalled a meeting with Sam Peckinpah when he was considered for a role in *Major Dundee* (1965). Peckinpah rejected him, saying, "The problem I'm having is that you aren't really a Negro. You're a mongrel." Strode simmered with anger over Peckinpah's goading. He later wrote, "After being colored for fifty years, I wasn't black enough to play a Negro" (Strode and Young 1990, 221).

The historical realities of Manifest Destiny complicated matters further, as Black people moving westward after the Civil War often had uneasy relations with Indigenous peoples into whose territories they were settling. Strode was considered Black by white society, but he was mixed in Black communities. He was therefore uniquely marked by the legacy of chattel enslavement and Indigenous genocide, a legacy that underscores his aged and rumbling delivery of his monologue in *Posse*. The Storyteller continues (figure 7.2):

> There's one thing about time. No matter how much or how little passes, it changes, see. People forget their past, they forget the truth. The pictures don't lie. . . . See people forget too that almost one out of every three cowboys was Black. Because when the slaves were freed, a lot of them headed out West, built their own towns. Shit, they didn't have much choice! In fact, over half of the original settlers of Los Angeles were Black. But, for some reason, we never hear their stories.

In fact, this is Strode's story. According to family lore, his great-grandfather escaped a plantation and married into a Creek tribe, and his grandmother was a full Blackfoot. His father moved to Los Angeles from Louisiana in 1900 "to escape the racial pressure" (Strode and Young 1990, 1–2). This hidden history is Strode's own (figure 7.2).

FIGURE 7.2. Strode as the Storyteller in *Posse* (Mario Van Peebles, 1993). Screenshot.

Posse ends by revealing that a small boy who survives a climactic battle in which one of those Black towns gets burned to the ground is in fact the Storyteller, who has been recounting his tale of Black cowboys to a trio of interviewers. The film fades out on Strode looking at a picture of the titular posse. As the end title music begins, text is superimposed on the photo: "The majority of Black towns were destroyed. . . . Often intimidated or lynched if they tried to own property, and discouraged from educating themselves, most of the early Black settlers were successfully kept from power. . . . Although ignored by Hollywood and most history books, the memory of the more than 8,000 Black cowboys that roamed the early West lives on." The credits roll over the hip-hop song "The Posse," by Tragedy Khadafi. Khadafi's lyrics describe Black people in the Old West, and the song incorporates samples from Ennio Morricone's score to *The Good, the Bad, and the Ugly* (Sergio Leone, 1966). Scenes from *Posse* are intercut with scenes from *The Bronze Buckaroo* and *Harlem Rides the Range* (both Richard C. Khan, 1939), two race films, Westerns starring all-Black casts. The credits then cut to an iconic shot of Strode from *Once upon a Time in the West*. The editing cleverly mixes real history with Hollywood history and asks cinephiles to consider their complicity in the whitewashed mythology of the Old West as portrayed in Hollywood Westerns.

It is fitting that Strode's final role in *The Quick and the Dead* (Sam Raimi, 1995) once again reveals a hidden history of Black people in the

West in another otherwise white Western. He plays the role of the undertaker in a town called Redemption. Whereas *The Cotton Club* laments racial inequity and celebrates Black music and dance, and *Posse* is a political film filled with righteous anger, *The Quick and the Dead* is a pastiche of various Hollywood and Spaghetti Western tropes and references. Strode has only one line, which comes just after the title sequence, as Ellen (Sharon Stone) rides into the town of Redemption. Strode's character, Charlie Moonlight, emerges from the left side of the shot, from behind a coffin he is hammering together. Wearing a black coat and hat, he grins up at her and calls out, "Five-foot-eight, am I right? Ha, I ain't never wrong!" This bit of gallows humor, as it were, speaks to yet another gatekeeping aspect of his role. Here he stands smiling at the border of the beyond. But he also reminds us of a history of death, of the Old West, of Black towns, of the Indigenous continent pre-European conquest. Subsequent scenes feature Strode in the background, standing in crowds watching shootouts, or at the edge of an interaction between lead characters, observing, doing bits of business with his hat or sanding a coffin. He is the sole Black presence, a smiling revenant of dead Black cowboys and soldiers (figure 7.3).[9]

Seeing Strode next to a coffin in *The Quick and the Dead* is reminiscent of Strode as Pompey, sitting in wake by the coffin of Tom Doniphon (John Wayne) in *The Man Who Shot Liberty Valance* (John Ford, 1962). Just a decade later, Strode did the same for Ford himself, sitting at his bedside, rationing his alcohol, and reading books together when he was ill. Strode was watching over Ford when he died in 1973, and, with Ford's son and sister, he draped him with an American flag and waited for the coroner (Eyman 1999, 557; Strode and Young 1990, 215–19, 249): Ford, the great mythologizer of America, who gave Strode what he considered the role of his life in *Sergeant Rutledge*, but who was unable to cast him as the Indigenous chief Little Wolf in *Cheyenne Autumn* (1964) because the producers insisted on Ricardo Montalbán.

Doorman, storyteller, undertaker. Cinephiles encountering Woody Strode in his later years see a synecdoche of Hollywood's troubled

9. There is one Indigenous character, Spotted Horse, played by the Lakota actor Jonothon Gill. Spotted Horse is a drunken gunman who, legend has it, cannot be killed by a bullet. He is eventually killed, but it takes several bullets.

FIGURE 7.3. Strode as Charlie Moonlight in *The Quick and the Dead* (Sam Raimi, 1995). Screenshot.

representation of history, the facts behind the legends. In a scene in *The Man Who Shot Liberty Valance* Ransom Stoddard (James Stewart) is teaching in the schoolhouse. Pompey sits with the children, and Stoddard asks him to recite the preamble of the Declaration of Independence. He stumbles on "self-evident, that . . . uh . . . that . . ." Stoddard, somewhat patronizingly, finishes for him. "That all men are created equal. That's fine, Pompey." Pompey looks up, his face in full close-up, and says, "I knew that, Mr. Rance, but I just plumb forgot it." Contrast that line with Strode's anecdote, early in his football career, of telling Kenny Washington, "Thank God we thought we were equal."[10] Pompey, the recently freed man and now manservant, occasionally forgot that he was equal in the revolutionary language of the Declaration of Independence. Strode never did.

10. Strode may finally be getting some deserved recognition as an actor. The Museum of the Moving Image in Astoria, New York, hosted a series "The Legend of Woody Strode" (February 11–March 6, 2022). The series screened *Pork Chop Hill*, *Tarzan's Fight for Life* (H. Bruce Humberstone, 1958); *The Last Voyage* (Andrew L. Stone, 1960); *Sergeant Rutledge*; *The Man Who Shot Liberty Valance*; *Once upon a Time in the West*; *Black Jesus* (*Seduta alla sua destra*, Valerio Zurlini, 1968); *The Professionals*; *Keoma* (Enzo Castelleri, 1976); and *Posse*.

Works Cited

Coppola, Francis Ford, dir. 1984. *The Cotton Club*. Beverly Hills, CA: MGM, 2001. DVD.

Coppola, Francis Ford, dir. 2019. *The Cotton Club Encore*. Santa Monica, CA: Lionsgate, 2019. Blu-ray.

Eyman, Scott. 1999. *Print the Legend: The Life and Times of John Ford*. Simon & Schuster.

Manchel, Frank, and Woody Strode. 1995. "The Man Who Made the Stars Shine Brighter: An Interview with Woody Strode." *Black Scholar* 25 (2): 37–46.

McBride, Joseph. 2001. *Searching for John Ford: A Life*. St. Martin's.

Nolley, Ken. 1998. "The Representation of Conquest: John Ford and the Hollywood Indian, 1939–1964." In *Hollywood's Indian: The Portrayal of the Native American in Film*, edited by Peter C. Rollins and John E. O'Connor, 73–90. University Press of Kentucky.

Raimi, Sam, dir. 1995. *The Quick and the Dead*. Culver City, CA: Sony Pictures Home Entertainment, 2018. Blu-ray.

Strode, Woody, and Sam Young. 1990. *Goal Dust: The Warm and Candid Memoirs of a Pioneer Black Athlete and Actor*. Madison.

Van Peebles, Mario, dir. 1993. *Posse*. Arlington, VA: Sandpiper Pictures, 2021. Blu-ray.

White, Armond. 2022. "Coppola's *Cotton Club Encore* Remakes American Entertainment." *National Review*, October 23, 2022. https://www.nationalreview.com/2019/10/coppolas-cotton-club-encore-remakes-american-entertainment/.

PART III

DEPARTING FROM THE YOUNGER SCREEN SELF

8

FROM ANGEL TO DEMON

The Italian Stardom of Alida Valli

Gloria Monti

Filmmakers have often recruited stars from past eras, whose careers have faded and yet who remain immediately recognizable to viewers. Italian director Bernardo Bertolucci was a notable practitioner of this approach, which he described as a benevolent and protective aura arising from the past, as a reassuring presence on the set (Olensky [1996] 2000, 239). His predilection for bringing back aging stars who are living quotations of a long cinematic history led him to cast melodrama star Yvonne Sanson in *Il conformista* (*The Conformist*, 1970); White Telephone films diva Alida Valli in *Strategia del ragno* (*The Spider's Stratagem*, 1970), *Novecento* (*1900*, 1976), and *La luna* (*Luna*, 1979); heartthrob Massimo Girotti, and two memorable protagonists of *Roma città aperta* (*Open City*, Roberto Rossellini, 1945), Maria Michi and Giovanna Galletti, in *Ultimo tango a Parigi* (*Last Tango in Paris*, 1972); matinée idol Jean Marais in *Io ballo da sola* (*Stealing Beauty*, 1996); and, finally, Italy's first star, Francesca Bertini, in *1900* (Gili [1978] 2000, 131).

While the returning divas who populate Bertolucci's filmography often appear in cameo roles, Valli played a significant part in the two films I will analyze, *The Spider's Stratagem* and *1900*. I argue that by casting Valli against type, the director cited earlier aspects of her star image while challenging rather than echoing her roles as an ingénue. This strategy of revisiting cinema history, while paying homage to it, effectively demonstrates how much Valli's roles and performances have changed over the years. In *The Spider's Stratagem*, Valli's character, Draifa, exudes confidence and authoritativeness:

she walks barefoot and identifies herself as the deceased local hero's official mistress. Bertolucci claimed that Draifa possesses a witchlike nature, displaying sudden contradictions, mood changes, playfulness, and anger (Chaluja, Schadhauser, and Mingrone [1970] 2000, 55). In *1900*, Valli plays Signora Pioppi, a feisty widow who dies a horrific death when opposing the local fascist henchman. Shown in close-ups that make her look almost demonic, her character morphs from Draifa's spiritedness, as she saunters through her house, to a ruthless defender of her home. These performances contradict Valli's iconic characters from the White Telephone romantic comedies of the 1940s that crowned her Italy's sweetheart and a fashion icon.

White Telephone Films

The term "White Telephone" films (Telefoni Bianchi) describes a genre popular between 1930 and 1945 that depicts a petit-bourgeois, conflict-free world filled with white decor where all dreams come true.[1] These studio productions, inspired by Hollywood's screwball and romantic comedies, located in imaginary spaces and centering on female protagonists, are marked by escapist narratives devoid of any references to the historical reality of the period.[2]

In her first White Telephone film, *Mille lire al mese* (*A Thousand Lire a Month*, Max Neufeld, 1939), only eighteen years of age, Valli plays a young woman who travels to a fictitious Budapest with her fiancé. Mario Gromo wrote in the daily *La Stampa* in 1939 that she was the film's revelation—"a surprise, delightful, fresh, poignant, casual, sweet" (quoted in Pellizzari and Valentinetti 1995, 42)—and *Mille lire al mese* became her star vehicle.[3]

1. Telephones in Italy were usually black, and a white telephone was considered a luxury item and an object of desire. These films adopted a monochromatic approach to their production design: all furniture, lamps, pianos, windows were painted white (Bíspuri 2020, 29).
2. Masi and Lancia state: "The white telephone films characterized the cinema of the fascist regime with settings and stories that were false, detached from reality, lavish and ostentatious, oozing with romantic froth" (1997, 28). Casadio attaches an even stronger political significance to this genre. He claims that the filmic dreams manufactured by the Cinecittà studios amounted to fascist propaganda, aimed at making the Italian public forget the suffering, grief, and tragedies that they had to endure in their daily lives (1991, 13).
3. Translations from Italian to English are mine.

Following the release of the film, a Valli-style fashion became popular: Young women imitated her long hair with a soft wave on the side (Gundle 2013, 235; Pellizzari and Valentinetti 1995, 43; Sollima 1947).[4] It was at this point that many Italian viewers began to suffer from "acute Vallitis" (Sollima 1947). "Valli's photogenic qualities were exceptional," as Stephen Gundle points out (2013, 226), and her "aloof, remote air and a vaguely central European configuration of the facial features bore no comparison with the other actresses of the time," a look that made her seem more foreign than Italian (583).[5] Raffaele De Berti's lengthy description of Valli's face captures many of her most arresting and extraordinary qualities:

> A perfect oval formed of two highly symmetrical halves, her face had a very high and slightly convex forehead that captured and made the light slide off it; her cheekbones were high and well defined, which, further underlined by make-up, created an undulating outline owing to the shadows cast on the lower half of her face. Lastly, we must not forget the long, slightly feline shape of her eyes . . . and their light colour, forming a point of attention in the morphology of her face. (2016, 22)

Valli's subsequent work with Neufeld confirmed her status as a box-office success.[6] She was mostly cast as sweet and simple characters: In *Ballo al castello* (*Ball at the Castle*, 1939), Valli plays a ballerina who is mistaken for a crown prince's lover; in *Assenza ingiustificata* (*Her First Love*, 1939), she plays a young wife who is unjustly suspected of infidelity; in *Taverna rossa* (*Red Tavern*, 1940), she plays a girl who marries a count after various misadventures and mistaken identities; in *La prima donna*

4. Gundle asserts that young women copied Valli's Veronica Lake–style parting of the hair. But Lake's peek-a-boo hairstyle became fashionable with the release of the film *I Wanted Wings* (Mitchell Leisen, 1941), two years after *Mille lire al mese*. Valli could not have been inspired by Lake (Gundle 2013, 235). As Sollima (1947) comments, the Valli-style hairdos preceded Veronica Lake's blond appearance on the Italian screens by a few years.

5. Costume designer Piero Tosi, who dressed Valli in *Senso* (*The Wanton Countess*, Luchino Visconti, 1954), remarks: "Photogenia is beauty, but especially the gaze. When the gaze reaches the film viewer, that is photogenia" (*Alida Valli: In Her Own Words*).

6. At the height of her stardom, Valli received more than three thousand fan letters a week (Vitella 2016, 95).

che passa (*The First Woman Who Passes*, 1940), she plays a young woman who is wrongly accused of being seduced by a duke. Ernesto G. Laura claims that these repeated roles of the ingénue did not do her justice because she possessed a multi-faceted personality capable of portraying many different characters (1979, 11).

Valli then expanded her acting repertoire and performed her most memorable dramatic roles to date, which earned her both critical acclaim and commercial success. In *Piccolo mondo antico* (*Old Fashioned World*, Mario Soldati, 1941), she plays a mother devastated by her daughter's death. Scholars argued this "role afforded her to display shades of introspection, stoicism, and even desperation" (Gundle 2012, 563), describing the performance as one "of subtle charm, reserved, devoid of prima donna exaggeration" (Laura 1979, 12). Valli acknowledged that with this film she felt the very first emotions of her career (Cristalli 1990, 8) and discovered the joy of acting (Verdesca 2020). She won the award for Best Actress at the 1941 Venice Film Festival for this role. In *Noi vivi* and *Addio Kira!* (Goffredo Alessandrini, 1942) Valli plays a self-sacrificing woman who gives herself to a man she does not love in order to secure money to pay for a cure for her true love's failing health.[7] Gundle writes: "Her eyes and face convey every shade of the inner torment of a woman. Never was melancholy made so compelling" (2013, 239; see figure 8.1).

Pellizzari and Valentinetti comment: "A beautiful—the most beautiful—Alida Valli, truly extraordinary in her role. Her eyes are boundless: romantic, languid, dreamy, but also anguished, desperate, lost" (1995, 86–87). Valli used her eyes—already remarked upon, light, long, slightly feline shaped, to convey both the lightheartedness of comedy and the desolation of tragedy. As had happened with *Mille lire al mese*, another Valli-style fashion became popular: the beret Kira wears (87).[8]

7. These two films were subsequently released in the US market in 1986 as a single film, *We the Living*.

8. The peak of Valli's success was between 1939 and 1943, ending with the Allied bombings of Rome that destroyed the Cinecittà studios, the armistice with the Allies, the German occupation, and a civil war. The Italian Social Republic, a puppet state led by Benito Mussolini and controlled by the Germans, was formed in the north, and a new studio, Cinevillaggio, was built in Venice. Valli refused to relocate and remained in Rome, despite receiving many offers from Fascist Party officers. She made four more films between 1944 and 1946, but her stardom had waned.

FIGURE 8.1. Alida Valli in *We the Living* (Goffredo Alessandrini, 1942). Screenshot.

Postwar Decline

The advent of Neorealism represented an uncompromising response to the escapism of the White Telephone films.[9] There was no space for Valli in this new filmic world that discarded glamour and created the image of the reverse-diva embodied by Anna Magnani in *Roma città aperta* (*Open City*, Roberto Rossellini, 1945) (Marcus 1986, 38). In 1995 Pellizzari and Valentinetti commented that "Valli suffered, more than anyone else, the rejection of stardom that Neorealism embraced, recruiting [actors] from the street, asking them to play themselves" (quoted in Gundle 2012, 566). She felt alien to Neorealism, declaring to journalist Sandro Cova in 1954, "Thinking again about the Neorealist films, what part could I have played? I don't see myself as a woman of the people, peasant, or pizza girl and I don't think the audience would have accepted me in those guises" (quoted in Gundle 2012, 580). At the age of twenty-five and after twenty-nine films, Valli signed a contract with producer David O. Selznick and left for Hollywood, where she enjoyed a brief spell of international success and

9. For further reading on Neorealism, see Christopher Wagstaff, *Italian Neorealist Cinema: An Aesthetic Approach* (University of Toronto Press, 2007); Mark Shiel, *Italian Neorealism: Rebuilding the Cinematic City* (Wallflower, 2006); and Marcus 1986.

appeared in canonical films such as *The Paradine Case* (Alfred Hitchcock, 1947) and *The Third Man* (Carol Reed, 1949).

Valli's stardom in her home country had faded by the time she returned to Italy in 1951. Her Hollywood experience was viewed less than kindly, as a waste of time (Pellizzari, Valentinetti 149–50), "erased almost entirely from the minds and memories of Italian spectators" (Gundle 2012, 582).[10] The poor distribution of her films did not help.[11] Valli belonged to a bygone era, and the film industry had moved on. The Italian cinema of the 1950s, like its Hollywood counterpart, thrived on what Gaylyn Studlar describes as "mammary madness," citing the voluptuous and hypersexualized femininity of Marilyn Monroe, Jayne Mansfield, Jane Russell, and Elizabeth Taylor (2013, 203). Valli did not share the physical appeal of popular stars like Sophia Loren, Gina Lollobrigida, or Silvana Mangano, and Italian cinema had very little to offer her, until she landed the lead role in *Senso* (*The Wanton Countess*), directed by auteur Luchino Visconti in 1954. But, regardless of her noteworthy performance, as "a free-thinking woman drawn into a murky adultery," Valli did not make another film for three years (Masi, Lancia 1997, 71).[12] She stated, with a mix of pride and bitterness, "I gave it my all when I played Contessa Serpieri, but despite the film's success my popularity did not return" (Pellizzari and Valentinetti 1995, 159). Then the opportunity to work with another auteur presented itself with *Il grido* (*The Cry*, Michelangelo Antonioni, 1957). Valli's

10. While in Hollywood Valli appeared on the cover of six Italian magazines, between 1947 and 1950: Two featured images from her films (*The Paradine Case* and *The Miracle of the Bells* [Irving Pichel, 1948]), and four included portraits of the star.

11. *The Third Man* was released in Italy two months after it was shown at the Cannes Film Festival, in September 1949; *The Paradine Case* was released in Italy in 1952, five years after it premiered in Los Angeles; *The Miracle of the Bells, Walk Softly, Stranger* (Robert Stevenson, 1950), and *The White Tower* (Ted Tezlaff, 1950) were released in 1951.

12. In 1954, Valli was involved a sex and drugs scandal surrounding a murder case: She provided an alibi for her lover who had been accused of homicide and was later acquitted. Her consequent "visibility" was not seen favorably by the press, the public, or film producers and had a negative effect on her film career. But she found a second career in the theater: In 1956 she made her debut and continued to work on the stage until 1995, alongside her return to the screen.

performance "conveys her pain, despair and emotional conflict in sharp, convincing style" (Weiler 1962). Even though she achieved critical success in these films, over the next ten years her home country seemed to have forgotten her. During this time, Valli worked predominantly in France, and also in Mexico. She admitted, "My name no longer thrills anybody" (Pellizzari and Valentinetti 1995, 242).

The Spider's Stratagem

In 1970, Bertolucci cast Valli as Draifa in *The Spider's Stratagem*, which signaled her return to the Italian screen in a role that challenged her earlier performances and renewed her celebrity after her stardom had dimmed for some thirty years.[13] Bertolucci recognized Valli's experience and status as a once great star by granting her the autonomy to make decisions about the film's style (*Alida Valli: In Her Own Words*).

Draifa sets the narrative in motion when she asks her dead lover's son to return to his hometown to investigate the father's murder, which occurred thirty years earlier. It is then that the young man discovers that his father's heroic antifascism and involvement in a plot—a stratagem—to assassinate Mussolini were both fabrications. In fact, the father turns out to have been a traitor who staged his own death and made it look like a murder carried out by the fascists in order to preserve the myth of his martyrdom.[14]

Valli makes an unsettling entrance in the film: Her appearance is heralded by the mention of her character's name, which is first articulated by the film's protagonist, Athos Magnani (Giulio Brogi, cast in the twin roles of father and son, both called Athos). After being asked about Draifa, a local resident of the town of Tara in the Po River Valley responds with a long pause before echoing the name, "Mmmm . . . Draifa!" This response acts as a

13. Pierini maintains that Valli was rediscovered by Bertolucci and his brother Giuseppe (2021, 122). Pellizzari and Valentinetti employ the same term, "rediscovery" (1995, 250). Falcinella posits that the film signaled Valli's comeback to the screen after a long absence from the limelight (2011, 80).

14. *The Spider's Stratagem* is a filmic adaptation of Jorge Luis Borges's 1944 short story "Tema del traidor y del héroe" ("Theme of the Traitor and the Hero"). A statue of Athos Magnani in the town's square displays a plaque that reads: "A hero cowardly murdered by fascist bullets."

warning.[15] It also provides an element of excitement before Valli makes her appearance onscreen standing underneath a colonnade. A star's entrance in a film is always heavily loaded and often features a build-up to anticipate her first image. Moreover, when a star enters a comeback film, this moment acquires an even greater importance—the anticipated desire to see a major star who has been out of the spotlight for some time is thus maximized. As Draifa begins to walk barefoot, the camera follows her in a lateral tracking shot. Although she sees Athos, she ignores him and walks offscreen, leaving the young man to trail behind in pursuit. She stops when he asks her name, but even then she does not turn around to face him. Instead, she faces the camera, which lingers to fix her image in the audiences' minds. Even in a long shot, her mischievous smile can be clearly discerned. Then she walks off toward the entrance of her house. It is only when she stops again that she finally turns to face her interlocutor. She then takes his hand and invites him inside. "Come, don't be afraid," she says ominously, but there is nothing reassuring about this remark. Given her peculiar behavior up until this point, anything could happen next. Yet, surprisingly, their visit poses no threat to the son and instead provides an insight into her mercurial personality.

While informing the young Athos that she was his father's acknowledged lover, Draifa also reveals that she is more jealous than Othello. She is now presented in closer shots and with camera movements that follow her as she paces around the room. Draifa is unashamed of her reputation, which she has maintained even after her lover's death, "as if nothing had changed." She also insists that she was never afraid of the fascists who controlled the village during the dictatorship (1922–45), and that she refused to run away.[16] As they sit down for a meal, she asks Athos whether he

15. Bolongaro affirms that "the expression on the townspeople's faces when her name was mentioned strongly suggested that she has a central role to play in the drama" (2005, 79).

16. Gavin has made the unsubstantiated remark that Valli's casting in the role of Draifa establishes a link between her, the father Athos, and Mussolini, "given that [she] had been Mussolini's mistress for a brief period in the 1940s" (2013, 16). Pellizzari and Valentinetti counter this slanderous accusation: The anonymous letters that denounced Valli's romantic involvement with Mussolini (and with his two sons, his nephews, fascist and Nazi party officials, as well as Goebbels) were written by a convicted felon. Valli always denied these allegations (*Il romanzo di Alida Valli*, 119–20). This incident is also discussed in *Alida Valli: In Her Own Words*.

thinks she is a bit loony. Shortly after, she collapses on the floor, only to refuse assistance when regaining consciousness, finally kicking her guest out of the house. However, in a later scene she proposes that Athos move in with her. Draifa's actions here exhibit the contradictions and mood changes that Bertolucci identified, noted above.

Many of Valli's arresting and extraordinary facial features still survived in 1970, as the image from *The Spider's Stratagem* indicates (figure 8.2): the exceptional symmetry of her forty-nine-year-old face, as well as its high forehead, well-defined cheekbones, and the cat-like eyes. Also, what is so interesting about Draifa beyond her unsettling and unpredictable nature is that she clearly contradicts those characters and performances that confirmed Valli's status as a star in Italy in the 1940s. Pellizzari and Valentinetti describe her as "the girl who combines exterior daring with a repressed sense of duty, desire for distraction with possible repentance, cheeky enterprise with a basic respect for hierarchy, and who manages to skirt convention while coexisting with it" (quoted in Gundle 2013, 228). In contrast, Draifa's exterior daring is immune to a sense of duty—hence the fact that she does not wear shoes, in violation of what would have been regarded as proper manners. She also disregards hierarchy, having been able to stand firm against the fascist state rather than fleeing the country. Moreover, she does not conform to convention, being unrepentant for what many of the townsfolk would have regarded as her sins. This is evident

FIGURE 8.2. Alida Valli in *The Spider's Stratagem* (Bernardo Bertolucci, 1979). Screenshot.

in her proud identification as the lover of a married man, an attitude that once again defies the established social and moral values of the time and place.[17]

This role, described as "made-to-measure" (Masi and Lancia 1997, 72), earned Valli praise from both the critics and the public. Vincent Canby wrote in *The New York Times*: "Of the players, I particularly liked Alida Valli, as the aging mistress, a tough, lean lady who lives in a style fitting an impoverished princess, but who walks around, barefooted and untidy, like a peasant" (1973). Her acting is described as "flawless in her splendid maturity" (quoted in Pellizzari and Valentinetti 1995, 250). She was grateful to Bertolucci for giving her the opportunity to discard her former screen image and help her transform from star-defining ingénue to grand dame (Parkinson 2021).[18] She wrote in her diary that Bertolucci was the first one who liberated her from that old and mythical image that was crushing her (Verdesca 2020).

This collaboration with Bertolucci set Valli's career on a new course: She became the godmother of emerging Italian filmmakers and continued to work for the next twenty-five years. She was cast in roles as diverse as a sexually liberated woman who becomes involved with a young man (*L'occhio nel labirinto* [*Eye in the Labyrinth*], Mario Caiano, 1972); a stern nanny in a family possessed by the devil (*L'anticristo* [*The Antichrist*], Alberto De Martino, 1974); and a murderous teacher at a ballet school (*Suspiria* [*Dario Argento's Suspiria*], Dario Argento, 1977). But she was cast most frequently as a mother: mean and petty (*La prima notte di quiete* [*Indian Summer*], Valerio Zurlini, 1972); overbearing (*Diario di un italiano* [*Diary of an Italian*], Sergio Capogna, 1973); jealous beyond reason (*Lisa e il diavolo* [*Lisa and the Devil*], Mario Bava, 1972); and foul-mouthed (*Berlinguer ti voglio bene* [*Berlinguer: I Love You*], Giuseppe Bertolucci, 1977). These portrayals are certainly very dissimilar from the iconic image Valli created in the White Telephone films.

17. This was not the only time Valli played a character who is involved in an extramarital affair, but while the "murky adultery" of *The Wanton Countess* is presented with melodramatic tones and a disastrous outcome, the infidelity of *The Spider's Stratagem* remains free from tragedy. Draifa was the official mistress.

18. Porro remarks, "Who else in the history of cinema has ever been able to flip like this: from the naïve student of *Schoolgirl Diary* to the trashy commoner of *Berlinguer: I Love You*?" (2021, 31).

1900

In 1976, Bertolucci cast Valli again. In *1900*, she plays Signora Pioppi, whose husband was forced into a predatory mortgage by the town's blackshirt foreman, a member of the armed squads of Italian Fascists who wore black shirts as part of their uniform. Following her husband's death, and deeply in debt, Signora Pioppi has not been able to repay the mortgage and as a result has endured constant aggravation, intimidation, and violence from the foreman, whose goal is to take possession of her home.

One night, she notices the foreman and his lover standing by the gate of her house and asks them inside. Despite her friendly manner, the woman describes Signora Pioppi's behavior as erratic ("She's really crazy. First she cuts me dead in public, then invites us for a drink"). If her offer and apparent contradictory actions might echo Draifa's in *The Spider's Stratagem*, she soon reveals her true nature: Signora Pioppi's kind disposition is a strategy to lure the couple indoors, where she promptly locks them in the living room, much to their astonishment. Again, her behavior is described as absurd ("I told you, she's mad"). But she is not mad, nor is she "a bit loony," like Draifa. Signora Pioppi then delivers her vengeful lines standing guard by the door, in a close-up that accentuates her fiendish expression (figure 8.3), her celebrated romantic, languid, and dreamy eyes now turned evil: "You have to listen to me. You have to sign a paper saying that this house

FIGURE 8.3. Alida Valli in *1900* (Bernardo Bertolucci, 1976). Screenshot.

will remain mine. You got that mortgage from my husband with threats and political blackmail. You tormented the poor man until he died. But now I have you trapped and I won't let you go. You're not leaving here. This house is mine and it'll stay mine." The foreman manages to break down the door and in doing so crushes Signora Pioppi against the wall. To complete his murderous action, he then skewers her body on the gate spikes.

Signora Pioppi is a more conventional character than Draifa. She is a married woman who becomes a widow in contrast to Draifa's publicly acknowledged role as the lover of a married man. Both characters live alone in a mansion, Draifa as an independent woman secure in her possession while Signora Pioppi has been left behind by her husband's passing and is menaced with the loss of her home. Whereas Draifa exhibits assertiveness, Signora Pioppi is in a position of weakness: First she unsuccessfully pleads with the town's wealthy landowner for financial help, then she shares with the parish priest the suffering she endures from the foreman who threatens her. But the priest does not believe her and instead declares that blaming others is a sin. If Draifa's peculiar exuberance remains a constant trait of her behavior in *The Spider's Stratagem*, Signora Pioppi's desperate situation forces a change in her character. She eventually finds the resolve to exact revenge against her tormentor. Her actions are mistaken for insanity, even deemed hysterical by the foreman's lover. On the contrary, she very lucidly arranges a merciless plan, luring the foreman and his lover into her villa and imprisoning them with the intent of obtaining a release from the mortgage in order to keep the house. But she pays with her life for this attempt to restore justice. Her role is described as the powerful display of an agonizing tragedy (Laura 1991, 21). Valli stated: "I like roles where they kill me, spiritually or physically. In *1900*, I was murdered both ways" (Pellizzari and Valentinetti 1995, 255).

Valli proved that her Italian career did not end with the waning of her White Telephone films' popularity. She returned to the forefront of Italian cinema after surviving Neorealism, mammary madness, auteur cinema, and film roles abroad. She reinvented herself and demonstrated her versatility as a performer by playing a variety of characters, channeling and exposing a much darker side to her persona. She became an inspiration for young directors who discovered her talent and saw in her a new creative muse. Giuseppe Bertolucci, Bernardo's brother, who directed Valli in six films, aptly stated, "Alida Valli is the mother of all actresses" (*Alida Valli: In Her Own Words*).

Works Cited

Amelio, Gianni, dir. 1976. *Bertolucci secondo il cinema*. YouTube video, 1:03:46. Posted January 26, 2019. https://www.youtube.com/watch?v=x33s4sjdHxU.

Bertolucci, Bernardo, dir. 1970. *Strategia del ragno / The Spider's Stratagem*. Featuring Alida Valli. RAI Radiotelevisione Italiana. 1:35:41. https://www.raiplay.it/video/2013/08/Strategia-del-ragno-9ba040a7-9686-4bdb-9d56-865df936c9b8.html.

Bertolucci, Bernardo, dir. 1977. *Novecento / 1900*. Featuring Alida Valli. Saint Charles, IL: Olive Films, 2012. DVD.

Bíspuri, Ennio. 2020. *Il cinema dei telefoni bianchi*. Bulzoni.

Bolongaro, Eugenio. 2005. "Why Truth Matters: Ideology and Ethics in Bertolucci's *The Spider's Stratagem*." *Italian Culture* 23:71–96.

Canby, Vincent. 1973. "Screen: Tangled Motives: '*Spider's Stratagem*' at the New Yorker The Cast." *New York Times*, January 6, 1973.

Casadio, Gianfranco. 1991. "Il cinema dei telefoni bianchi." In *Telefoni Bianchi: Realtà e finzione nella società e nel cinema italiano degli anni Quaranta*, edited by Gianfranco Casadio, Ernesto G. Laura, and Filippo Cristiano, 11–30. Longo Editore.

Chaluja, Elias, Sebastian Schadhauser, and Gianna Mingrone. [1970] 2000. "A Conversation with Bertolucci." In *Bernardo Bertolucci Interviews*, edited by Fabien S. Gerard, Jefferson Kline, and Bruce Sklarew, 51–62. University of Mississippi Press.

Cristalli, Paola. 1990. "Alida dai cento volti." *Cineteca* 6 (2–3): 8–9.

De Berti, Raffaele. 2016. "Biografie di una 'stella di casa nostra': Alida Valli da giovinetta a mamma." *Bianco e Nero* 586 (77): 22.

Falcinella, Nicola. 2011. *Alida Valli: Gli occhi, il grido*. Le Mani.

Gavin, Dominic. 2013. "Myths of the Resistance and Bernardo Bertolucci's *Strategia del ragno*." *California Italian Studies* 4 (2): 1–29.

Gili, Jean. [1978] 2000. "Bernardo Bertolucci." In *Bernardo Bertolucci Interviews*, edited by Fabien Fabien S. Gerard, Jefferson Kline, and Bruce Sklarew, 108–33. University of Mississippi Press.

Gundle, Stephen. 2012. "Alida Valli in Hollywood: From Star of Fascist Cinema to 'Selznick Siren.'" *Historical Journal of Film, Radio, and Television* 32 (4): 559–87.

Gundle, Stephen. 2013. "The Photogenic Beauty: Alida Valli." In *Mussolini's Dream Factory: Film Stardom in Fascist Italy*, 224–43. Berghahn.

Kolker, Robert Phillip. 1985. *Bernardo Bertolucci*. Oxford University Press.

Lai, Sandro, dir. 2002. *Bernardo Bertolucci: A cosa serve il cinema? / Bernardo Bertolucci: Reflections on Cinema*. Saint Charles, IL: Olive Films, 2012. DVD.

Laura, Ernesto G. 1979. *Alida Valli*. Gremese Editore.

Maina, Giovanna. 2016. "Vallinferno: Interpretazioni di genere di una diva 'del passato.'" *Bianco e Nero* 586 (77): 79–91.

Marcus, Millicent. 1986. *Italian Film in the Light of Neorealism*. Princeton University Press.

Masi, Stefano, and Enrico Lancia. 1997. *Italian Movie Goddesses: Over 80 of the Greatest Women in Italian Cinema*. Gremese Editore.

Olensky, Allen. [1996] 2000. "Tiptoeing in Tuscany." In *Bernardo Bertolucci Interviews*, edited by Fabien S. Gerard, Jefferson Kline, and Bruce Sklarew, 235–40. University of Mississippi Press.

Parkinson, David. 2021. Review of *Alida Valli: In Her Own Words*. Parky at the Pictures, December 12, 2021. https://www.parkyatthepicures.com/post/parky-at-the-pictures-12-11-2021.

Pellizzari, Lorenzo, and Claudio M. Valentinetti. 1995. *Il romanzo di Alida Valli: Storie, film e altre apparizioni della signora del cinema italiano*. Garzanti.

Pierini, Mariapaola. 2021. "'Dare la parola a un cast di attrici.' *Segreti Segreti* e la recitazione del femminile tra storia italiana e memoria del cinema." In *Il dolce rumore della vita: Giuseppe Bertolucci tra cinema, teatro, televisione e poesia*, edited by Franco Prono and Gabriele Rigola, 117–29. Edizioni Cineteca di Bologna.

Porro, Maurizio. 2021. "Maria Altenburger probabilmente: Il lato oscuro di Alida Valli." *Cineforum*, no. 2:26–31.

Sarazani, Fabrizio. 1939. Review of *Mille lire al mese*. *Il Giornale d'Italia*, January 15, 1939.

Sollima, Sergio. 1947. "Le attrici del giorno: Alida Valli." *Rivista del Cinematografo* (May 1947), reprinted on cinematografo.it, April 21, 2021. https://www.cinematografo.it/news/alida-valli-secondo-sergio-sollima/.

Studlar, Gaylyn. 2013. *Precocious Charms: Stars Performing Girlhood in Classical Hollywood Cinema*. University of California Press.

Verdesca, Mimmo, dir. 2020. *Alida Valli: In Her Own Words*. Rome: Istituto Luce Cinecittà, 2021. DVD.

Vitella, Federico. 2016. "'Mia carissima Alida.' Le lettere degli ammiratori nell'Italia Mussoliniana." *Bianco e Nero* 586 (77): 92–114.

Weiler, A.h. 1962. "Screen: Antonioni's '*Il grido*' Arrives: '57 Film a Forerunner of '*L'Avventura*' Steve Cochran Enacts Quest for Love." *New York Times*, October 23, 1962.

9

AMITABH BACHCHAN'S REVIVED STAR TEXT IN BOLLYWOOD CINEMA

Sony Jalarajan Raj and Adith K. Suresh

The Indian popular film industry, known internationally as Bollywood, is home to big superstars who embody active masculine corporealities that define their larger-than-life star identities onscreen. Here, stars live in the realm of imagination, where their star text is constructed, historicized, and reproduced for a long time, thus extending the image of the star to multiple contexts that signify different aspects of stardom. The transformations a star has to undergo are crucial in deciding their fate. A star's identity that was established in a particular era is often threatened when circumstances change. In order to survive in a new era, stars adopt new vehicles to renegotiate themselves by either abandoning their past glory or carrying a different version of it to the present. Among the many Indian superstars, Amitabh Bachchan can be identified as a classic example of a surviving star.

With a career that spans more than five decades and two hundred movies, Amitabh Bachchan is considered one of the greatest actors in Indian cinema and a popular cultural icon. Famously endowed with titles such as "Star of the Millennium," "Big B," and "One-Man Industry," Bachchan's exceptional celebrity status as an actor, a producer, and a former politician in India is unparalleled, even expanding its impact to global levels and becoming a recognizable cinematic identity from the Asian diaspora. From the 1970s–1980s golden era that established him as the Indian "Angry Young Man" superstar persona to the short and failed political career surrounded by controversies and allegations of corruption, Bachchan's on- and offscreen performances have been an important subject for both public debates and critical discourses. After a semiretirement from acting, Bachchan revived his career in the 2000s, when he started to appear in films that reflect the identity of an "aging star."

The box-office hit *Mohabbatein* (*Love Stories*, Aditya Chopra, 2000) marked Bachchan's official return to Bollywood as an elder star. This chapter examines how *Mohabbatein* establishes itself as the comeback vehicle of Bachchan's revived career through which the faded star charisma of one of Bollywood's biggest stars is renegotiated. In the film, he plays the role of the "Angry Old Man," the traditional Hindu patriarchal figure, that resembles his past superstar image in a subversive way. The connection and contrast between a radical iconoclast who challenges a corrupt system and a stubborn conservative obsessed with the protection of traditional values reveal how Bachchan's comeback is more of a role reversal than an ingenious transformation. It proposes that if the Angry Young Man period of Bachchan's superstardom was a reaction to the sociopolitical insecurities of a traditional India, the comeback of Bachchan can be viewed as a reaction to a modern postliberalization India. This study argues that the star text of Bachchan's comeback reprises the fundamental quality of dissent with which his star iconography is defined and has evolved over time, and it has the ability to strategically change in accordance with other changing coordinates of stardom. This chapter analyzes how an aged Bachchan disrupts the natural order by departing from the position of his younger screen self, and how he adapts to maintain the essence of his former stardom in new contexts. It critically investigates how this role reversal commemorates his reception in a new-generation audience who perceives the revived cinematic spectacles of an old superstar in a new form that actively engages with the cinematic, cultural, and political ethos of the time.

The Aging Star

In his early years, Bachchan was known as the embodiment of the Angry Young Man, due to a series of action hero roles he played in popular movies of 1970s Bollywood. The Angry Young Man reflected a vibrant and hyperactive version of Bachchan's corporeality where recognizable body features such as his six-feet height and strong, lean body made him look like an alpha male iconoclast who wanted to disrupt the normative discourse of social order. Bachchan's earlier star image, therefore, set the archetype of a mighty social hero capable of transgressive acts that not only painted a picture of the social structure in which such a character type is accepted and celebrated but also became a new reference figure for younger audiences. The emotional outbursts of Bachchan's characters in films like *Zanjeer* (*Shackles*, Prakash Mehra, 1973); *Sholay* (*Embers*, Ramesh Sippy, 1975); and *Deewaar* (*The Wall*, Yash Chopra, 1975) established anger as a popular character trait that violated the typical romantic hero narratives of Bollywood. "As an actor, Amitabh's anger was never ugly. Other actors mix anger with arrogance. But Amitabh's anger was mixed with hurt and tears," stated Javed Akhtar, the writer of *Zanjeer*, the film that popularized Bachchan's image as the Angry Young Man (Kabir 1999, 88).

According to Richard Dyer, stars are the outcome of a range of discourses from which a specific image of the star is constructed, highlighted, and reproduced: "From the structured polysemy of the star's image certain meanings are selected in accord with the overriding conception of the character in the film" ([1979] 1998, 127). The type of stardom Bachchan encapsulates emerged from a generation rife with political turmoil and systemic inequalities. It was a period when India was heading toward modernity However, as a country haunted by its oppressive colonial past, traumas of Partition, internal insurgencies, and border conflicts, the complexities of Indian politics were too extreme, and finding easy solutions to social problems became difficult. In addition, the tensions between different cultures, traditional beliefs, and religious superstitions made it impossible for India to function in its role as the largest democracy in the world. When corrupt political leaders and bureaucratic officials controlled centralized power and nurtured injustice as the natural order, the population was the first to suffer. The Angry Young Man was the symbolic manifestation of the rebellious other that emerged from the imagination of the masses and their hope for sudden change through heroic action. The Angry Young Man films used the idea of "*virtuous anger*—a concept with the potential to emotionally reintegrate the disappointed and dispelled masses into a popular national ideology" to find commercial success (Rajamani 2012, 70). Bachchan's characters could single-handedly eradicate problems by eliminating antagonists, often beating them up or killing them at the climax of the film.

Since Bachchan's status as a rebellious hero in his younger years was integral to the construction of his star text, which allegorically resonated with the sociopolitical ethos of his time, the evolutionary transformation of Bachchan's aging star image depends on how this Angry Young Man prototype is renegotiated in a new phase. Stardom is a time-bound phenomenon that thrives on a particular image or phase of an actor's career, and the inevitable change in time forces the star to either abandon their former stardom to find a new one or revive it in new ways to appropriate the star identity to formats that are suitable to a changed scenario.

The aging star in this context is a concept with different meanings. It primarily refers to the image of an actor who has become literally too old and weak to compete with the more charismatic younger generation of actors; their star image has faded and become irrelevant to contemporary times. An aging/aged star is often identified as a "has-been," a pejorative term that emphasizes the past glory of an actor who is now lost or unacceptable. However, an aging star is also a veteran actor who is still present and available to play new roles that specifically demand their experience and skills. Bachchan's old man image started to dominate in the early 2000s, when he came back from a then supposedly failed career to a new phase of acting that required more of his contributions as a character actor than an action star.

The meaning of a star's image depends on the performance style they develop over a number of films through which the star is rendered familiar through their physical appearance (Dyer [1979] 1998, 142). When film actors become stars, the demarcation between the "star" and the "character" often collapses, so that the actor's performance is recognized for their star and cultural status as a known figure rather than for the character roles played on screen. For Paul McDonald, "the basic contradiction of film star acting" is formed by "the tension between story and show, or between the representation of character and the presentation of the star" (2012, 170). The fundamental difference between the character and the performance of the star is that a character is more confined within the narrative as an agent who specifically adapts to the requirements of the story while the star uses the narrative as a medium to showcase their stardom to a wide audience. If the marketability of a star is what defines star performance, the narrative's overall structure gives significance to character acting.

In the case of Bachchan, his Angry Young Man characters contributed to the development of his performance style as a star, and films were specifically made with the intention to market this particular image. However, when the repetitive reproductions of the Angry Young Man trope were no longer commercially successful, filmmakers started to use Bachchan's veteran actor image in their films. This marked a fundamental transformation in his acting approach that helped him replace the faded hyperactive and aggressive action star of yesteryear with new challenging character roles. This comeback produced a new star text for Bachchan that reflected the differences and similarities with his past stardom, renegotiated his position and role among a new era of film stars, and established his return as a captivating actor who has authority, relevance, and future.

The Return: *Mohabbatein* as a Comeback Vehicle

Bachchan's characters are adamant about the moral values they believe in, and their actions vehemently reveal the need for a higher social and cultural order that must replace the existing one. His Angry Young Man masculinity refers to the construction of the Bollywood hero as an agent who protects the law often by changing his identity from idealist to outlaw to cater to the public rage against the system (Chakravarty 2000, 216). In films like *Zanjeer*; *Adalat* (*Court*, Narendra Bedi, 1976); *Deewaar*; and *Trishul* (*Trident*, Yash Chopra, 1978), he plays the role of a national hero who upholds the notion of justice, for which he engages in violent action that shares the collective nationalistic sentiments of a generation of disillusioned masses (Kishore 2011, 3). One of the important aspects of Bachchan's "return" is the reproduction of this moralistic angle through which he reconstructs certain character types.

Mohabbatein was the biggest project that jump-started Bachchan's second film career. An instant blockbuster, it became one of the best examples of a typical Bollywood romantic drama that relies on the spectacles of song-and-dance, melodramatic dialogue, and over-the-top color and sonic aesthetics.[1] Director Aditya Chopra who established his name in Indian

1. The ability to create spectacles defines the popularity of Bollywood cinema among a large audience and their fan cultures. The stars of Indian popular cinema are objects of desire in these spectacles. According to Nair, "The [star] celebrities circulate in two ways—as a perpetual *spectacle* and as an *extended* celebrification. Celebrification and its spectacle is perhaps the core process, the DNA, of celebrity ecology" (2009, 68). The spectacles in *Mohabbatein* are controlled by Shah Rukh Khan, who, therefore, has more visibility in the film as a star than Bachchan.

popular cinema with *Dilwale Dulhania Le Jayenge* (*The Big-Hearted Will Take the Bride*, 1995), the film that brought Bollywood superstar Shah Rukh Khan his transnational stardom, uses the same tropes and themes in *Mohabbatein*. For instance, the narrative is centered around the sanctity of romantic love and its inevitable triumph at the end. In *Mohabbatein*, Bachchan plays the character of Narayan Shankar, the strict principal of Gurukul, a reputed all-boys college that follows the motto of "honor, tradition, and discipline." The narrative follows the conflict between Narayan Shankar and Raj Aryan Malhotra (Shah Rukh Khan), the newly appointed music teacher, who tries to challenge Shankar's conservative views on love and romantic relationships that, in the past, led to the tragic suicide of Shankar's daughter, Megha (Aishwarya Rai). It is revealed that Raj Aryan was a former student of Gurukul and was in love with Megha, a relationship Narayan Shankar opposed by evicting Aryan from Gurukul, thus resulting in the suicide of a heartbroken Megha. Tormented by the past, Narayan Shankar lives a secluded life dedicated to the protection of Gurukul's traditional values and legacy.

As Bachchan's comeback vehicle, *Mohabbatein* launches the aged star's image throughout the film's three-and-half-hour duration. Narayan Shankar is a fifty-five-year-old patriarchal authority figure with twenty-five years of experience who literally stands tall in front of everyone and controls everything with his commanding power. At the very beginning of the film, Bachchan's character stands near the river doing *sooryanamaskar*, the morning religious ritual of worshipping the sun, looking directly at the sun, chanting mantras, while the camera slowly approaches him from a distance. Suddenly he turns back and walks toward the camera in typical Bollywood hero introduction style with drums playing in the background. Now we are introduced to "the one and only Mr. Narayan Shankar," says one character in admiration and respect. In the very next scene, Bachchan is pictured against the background of a wall that has Gurukul's emblem, the shining sun, in which the sun's yellow spikes appear to project from behind his head, symbolically suggesting Bachchan's status as a demigod. Bachchan's character is introduced with medium-to-long shots, slow zoom-ins, close-ups, and low angles to establish his authority not only as a character but also as a veteran star who has been in show business for a long time.

Star images are characterized by "inconsistency, change and fluctuation," and whenever an aging star makes a comeback, factors like change in physical appearance are explicitly visible and they affect the previously established star appeal of the actor (Mayne 1993, 128). Bachchan's comeback in *Mohabbatein* also reflects this transformation in framing the character as a recognizable identity, but in new attire, form, and context. Before the audience starts to reminisce about the golden years of Bachchan's superstardom and tries to apply its signs to the aging yet charismatic body of the new Bachchan through Narayan Shankar, the film presents the aging star to a younger generation. Narayan Shankar reminds his new students who have just been admitted to Gurukul: "Tradition, honor, and discipline. These are the three pillars of Gurukul. These are the values with which we shape your future. Those who have gone before you have set very high standards for you. Today, all of them are successful men in their own respective fields. . . . Today, you have the opportunity to be part of this great lineage."

Here, the film introduces Bachchan's new image, the patriarchal father figure from the past while reminding the audience of how Bachchan as an actor is fit for his current role. When reintroducing someone "great" from the past, it is essential to point out how some fundamental aspects do not change when put to the test of time. Dyer observes that "stars represent typical ways of behaving, feeling and thinking in contemporary society, ways that have been socially, culturally, historically constructed" (2004, 15–16). The conservative attitude of Bachchan's character does not just define his new introduction but specifically reminds the viewer of the longevity and experience of a veteran actor. According to Susmita Dasgupta, Amitabh's new appearance in a new age reprises his identity as an "icon of the past" and "serves to provide a semblance of continuity and familiarity" (2006, 147). The central conflict in *Mohabbatein* emerges from this sense of continuity that challenges or is challenged by a new-era star like Shah Rukh Khan, who, a vulnerable and sensitive star in comparison with Bachchan, is observed to have restructured the male stardom in Hindi cinema (Gopinath 2018, 312).[2] David Chute observes that "it actually works for the

2. Shah Rukh Khan renegotiated stardom in the context of globalization. Khan's "comedy-laced and yet tear-jerking balance of modern life and traditional commitments" exemplifies a mode of transnational stardom where global modernity is understood as a "major transformation in the textures and sensations of everyday life" rather than as a category of social, political and economic structures (Meeuf and Raphael 2013, 6).

movie that Bachchan looks like a strange visitor from another era, the ne plus ultra of all the stern father figures his Vijay Angry Young Man characters rebelled against in the Seventies" (2005, 55). The "fight" between Narayan Shankar and Raj Aryan becomes the context in which the yesteryear stardom of Bachchan is remolded through Khan's star text.

The way *Mohabbatein* reintroduces Bachchan has much to do with his new role in cinema as a character actor rather than a star phenomenon. Since stars in cinema have the freedom to control the narrative in favor of their performative preferences, and characters are more bound to the narrative, Bachchan had to abandon his earlier star image as an action "all-rounder" to settle for his new one as the aging father who barely engages in action.[3] The popular template of Bollywood dramas relies on how spectacles are produced, mainly song-and-dance sequences that celebrate various emotional points in the narrative.[4] This cinematic extravaganza highlights the charismatic presence of a star whose involvement elevates the visual appeal in such scenes. *Mohabbatein* presents five extended song-and-dance sequences that deny Bachchan's character narrative space because he has become a strict old patriarch who resents youth and their energy. His role is that of an observer.

The film deliberately excludes Bachchan's Narayan Shankar from any situation that demonstrates the flexibility of a star actor. Instead, he is always introduced as a *rigid* figure because he embodies a character type who is limited in movement, expression, and action. However, the character of Shah Rukh Khan does the opposite, as the film allows his young body to represent an emotionally vulnerable romantic ideal against Bachchan's emotionally cold, traditional archetype. When Shankar meets Aryan for the first time, which is also Khan's introduction scene in the film, Aryan is playing the violin, an activity that disturbs Shankar because it explicitly challenges his rules of conduct. This difference in attitude is

3. Bachchan was an established all-rounder in producing spectacles in his Angry Young Man days, when he would engage in acrobatic action set pieces, song-and-dance sequences, and emotionally dramatic situations—a reflection of the star's highly active presence. In his comeback era he often became an observer of the spectacles performed by younger actors.

4. "Spectacles" refer to visually striking sequences—often exaggerated, overdramatic, and unrealistic—that create an extravaganza onscreen and that the audience can find visually and emotionally appealing. See Nair (2009, 69).

visible in every confrontation scene between Bachchan and Khan, where the young star engages in new activities, such as encouraging his students to pursue their desires and fall in love—transgressions in the eyes of the old star. It is apparent that the young star has more authority in the film than a comeback star.

Bachchan's image of the old man is the antithesis of the Angry Young Man in the past because he is in the presence of a new, young generation actor whose star value is already solidified in popular cinema. Bachchan's role in *Mohabbatein* is not that of a hero who can single-handedly solve everything on his own. Therefore, to maintain his star value, which is now compromised and needs new methods to be visible, Bachchan prefers an antagonistic stance that balances the other heroic star configurations. Bachchan continued this strategic renegotiation in the following years, in films such as *Ek Rishta: The Bond of Love* (*A Relationship: The Bond of Love*, Suneel Darshan, 2001); *Kabhie Khushi Khabhi Gham . . .* (*Sometimes There Is Joy, Sometimes There Is Sorrow . . .* , Karan Johar, 2001); and *Armaan* (*Desire*, Honey Irani, 2003). The aged Bachchan's actions do not rely on the authority of violence but constitute "a medley of emotions, song and dance, dialogues, and online entries and persona" that "help to construct and maintain his ongoing and aging stardom" (Dudrah 2021, 142).

Renegotiating Dissent: Bachchan's Role Reversal and the Revival of a Glorious Past

The box-office successes of films that depend on Bachchan's "stern, but loving patriarch" role in the twenty-first century prove that his identity as an old star still holds a certain power in the Bombay industry (Ganti 2004, 121). When stars return after taking a break from their career, they enter a new phase where they often consider role reversals to adapt to a new environment. Bachchan's role reversal, from an iconoclast to a conservative in modern cinema, is symbolic of the change in the social, political, and cultural ethos of contemporary India. According to Aparna Sharma, Bachchan recently renegotiated his star image with the neoliberal values of India, and the sustainability of his stardom has everything to do with his ability to align with contemporary dominant cultural and political attitudes (2016, 23). Similarly, Sreya Mitra argues that the new star persona of Bachchan is that of a "benevolent patriarch" who is vulnerable when his traditional beliefs are contested by modern aspirations; it delineates a shift from India's earlier socialist ideals to new, consumerist, neoliberal goals (2020, 63). In *Mohabbatein*, the shift from the Angry Young Man to an orthodox father figure represents this political change, as Mitra observes: "Bachchan's on-screen character is configured as the prototype of discipline, restraint, and order—encapsulating the self-imposed barriers of socialist India—while Khan's Raj Aryan is the harbinger of change, modernity, love, and uninhibited acceptance and openness, signifying the 'new' India, willing to explore and lay its claim on a global citizenship" (2020, 66).

India opened the doors to neoliberalization in 1991 with new economic policies, and the country prepared to utilize the possibilities of globalization and development. Parallel to this change, there emerged in India a revival of religious and nationalistic sentiments through which Hindu fundamentalism tried to grab political power by accusing Western influences of replacing Indian values. In response to this crucial change, new icons were created to influence people to go back to their "roots" and find an imagined glorious past to authenticate their national and cultural identity. This was a new context for Bollywood, to construct characters who defend the past; such portrayals uphold and revive political and historical formats of nationalism and religious fundamentalism through the glorification of traditional values and cultural practices. This was an opportunity for Bachchan to depart from his Angry Young Man films—in which his rebellious characters fight internal insurgencies—to find a new space to defend Indian values against Western agencies.

In *Mohabbatein*, Narayan Shankar is portrayed as a Hindu patriarch who strictly follows religious scriptures and rituals, which he also imposes on everyone else. It is not coincidental that Shankar is the principal of Gurukul, which refers to *gurukulam*, the ancient Indian educational system and a part of the history of Hindu philosophical lineage. In his opening speech, Narayan Shankar proclaims his preference for values such as *parambara* (tradition), *prathishta* (honor), and *anushasan* (discipline), which retained the pristine glory of Gurukul for the past twenty-five years, and frequently reminds Raj Aryan that he does not like *parivarthan* (change). Bachchan's comeback, in this sense, becomes symbolic of the comeback of a past and its continuation in the present. Therefore, Bachchan's star text, which was previously based on dissent, a quality epitomized in the onscreen image of the Angry Young Man, now renegotiates itself, reprising it in a new way, that is, redirecting it to dissent against the desecration of the past and its glory. This is revealed in a confrontational scene with Raj Aryan where Narayan Shankar states:

> You have given a fifty-five-year-old tired man a reason to fight again. He has to prove all over again that for twenty-five years whatever he has stood for and believed in still holds true. You were right about me, Mr. Aryan. Like you, even I love challenges. So, now you do what you have to, and I'll do what I have been doing for the last twenty-five years. The foundation of this structure is so strong that no Raj Aryan with a violin in his hand and a smile on his face will ever dare to walk in here to change things around. Never, Mr. Raj Aryan. Never.

These words romanticize the glory of both Bachchan's past stardom and India's cultural past and announce that Raj Aryan, the newcomer as an adversary, will not be able to destroy what has been there for a long time. Narayan Shankar is happy that his intervention brought back the "winds of Gurukul" to normal, which, for years, "have been blowing from the East" but "recently began to blow from the West." The insinuation here is obvious: The actions of Shankar and Aryan ultimately signify the conflict between Eastern and Western ideologies. This is true even at the end of the film, where Narayan Shankar becomes guilty of his own actions, admits his past mistakes, and starts to make amends with Raj Aryan by naming Aryan as the new principal of Gurukul. Here, the "change" does not negate any of the fundamentals through which Bachchan reconstructed his authoritative role. Raj Aryan does not replace Narayan Shankar at the end but, on the contrary, literally touches his feet to seek blessings in the traditional Indian way. The film emphasizes that the comeback of Amitabh Bachchan ultimately means an essential revival of the past and its continuation in the image of an iconic star who demands nothing but respect and validation.

Works Cited

Chakravarty, Sumita S. 2000. "Fragmenting the Nation: Images of Terrorism in Indian Popular Cinema." In *Cinema and Nation*, edited by Mette Hjort and Scott MacKenzie, 209–23. Routledge.

Chopra, Aditya, dir. 2000. *Mohabbatein / Love Stories*. Mumbai: Yash Raj Films. DVD.

Chute, David. 2005. "The Big B: The Rise and Fall and Rebirth of Bollywood Superstar Amitabh Bachchan." *Film Comment* 41 (2): 50–52, 54–56.

Dasgupta, Susmita. 2006. *Amitabh: The Making of a Superstar*. Penguin.

Dudrah, Rajinder. 2021. "The Geri-Actions of the Aging Amitabh Bachchan." *Journal of Popular Film and Television* 49 (3): 136–43.

Dyer, Richard. [1979] 1998. *Stars*. British Film Institute.

Dyer, Richard. 2004. *Heavenly Bodies: Film Stars and Society*. Routledge.

Ganti, Tejaswini. 2004. *Bollywood: A Guidebook to Popular Hindi Cinema*. Routledge.

Gopinath, Praseeda. "'A Feeling You Cannot Resist': Shah Rukh Khan, Affect, and the Re-Scripting of Male Stardom in Hindi Cinema." *Celebrity Studies* 9 (3): 307–25.

Kabir, Nasreen Muni. 1999. *Talking Pictures: Conversations on Hindi Cinema with Javed Akhtar*. Oxford University Press.

Kishore, Vikrant. 2011. "Amitabh Bachchan: From 'Angry Young Man' to 'Flirtatious Old Man': Changing Representations of Masculinity in Bollywood." *International Journal of Communication Development* 1 (1): 3–9.

Mayne, Judith. 1993. *Cinema and Spectatorship*. Routledge.

McDonald, Paul. 2012. "Story and Show: The Basic Contradiction of Film Star Acting." In *Theorizing Film Acting*, edited by Aaron Taylor, 169–83. Routledge.

Meeuf, Russell, and Raphael Raphael. 2013. "Introduction." In *Transnational Stardom: International Celebrity in Film and Popular Culture*, edited by Russell Meeuf and Raphael Raphael, 1–16. Palgrave Macmillan.

Mitra, Sreya. 2020. "From 'Angry Young Man' to 'Benevolent Patriarch': Amitabh Bachchan, Bollywood Stardom, and the Remaking of Post Liberalization India." *South Asian Popular Culture* 18 (1): 63–77.

Nair, Pramod K. 2009. *Seeing Stars: Spectacle, Society and Celebrity Culture*. Sage.

Rajamani, Imke. 2012. "Pictures, Emotions, Conceptual Change: Anger in Popular Hindi Cinema." *Contributions to the History of Concepts* 7 (2): 52–77.

Sharma, Aparna. 2016. "From Angry Young Man to Icon of Neo-Liberal India: Extra-Cinematic Strategies That Make Amitabh Bachchan India's Lasting Super-Star." In *Lasting Screen Stars*, edited by Lucy Bolton and Julie Lobalzo, 11–25. Palgrave Macmillan.

10

THE STAR AT SUNSET

The Return of Jean-Pierre Leaud

STUART BELL

On May 16, 2022, Jean-Pierre Léaud was awarded an honorary Palme d'Or at the Cannes Film Festival, presented to him by director Arnaud Desplechin. A lifelong admirer of Léaud, Desplechin later told the press that he found himself too nervous on stage to read aloud the homage that he had prepared. Instead, he read it on French radio four days later:

> I am going to talk to you about Jean-Pierre Léaud. In the final shot of *The 400 Blows*, your first ever film, Jean-Pierre, you turned around to look us straight in the eye. You were fourteen. You were at Cannes and Jean Cocteau held you in his arms. Léaud has given his entire life to cinema. It's unique. And tonight cinema pays tribute to him. (2022)

Desplechin's words echo those of Léaud's discoverer and adopted cinematic father, François Truffaut, who said of his actor protégé back in 1973: "Jean-Pierre Léaud is among those actors, like Jeanne Moreau, who are so generous that sometimes they can be led to give too much, or to portray things the wrong way, and when that happens we lash out at them. But the fact that they can give so much is what makes them so rich" (Gillain 1988, 308).

Speaking in 2022, Desplechin reaffirmed what Truffaut had realized some forty-nine years earlier: Léaud already was, and would remain, a star willing to give himself over completely to cinema. Already a sensation in

1959, he would go on to star in a number of French films throughout the 1960s and 1970s, his persona a "site of privileged terrain" (Marie 2013, 310) for directors Jean-Luc Godard, Jean Eustache, and, naturally, Truffaut himself. Léaud is best known for his performances as Truffaut's "alter ego" (Hoberman 2017, 15) Antoine Doinel, first introduced in *Les quatre cent coups* (*The 400 Blows*, 1959), ultimately departing in Truffaut's final Doinel cycle film, *L'amour en fuite* (*Love on the Run*, 1979). Having played Doinel for the final time, Léaud took a break from the cinema. This was the start of an eleven-year hiatus during which he had no major roles, making only brief screen appearances. When he eventually did reappear as headlining star, in *I Hired a Contract Killer* (Aki Kaurismäki, 1991), it was a very different Léaud on screen. This comeback was followed by starring roles in the films *Irma Vep* (Olivier Assayas, 1996); *Le pornographe* (*The Pornographer*, Bertrand Bonello, 2001); and *La mort de Louis XIV* (*The Death of Louis XIV*, Albert Serra, 2016). While the earlier among these may appear, at least temporally, to be Léaud's most obvious comeback vehicles, this chapter focuses on the later film *The Death of Louis XIV*, arguing that this titular role constitutes the true comeback of Truffaut's former child star, albeit reincarnated in a strikingly different form, having departed radically from his younger screen self.

The Hiatus

Chris Darke argues that in the early 1990s both Léaud's real-life and onscreen persona were characterized by a "barely suppressed madness," partly induced by the sudden death of Truffaut in the mid-1980s. Darke writes:

> With Truffaut's death in October 1984, Léaud lost his mentor and protector. . . . Unsurprisingly, a period of psychological turmoil followed the filmmaker's death. Neighbours in Léaud's Parisian apartment block were said to have seen him standing naked in the courtyard waving a crucifix and bawling "Back, Satan!" while in 1987 he assaulted an elderly woman he believed was spying on him with a flowerpot. He was given a three-month suspended sentence; the psychiatric report stated that he was depressed following Truffaut's death. (2006, 39)

Depression and madness underpin Léaud's performances in *Irma Vep* and *The Pornographer*. In each he plays a tortured film director, emulating Truffaut's self-parody in *La nuit américaine* (*Day for Night*, 1973), a film in which Léaud also costarred. Both films stage Léaud as a melancholy, solitary figure. Indeed, five years prior to *Irma Vep, I Hired a Contract Killer* had already captured Léaud as a depressed Frenchman living in London who makes various failed attempts to commit suicide before hiring a team of hitmen to execute him. In each film there is a palpable sense that the Léaud character cannot go on living.

When Léaud returned to starring roles, he reappeared as Truffaut reincarnated. Not only did he follow his mentor by playing exasperated film directors and middle-aged men facing tragic untimely deaths, he also gestured to Truffaut via onscreen explorations of paternal-filial relations. Throughout *The Pornographer*, for example, questions of fatherhood are explored when Léaud's character (Jacques Laurent) attempts to make amends with his long-estranged son, who disapproves of his father's profession as a porn filmmaker. In this film it falls to Jacques to nurture and guide the younger man in his life—in this case, his diegetic son—just as Truffaut had done for Léaud.

If *I Hired a Contract Killer*, *Irma Vep*, and *The Pornographer* cannot be the true comeback vehicles of Léaud's cinematic return, this is because they testify to two realities: first, they expose the depressive madness that characterized Léaud's star persona in the wake of Truffaut's death; and, second, they affirm the end of Léaud's New Wave heyday as an actor of "privileged terrain" (Marie 2013, 310) over which directors once fought. The period 1991–2015 can be seen as a filmic documentation of Léaud's attempts to negotiate the loss of a man with whom he felt so deeply imbricated that he claimed he physically resembled Truffaut, stating: "We look like the people we love" (Truffaut and Léaud, 1965).

Inspired by Darke's emphasis on the melancholia that pervades the 1991–2015 film roles, I argue that *The Death* is Léaud's veritable comeback film, which sets the stage for the return of Antoine Doinel, even if the iconic youth is scarcely discernible. If Darke is right about Léaud's post-1991 films when he writes, "Léaud's old intensity is still intact, but is focused on the wrong object, the wrong job," *The Death*, then, is the film to right this wrong: it is the role of the fading Sun King that allows Léaud to come back proper, to self-stage as a star that outshines all others and, in so doing, fulfill his cinematic life's work (2006, 39).

The Death of Louis XIV

During a press conference at the 2017 New York Film Festival, the director of *The Death*, Albert Serra, was interviewed alongside Léaud. Serra explained how the idea for the film originated in his discovery that Léaud was tipped to play Louis XIV in a live "durational performance" (Nadal-Melsió 2021, 268) at the Centre Georges Pompidou in Paris. Ultimately canceled due to budget constraints, this installation piece was designed to exhibit the king's final days, restaged in agonizing detail. In transposing Léaud from a case made of glass to the screen, Serra frames him unapologetically as the film's gravitational center. Léaud sits at the center not only of the diegesis but also the mise-en-scène. He is the star that Serra and his crew orbit: "All the dramaturgy of the film is created naturally because of a presence in the centre: the presence of Jean-Pierre. . . . To put him in the centre, and to wait a little bit, this was my point, that the dramaturgy would be created as naturally as possible" (Serra and Léaud, 2017).

The Death is a film about looking at Léaud. The consistent use of long takes without dialogue invites quiet contemplation of Léaud not only as Sun King but also as a comeback star. What separates *The Death* from Léaud's 1991–2015 work is the agency that the film restores to him; the role of Louis becomes the ultimate platform for Léaud to self-stage freely. Akin to Truffaut, who famously allowed the boy Léaud to improvise while filming *The 400 Blows*, Serra too found that Léaud is a star willing to give himself over completely and authentically to the camera, allowing for the emergence of an organic, infantile quality. Serra stated: "Even if he knew a lot about Louis XIV and he was really interested in the character, in the end there is some kind of innocence, inside him, that makes this really alive. . . . I love the way he escaped cliché, totally naturally. I think it's due to this total innocence" (Serra and Léaud, 2017).

Serra sets the conditions for (re)capturing the child star essence of Léaud. The majority of filming takes place in the king's bedchamber, where Léaud reclines on the bed, dying with an untreatable gangrenous leg. Serra decided to fix several cameras around the bed, heightening the sense of exhibition and voyeurism. Léaud's role is to lie in wait. As J. Hoberman puts it: "Léaud appears as a holy relic . . . and as always, as himself" (2017, 17). Yet his presentation of self uniquely combines past and present. This is captured via three distinct tributes to Antoine Doinel that document his long-awaited screen return: breaking the fourth wall, the reclining star body, and a staged reunion with the lost experience of childhood.

Breaking the Fourth Wall

In his edited collection *The Companion to François Truffaut*, Dudley Andrew writes of the "remarkable, indeed revolutionary" shots of Léaud in *The 400 Blows* that were entirely improvised, moments spent: "speaking directly into the camera . . . without a single reverse shot intervening" (2013, 228). The final shot captures what Angela Dalle Vacche—also writing in Andrew's volume—sees as "one of the most startling film endings ever accomplished in freeze-frame" (405): the final moment when Léaud looks into the camera and is immortalized in the flash of a snapshot (figure 10.1). While the role of the opportunistic runaway Doinel appears, at first, as totally antithetical to that of the Sun King, Léaud nevertheless succeeds in rechanneling this moment in the ailing body of the monarch, rediscovering the freedom in performance once enjoyed with Truffaut, now revisited and reenacted in Serra's film.

Toward the end of *The Death*, the king is stretched out in bed, propped up with ornate cushions. He is wearing a golden robe, nestled in ruby patterned bedcovers. He clutches a glass of wine that he struggles to carry to his lips, spilling the liquid over his mouth and chest. Léaud

FIGURE 10.1. Jean-Pierre Léaud in *The 400 Blows* (François Truffaut 1959). Screenshot.

looks in frustration into one of the surrounding cameras: it is a direct gaze, held in the center of the frame (figure 10.2). The prolonged stillness of this shot takes on the aspect of a tableau vivant. Léaud glances at the camera, then holds the spectator in direct fourth-wall address. This long take, lasting three minutes and four seconds, serves two purposes. First, it restores the intensity and interactivity of the live art installation at the Pompidou that never happened, and, second, and more movingly, it restages the end of *The 400 Blows*. Léaud is now old, scarcely recognizable. In playing the dying king, he is heralding the start of his own cinematic eclipse. Just as the final shot of *The 400 Blows* signals the end of the beginning (Léaud would star in a number of films portraying Doinel's adventures), Léaud as Louis XIV in *The Death* would signal the beginning of the end of an iconic career and life lived on film. Akin to an artwork, the reclining star invites still reflection, quiet contemplation. At the 2017 press conference, a delegate asked Serra about this configuration. He explained that it was curated by Léaud:

> We shot it two or three times. One of the reasons was music. Jean-Pierre wanted to listen to music. He wanted Monteverdi but we didn't have Monteverdi because the composer was not chronological. He was born after the rule of the King. . . . Usually when somebody looks at the camera, you know, it puts you out of the film. Because you realise that this is a film. But here I don't know why it worked. . . . Paradoxically in this scene, when they look at you, you get more into the film. (Serra and Léaud, 2017)

FIGURE 10.2. Jean-Pierre Léaud in *The Death of Louis XIV* (Albert Serra 2016). Screenshot.

Several points are of interest here. First, Léaud's request to have classical music played on set is a further nod to the ending of *The 400 Blows*, where violin strings famously accompany the final shot of Doinel. It is as if Léaud's request looks to create the affective conditions for a cinematographic restaging of this legendary moment. Second, Serra's overcoming his initial reluctance to have his star break the fourth wall further cements the sense that during filming, Léaud was truly allowed to self-stage, to curate his own authentic cinematic moment. And, third, Serra's discovery that Léaud's fixed stare actually works to draw spectators into the film, while a point well made, it perhaps does not go far enough. Not only does the direct address of the gaze in *The Death* bring spectators into this film narrative specifically, it also ushers them into a space for considering Léaud as comeback star, a space in which the very genesis of his fame is suspended and mutely commemorated. Serra gifts Léaud and the spectator three full narrative minutes to pause and coexperience the onset of approaching death as the end of a filmic era, just as Truffaut documented its beginning in 1959.

The Reclining Star

Looking back over the Doinel cycle, some of the most iconic and enduring images of Léaud are those in which he is lying down. In *The 400 Blows*, Doinel reads Balzac while smoking and relaxing on his bed. In *Baisers volés* (*Stolen Kisses*, 1968), he is again lying in bed, hiding under the covers during the key narrative moment when his much older love interest, Fabienne Tabard (Delphine Seyrig), propositions him. In *Domicile conjugal* (*Bed and Board*, 1970) he sits propped up in bed beside his wife, Christine (Claude Jade), reading books about Japanese women and the dancer Rudolf Nureyev. Bedroom scenes are indeed central to Truffaut's figuration of Doinel. In curating a film decades later that captures Léaud reclining in almost every scene, *The Death* sets up an intimate space for the retrospective contemplation of Doinel in familiar and nostalgic poses, most specifically as put-to-bed child and as philandering young lover.

In *The 400 Blows*, Doinel runs away, spending the night sleeping rough in a printing factory. When his mother (Claire Maurier) finds him and brings him home, she puts him in the bath, dries him off, then puts him to bed. Head resting on his arm, he looks up as she sits beside him on the bedcovers, telling anecdotes of her own childhood escapades (figure 10.3).

FIGURE 10.3. Jean-Pierre Léaud and Claire Maurier in *The 400 Blows* (François Truffaut 1959). Screenshot.

This moment is later restaged in *Stolen Kisses*, when Fabienne Tabard, an Oedipal mother substitute, sits in exactly the same position on the bed, offering herself sexually to him. Later, in *The Death*, Léaud restages himself in bed, yet this time his elder female companion is Madame de Maintenon (Irène Silvagni), Louis XIV's wife. In true mimetic style, Maintenon sits on the same side of the bed as Madame Doinel (figure 10.4). As if the most enduring moments of Léaud's filmography are being relived in such moments, the reclining star is enacting the end of a lifelong continuum of staged moments of vulnerability, a filmed trajectory of being watched over in bed by an older mother/carer figure. Once again, in *The Death* spectators are invited to tap into Serra's sense of the "total innocence" (2017) of the Léaud star persona. This persona, at its origin, was that of a young man, surprisingly self-sufficient, yet nevertheless yearning for the attentions and acceptance of the (m)other. In *The Death*, Doinel is remediated as a royal infant: still a vulnerable child at heart, even if now metamorphosed into an end-of-life gilded ruler. As Darke has argued: Léaud's 1991–2015 films focused on "the wrong object, the wrong job." In presenting a radically reinvented Doinel in ultimate need of care, this film has relocated the "right" object (2006, 39).

A Childhood Reunion

At the midway point of *The Death*, the King is joined by his great-grandson, soon to be his successor. The scene begins with the child already placed on

FIGURE 10.4. Jean-Pierre Léaud and Irène Silvagni in *The Death of Louis XIV* (Albert Serra 2016). Screenshot.

the bed, sitting upright in silence, listening obediently to his dying great-grandfather. Léaud speaks to the child in low murmurs, telling him to live his life differently, fulfilling his duty to give back to God. During this short monologue, the King looks back over his life, regretful of his "love of buildings" and "love of war." He tells the child to govern peacefully, then embraces him, pressing his cheek against the boy's own and enveloping him in his arms. The close-up on Léaud's face accentuates his loose, aged skin.

A striking characteristic of Léaud's 1991–2015 films is their markedly adult themes and the narrative absence—almost exclusively—of children. *The Death* provides the platform for Léaud to self-stage, via this child's innocence, his own cinematic beginning and end. The young boy, filmed only from behind, recalls the precocious if not brutish innocence of Doinel. As the spectator witnesses Léaud looking into the child's eyes, it is as if a cinematic mirror were held up connecting the present moment of the star's approaching death to the past moment of his screen début. As the King tells his successor what a ruler must not do, Léaud too appears to be reflecting on the turmoil of his own life, documented almost in its entirety on film, as Darke and Hoberman remind us (2006, 2017).

Sun King: Fading Star

During the New York Film Festival Press conference, Léaud quoted a line from Jean Cocteau: "Cinema is the only art that can capture death at work." He explained: "It was my own death that was being filmed while

I was interpreting Louis XIV's death. It was a completely unique, intimate and personal experience to be filmed in such a way. I can't imagine another actor that could go to the same extent, to go to such depth, in interpreting this character, the death of Louis XIV, as I did" (Serra and Léaud, 2017).

Léaud's self-directed words here anticipate the homage that Arnaud Desplechin would pay him at Cannes five years later. As a star born to the screen at the end of the 1950s, Léaud faded increasingly from view as the decades passed. His veritable comeback called for a restaging of the self through a return to the very filmic conditions that paved the way for his initial rise: an uninhibited staging of the self, free from the agony of Truffaut's loss. The footage of the fourteen-year-old Léaud auditioning for the part of Doinel shows that what underpins his stardom is a simple, if not fragile, formula: within a given role, Léaud must be allowed to freely exhibit himself. In *The Death* he does just this. Regal and reinvented, he returns to pay silent tribute to Doinel: he looks the spectator in the eye one last time, reclining as he always did, under the watchful guard of the beloved (m)other, narrating his own life story to a(nother) child, who, like him, is predestined to live a life under the gaze of the world. In *The Death*, Léaud the star returns to die on the same cinematic screen that birthed him. Both Truffaut and Desplechin speak truthfully when they claim that Jean-Pierre Léaud has given himself, and his entire life, to cinema—perhaps to the point of giving too much—unlike any other French star before him.

Works Cited

Andrew, Dudley. 2013. "Every Teacher Needs a Truant: Bazin and *L'Enfant Sauvage*." In *A Companion to François Truffaut*, edited by Dudley Andrew and Anne Gillain, 221–39. Wiley-Blackwell.

Dalle Vacche, Angela. 2013. "Directing Children: The Double Meaning of Self-Consciousness." In *A Companion to François Truffaut*, edited by Dudley Andrew and Anne Gillain, 403–19. Wiley-Blackwell.

Darke, Chris. 2006. "Jean-Pierre Léaud: Lord of the Left Bank." *Sight and Sound* 16 (10): 36–39.

Desplechin, Arnaud. 2022. "Jean-Pierre Léaud, vous avez changé ma vie, sans vous, j'aurais été tellement seul." Broadcast on France Inter, May 20.

https://www.radiofrance.fr/franceinter/arnaud-desplechin-jean-pierre-leaud-vous-avez-change-ma-vie-sans-vous-j-aurais-ete-tellement-seul-7798620.

Gillain, Anne. 1992. *Le cinéma selon François Truffaut*. Flammarion.

Hoberman, James. 2017. "From Teenage Rebel to Dying King, Jean Pierre Léaud and a Life Lived Onscreen." *New York Times*, March 26, 2017. https://www.nytimes.com/2017/03/24/movies/jean-pierre-leaud-and-a-life-lived-on-film.html.

Marie, Michel. 2013. "Cain and Abel: Godard and Truffaut." In *A Companion to François Truffaut*, edited by Dudley Andrew and Anne Gillain, 300–316. Wiley-Blackwell.

Nadal-Melsió, Sara. 2021. "The Dead Ends of Photogénie. From Cinephilia to Cinephobia and Back: Albert Serra's *La mort de Louis XIV* and *Roi Soleil*." *Journal of Spanish Cultural Studies* 22 (2): 261–71.

Serra, Albert, dir. 2016. *La mort de Louis XIV / The Death of Louis XIV*. Paris: Capricci Films, 2016. DVD.

Serra, Albert, and Jean-Pierre Léaud. "The Death of Louis XIV," press conference, New York Film Festival 2017. YouTube video, 28:05, March 28, 2017. https://www.youtube.com/watch?v=USDfTbhZ9E8.

Truffaut, François, and Jean-Pierre Léaud. "Cinéastes de notre temps: François Truffaut ou l'esprit critique." Interview by Janine Bazin, André Sylvain Labarthe, and Jean-Pierre Chartier, 1965, YouTube video, 17:19, April 28, 2017. https://www.youtube.com/watch?v=0A3tbrofEcA.

Truffaut, François, dir. 1968. *Baisers volés* [*Stolen Kisses*]. Paris: Les Films du Carrosse, 1968. DVD.

Truffaut, François, dir. 1959. *Les quatre cent coups* [*The 400 Blows*]. Paris: Les Films du Carrosse, 1959. DVD.

11

REMAKING HIS WAY WITH ZEN

Sessue Hayakawa and the Zen Boom

DAISUKE MIYAO

Aging Star from the Silent Era

"There are times . . . when suddenly you realize you're nearer the end than the beginning. And you wonder, you ask yourself, what the sum total of your life represents. What difference your being there at any time made to anything—or if it made any difference at all, really." In *The Bridge on the River Kwai* (David Lean, 1957), an epic war film set in a Japanese prison camp in the jungles of Southeast Asia during World War II, Major Nicholson (Alec Guinness), a British prisoner of war, makes this speech to Colonel Saito (Sessue Hayakawa), a refined but merciless Japanese commander (figure 11.1). Throughout the film, Nicholson has been tortured by Saito for not being obedient. Nicholson is locked up in a small cell under the sun, "an oven," when he rejects Saito's order to engage in manual labor, insisting that the code of the Geneva Convention prohibits officers from being forced to do it. Saito shouts at Nicholson, "What do you know of the soldiers' code, Bushido? Nothing! You are unworthy of command!"

In the end, however, it is Saito who turns out to be "unworthy of command." Being unsuccessful in building a bridge over the River Kwai, he has no choice but to permit Nicholson to reorganize the plan for constructing the bridge under the British command. When the construction is complete, Nicholson and Saito meet on the bridge at sunset. Saito observes the bridge and sadly praises Nicholson's accomplishment: "Beautiful. Yes, a beautiful creation." This is the time when Nicholson eloquently talks about

FIGURE 11.1. Alec Guinness makes a speech to Sessue Hayakawa on a newly built bridge in *The Bridge on the River Kwai* (David Lean, 1957). Screenshot.

his twenty-eight-year career with the British army. Saito stays silent. Saito's back is captured on the right edge of the frame in the long shots that center on Nicholson talking. He has turned into a passive listener, an incompetent supporting character who initiated this mission but commanded it unsuccessfully. This is the time when Saito decides to end his life.

Both Saito and Hayakawa failed in their missions—Saito in the jungle of Ceylon, and Hayakawa at the 30th Academy Awards Ceremony. *Kwai* became the highest-grossing film of 1957 and was nominated in eight categories, including Best Supporting Actor for Hayakawa. The film won seven Oscars, except in one category: Best Supporting Actor. Ironically, the award went to Red Buttons for his role in *Sayonara* (Joshua Logan, 1957), a film that was set in Japan. It must have been extremely disappointing for Hayakawa. However, he decided to use his failure to win an Oscar to forge a new international star image of the role he played in *Kwai*: a samurai.

Popular film audiences in 1957 heard the name Sessue Hayakawa for the first time. Yet he was a star in Hollywood and the only Asian matinee idol of the silent era. His astounding performance as a sexy villain in *The Cheat* (Cecil B. DeMille, 1915) propelled him to superstardom. As early as May 1916, only five months after *The Cheat* was released, Hayakawa was ranked number one in the *Chicago Tribune* popular star contests (1916). While the art and culture of Japan were fascinating to many Europeans and Americans in the name of Japonisme, at the same time the general public in the United States supported segregation, and interracial marriages were illegal in many states. Hayakawa was keen enough to balance two images to sustain and enhance his stardom: an attractive foreigner with an exotic cultural background, and an Americanized gentleman who would not endanger the moral code of the United States. When he established his own production company, Haworth Pictures Corporation, in 1918, for instance, Hayakawa stated, "Such roles [in a film like *The Cheat*] are not true to our Japanese nature . . . They are false and give people a wrong idea of us. I wish to make a characterization which shall reveal us as we really are" (Kingslay 1916, 139). But he also knew that too faithful an adherence to Japanese realities would not please his American fans who were expecting mysticism (Miyao 2007, 153). Hayakawa's strategy was a simultaneous campaign of winning the hearts of American audiences by upholding his already established exotic star image and convincing the viewers in Japan as well as in Japanese American communities of his more authentic depiction of Japanese characters. He was very good at sensing the perfect timing and packaging himself as a celebrity. His tactics were successful, and he was able to maintain his stardom for another four years in Hollywood and then much longer in France and Japan.

Hayakawa's popularity declined along with the rising anti-Japanese sentiment on the West Coast in the early 1920s. He left Hollywood in 1922, and his name was forgotten in the United States. But with the success of *Kwai*, Hayakawa gained a high level of international exposure in this film and at the Oscars ceremony. The nomination was an honor even though he did not win. *Kwai* was his comeback film, with which he attained the celebrity and media spotlight for the first time in more than three decades.

Two Autobiographies: Samurai Warrior or Zen Priest?

Hayakawa reformulated his star image around the famed character of Colonel Saito, the defeated samurai. To revitalize his stardom, Hayakawa connected this image of a samurai to another image of traditional Japanese culture that was in vogue at that time: a Zen Buddhist. That was how Hayakawa's role in *Kwai* marked a departure from his work as a silent film star in Hollywood in the 1910s–20s. It was his challenge to transform his star image from a matinee idol during the silent era to an aging star who realized he was "nearer the end than the beginning." Perhaps Hayakawa asked himself, following the line of Alec Guinness in *Kwai*, "what the sum total of [his] life was representing," or what he wanted his life to represent. Zen was his answer, capitalizing on its popularity in the United States in the 1950s.

In the two years after the Oscars, in 1959 and 1960, Hayakawa published two autobiographies back-to-back—first in Japanese and then in English. The obvious assumption is that the latter is a translation of the former. But it is not. The two are almost completely different books. In each volume, Hayakawa mentioned many identical incidents that he encountered in the United States, Japan, and France. But he contextualized those episodes and their approaches differently. While the Japanese book is light and cheerful, the English book is meditative and serious.[1] The former could be seen by some as gossipy, while the latter could be taken as a guidebook to live a good life. The Japanese book's title is *Musha shugyō sekai o yuku* (Training in Warriorship in the World) while the English one is titled *Zen Showed Me the Way . . . to Peace, Happiness, and Tranquility.* Why the difference?

Was Zen Important for Hayakawa?

The biggest difference between Hayakawa's two autobiographies is how he dealt with Zen Buddhism, which plays an essential role in *Zen Showed Me the Way*, as its title indicates. Hayakawa selected the term *musha shugyō* as the title of the Japanese book, a decision that was arguably inspired by Zen monks who would engage in ascetic wanderings before attaining enlightenment. But, in the book, he mentioned Zen only once, and frivolously (1959, 197).

While in *Musha shugyō* Hayakawa devoted almost no space to the time prior to his arrival in the United States (only ten pages) from his native country of Japan, in *Zen Showed Me the Way* he did not mention setting foot on American soil until after eighty-four pages. What did he do in those pages? First, Croswell Bowen, the editor of the book and an award-winning biographer, contributed a ten-page introduction to *Zen*. Then, Hayakawa started the book by describing the character of Colonel

1. The Japanese book contains chapters titled "Bijin dangi" (Discussing Beautiful Women) and "Onna ni moteru gijutsu" (Techniques to Flirt with Women), in which Hayakawa discussed his experiences with women. Throughout this chapter, the translation from Japanese to English is mine.

Saito as a defeated samurai and how he played the role during the production of *Kwai*. He wrote:

> As I sat before the camera in the character of Colonel Saito, . . . the past and the present became one. The real and the unreal fused together. Time stood still; eternity yawned. . . . What was present in Ceylon became the past in another place, in another time, more than fifty years ago, when an eighteen-year-old youth knelt in a pool of soft light from white candles and composed a poem he prayed would explain why, minutes later, he would raise an ancient dagger against himself in protest against his destiny. (1960, 30)

This is a description of a scene that follows Nicholson's speech stressing how "honorable" the British soldiers are. The shot of Nicholson's speech is crosscut with a high-angle long shot that captures the back of Saito, making him look small and defeated, completing a document in Japanese and ritualistically cutting a few of his hairs with his knife (figure 11.2). The shot alone does not clarify what the document is, but it is most likely his suicide note because earlier in the narrative he declared, "I'll have to kill myself," in case he failed to accomplish his mission. Saito commits hara-kiri out of shame to protect his honor as a samurai. Such an image of a samurai follows how the American cultural anthropologist Ruth Benedict characterized the Japanese culture in *The Chrysanthemum and the Sword: Patterns of Japanese Culture* (1946), arguably the most influential book on Japan during the Cold War. Benedict called Japan the "culture of

FIGURE 11.2. Completing a document in Japanese, Sessue Hayakawa takes out a knife ritualistically in a high-angle long shot in *The Bridge on the River Kwai* (David Lean, 1957).

shame" and explained such a fantastical connection between the samurai and self-sacrifice. She wrote: "Though every soul originally shines with virtue like a new sword, nevertheless, if it is not kept polished, it gets tarnished. This 'rust of my body,' as they [Japanese people] phrase it, is as bad as it is on a sword" (1989, 198). Conscious of Benedict's work or not, Hayakawa wrote, "*Renchi-shin*, the sense of shame is called in Japanese. Sense of shame has an intense effect on samurai. . . . A person reared by the *Bushido* code, such as I was, is required to know what will bring shame and to avoid it" (1960, 52; italics in the original).

Hayakawa connected Saito to his youth when he similarly committed hara-kiri out of shame. As the son of a samurai, Hayakawa's boyhood dream was to become an admiral of the Japanese Navy, but he was dismissed from the Naval Academy because of an unexpected accident in the summer of 1907. During the summer break, he went back to his native village of Nanaura in Chiba prefecture and dove too deep for abalone (Nanaura's major business), bursting his eardrum. It made him ineligible for naval service. According to Hayakawa, his failure was his father's dishonor (1960, 48). Committing hara-kiri, using a dagger, a samurai weapon, that was passed down in his family for many years was the only choice for him to save his father, who was the governor of a province, from disgrace. Hayakawa composed a farewell poem, brushed it upon white rice paper, and drove the point of the dagger into his belly in protest against his destiny (33–36).

But he did not die. Instead of going home, he turned to a Zen Buddhist temple, where he met a priest Eichi (Hayakawa 1960, 53). It was Eichi who told Hayakawa about Zen being "the religion of life, essentially the acquisition of a new point of view on life which accepts the unity of all living things" (62). It was easier for Hayakawa to listen to Eichi's introduction to Zen because he also told him that Zen is the religion of the samurai. Eichi said, "The strength of the samurai lies in an attitude of mind as it puts the consciousness of self second to the task at hand. And what is the source of such an attitude of mind? Zen." Hayakawa listened to what Eichi told him "as if in a trance" (58).

As he sat thinking about Zen, he saw a ship plunging into a rock and listing to one side. According to Hayakawa, he forgot himself and rushed down the mountainside to help passengers on the sinking ship (1960, 72–73). The US steamship *Dakota* collided with a reef off the coast of Chiba prefecture in 1907. In both autobiographies, Hayakawa wrote that he played an active part as an interpreter during the rescue mission. He said that this incident and his conversation with the passengers in English stirred up his desire to go to the United States. But only in *Zen Showed Me the Way* did he explain what happened to him in connection to Zen: "Perhaps it was meant to be—this sudden flight back to the world of men from the content I was finding in my pursuit of self. Why did the ship strike the rock? Why did I see it? Why did I instantly rush to help total strangers?" (77).

Hayakawa's older brother Otojirō had been engaged in abalone fishing in California. After the 1868 Meiji Reconstruction, the Japanese government subsidized Kodani Gennosuke and Kodani Chūjirō from Chiba prefecture to help them engage in abalone fishing in California. The Kodani brothers facilitated Hayakawa's trip to the United States (Ōba 1995, 57–58). In *Musha shugyō*, Hayakawa did not mention anything about his attempted hara-kiri, his meeting with Eichi, his learning of Zen, or his eureka moment of witnessing the *Dakota* accident. He simply wrote that he engaged in the rescue mission and decided to go to the United States. Thus, in *Zen Showed Me the Way*, Hayakawa reframed his past in Japan and the present of *Kwai* with the notions of karma and oneness of Zen by way of the act of hara-kiri, a real-life experience of a fictional role (*Kwai*) and an autobiographical experience whether real or not that occurred in the past. "At the root of my portrait of Colonel Saito, is Zen," argued Hayakawa. "His destiny was to battle within himself and lose. It was my destiny to portray him, and by my portrait to open my future to greater vistas. Saito and I became invisible. The Zen state of *muga* made us one and the same. . . . I had come full cycle" (1960, 252, 254; italics in the original).

Hayakawa never referred to Zen during his silent film stardom in the 1910s–20s. For instance, an article in the *Literary Digest* in November 1917 articulated Hayakawa's star persona based on his Japanese cultural background. According to Hayakawa, "An old Samurai who had really studied ju-jutsu," a Japanese martial art, could make someone who pointed his revolver at him put it down just by his "mysterious force" because "to a Japanese death is nothing and is welcomed joyously" (1917, 70, 72). Curiously, in *Zen Showed Me the Way*, Hayakawa described an episode during which he was attacked by a person with a revolver when he first arrived in San Francisco. He emphasized the significance of his Zen practice, and not ju-jutsu, when he escaped from the attacker.

Zen Boom in the United States in the 1950s

After the success of *Rashomon* (Akira Kurosawa, 1950) at the Venice International Film Festival, the Japanese film industry became involved in international distribution. Cultural motifs such as samurai, geisha, *noh* and kabuki drama, and Zen Buddhism were self-consciously marketed as "traditional Japanese" in the films for export. The emphasis on exotic Japaneseness was thus strategically chosen as a commodity for foreign audiences and a renewed symbol of a national identity of postwar Japan that would be approved internationally. Hayakawa was aware of this trend. In this context, Hayakawa wrote *Zen Showed Me the Way*. But why Zen in particular?

In the 1950s, the so-called Zen boom grew in the United States. Japanese Zen Buddhist scholar Daisetsu Teitarō (D. T.) Suzuki gave a series of lectures at Columbia University as a visiting professor in 1952 and made it available to a wide number of people, including the Beat poets, who formed the core of the Zen boom, regarding Zen as a counterculture (Shigematsu 2020, 144).

Suzuki's influence was visible in Hayakawa's description of Zen in *Zen Showed Me the Way*, especially in its early section, where he wrote about his time with Eichi. Hayakawa found "stories of experiences of *satori*, the Japanese term for enlightenment, or awakening" in the books that Eichi gave him (1960, 59; italics in the original). Hayakawa wrote: "Satori is the criterion of Zen—a spiritual experience so definite one is never mistaken in experiencing it. It is the sudden realization of the truth of Zen. It cannot be explained by the intellect. It cannot be brought about by intellectualizing. Logic has no place (60)." The concept of *satori* occupies the core of Suzuki's presentation of Zen. His essay "On Satori" was first published in English in 1927 but was included in William Barrett's 1956 anthology of Suzuki's writings, *Zen Buddhism: Selected Writings of D. T. Suzuki*, and was widely read in the Zen boom. In the essay, Suzuki states: "Satori is the raison d'être of Zen, and without which Zen is no Zen. Therefore every contrivance (*upāya*) disciplinary or doctrinal is directed toward the attainment of satori. Satori is the most intimate individual experience and therefore cannot be expressed in words or described in any manner" (2014, 35, italics in the original). It is thus obvious that Hayakawa was referring to Suzuki's definition of the notion of *satori*.

Eric Cunningham argues that for Americans seeking the convenience of "instant enlightenment" during the Zen boom, the Zen popularized by Suzuki was "highly accessible, enriching, and even entertaining" (2015, 45). Suzuki's Zen has been criticized by Buddhists and scholars of Buddhism in Japan for its accessibility and entertaining aspect. For instance, Zen priest Minami Jikisai criticized Suzuki's emphasis on empiricism in the notion of *satori*. He wrote: "If you practice zazen or meditation based on a certain method, our normal consciousness transforms. Our daily 'self' is lost, and many people feel 'being united with the world.' Such an experience is often accompanied by strong 'ecstasy.' Zen warns against such ecstasy by calling it 'Zen sick' or 'Zen evil.' It is an obsession with liberating consciousness and pursuing pleasure. I criticize it as 'no satori'" (2017, 119–20).

Hayakawa probably did not care about such criticism of Suzuki's Zen. Instead, it was more important for him to utilize the accessible and entertaining aspect of Suzuki's Zen, especially when he narrated the early story of his life and reframed the 1907 *Dakota* incident as his moment of *satori*. So, in his 1960 description of his life to English-language readers, an enlightened Hayakawa traveled to the United States and became a Hollywood star. In contrast, for the Japanese readers of his 1959 autobiography, he was not. He was simply "inspired by" his experience as an interpreter during the *Dakota* incident and became eager to experience the American way of life (Hayakawa 1959, 22).

Remaking His Stardom with Zen

Thus, how Hayakawa presented himself differently in the two autobiographies that were published in the wake of *Kwai* suggests that he was a shrewd manipulator of the media and a canny self-publicist. He aligned himself with the character of Colonel Saito of Kwai in the English version of his autobiography and used Saito's sense of shame at the climax of the film to offset his own disappointments (failures at the Naval Academy and at the Oscars). Hayakawa tried to turn his defeat into his triumph by using publication media and repackaging his star image. He engaged with the task of mythmaking of his star persona again. This time, though, he was not trying to become a sex symbol but was regarding himself as a Zen practitioner. A Japanese weekly magazine *Shūkan Yomiuri* quoted

Hayakawa in its September 20, 1959, issue: "American people think that there is something mysterious in me," and he completed a book on his "spiritual journey" for an American publisher to cater to such expectation (1959, 47). Hayakawa thus revived his stardom after *Kwai* by strategically reinventing himself as a Zen priest amid the Zen boom. Thus, Hayakawa remade his way with Zen.

Works Cited

Benedict, Ruth. 1989. *The Chrysanthemum and the Sword: Patterns of Japanese Culture*. Mariner.

Cunningham, Eric. 2015. "D. T. Suzuki: A Biographical Summary." *Education About Asia* 20 (2) (Fall): 42–45.

"Hayakawa, Japanese Screen Star." 1917. *Literary Digest*, November 3, 1917.

Hayakawa, Sesshū. 1959. *Musha shugyō sekai o yuku*. Jitsugyō no Nihon sha.

Hayakawa, Sessue. 1960. *Zen Showed Me the Way . . . to Peace, Happiness, and Tranquility*. Bobbs-Merrill.

Kingsley, Grace. 1916. "That Splash of Saffron: Sessue Hayakawa, a Cosmopolitan Actor, Who for Reasons of Nativity, Happens to Peer from Our White Screens with Tilted Eyes." *Photoplay* 9 (4) (March): 139–41.

Lean, David, dir. 1957. *The Bridge on the River Kwai*. Culver City, CA: Sony Pictures Home Entertainment, 2000. DVD.

Minami, Jikisai. 2017. *"Satori" wa hirakenai*. Besutoserāzu.

Miyao, Daisuke. 2007. *Sessue Hayakawa: Silent Cinema and Transnational Stardom*. Duke University Press.

Ōba, Toshio. 1995. "Hayakawa Kintarō (Sesshū) no tobei kankyō to ryoken ni tsuite." *Bōsō no kyōdo shi*, no. 22:57–58.

"Sekai o butai ni suru otoko Hayakawa Sesshū shi." *Shūkan Yomiuri* (20 September 1959): 43, 47.

Shigematsu, Sōiku. 2020. "'Emason no zengakuron' o meguru shiteki zakkan." *Gendaishisō* 48 (15) (November): 138–45.

Suzuki, Daisetsu Teitarō. 2014. *Selected Works of D. T. Suzuki*. Vol. I, *Zen*, edited by Richard M. Jaffe. University of California Press.

"Vote for the Picture of Your Favorite Player." 1916. *Chicago Tribune*, May 14, 1916.

12

BURT REYNOLDS AND THE REDEMPTION OF THE GOOD OL' BOY IN *THE LAST MOVIE STAR*

JENNIFER LOUISE FIELD

At the height of Burt Reynolds's popularity, his star image as a good ol' boy was an irresistible juxtaposition of swagger and self-deprecating charm. Though his breakthrough role in *Deliverance* (John Boorman, 1972) established him as a southern star, it was his late-night talk show persona and nude *Cosmopolitan* centerfold that catapulted him to sex symbol status and opened the doors to box-office hits such as *The Longest Yard* (Robert Aldrich, 1974); *Smokey and the Bandit* (Hal Needham, 1977); *Smokey and the Bandit II* (Hal Needham, 1980); *Smokey and the Bandit Part III* (Dick Lowry, 1983); and *Cannonball Run* (Hal Needham, 1981). After a five-year reign as box-office king from 1978 to 1982, Reynolds's star faded through the 1980s as his southern folk hero roles took a backseat to his personal tribulations. It was the role of pornography auteur Jack Horner in *Boogie Nights* (Paul Thomas Anderson, 1997) that would present Burt Reynolds with a comeback opportunity. At age sixty-two, Reynolds embodied a brand of masculinity in the role that was less brash and more paternal. He shone precisely because of the similarities between Reynolds and Horner: Both men believe deeply in their artistic vision and talent but find themselves on shaky footing in a world that's swiftly leaving them behind. Though Reynolds won a Golden Globe Award for his performance, it hardly materialized into the comeback he had hoped for. His involvement in the remakes of *The Longest Yard* (Peter Segal, 2005) and

The Dukes of Hazzard (Jay Chandrasekhar, 2005), as well as a role playing a hyperrealized version of himself in the television series *Archer* (Adam Reed, 2012), all cash in on his 1970s good ol' boy persona. That was until 2017, when writer-director Adam Rifkin lovingly crafted the character of Vic Edwards in *The Last Movie Star* for the eighty-two-year-old actor. This second comeback opportunity offered Reynolds a departure from the good ol' boy, allowing him instead to showcase the toll of this youthful persona on his body, personal life, and career. This chapter will focus on *The Last Movie Star*'s intertextual use of Reynolds's films *Smokey and the Bandit* and *Deliverance*, which place his younger self in direct dialogue with his older self. This technique effectively breathes authenticity into Vic Edwards's redemptive odyssey by way of Burt Reynolds's own redemptive pursuit to shake off his good ol' boy image and finally be regarded as a serious actor.

Burt Reynolds's Good Ol' Boys

At the peak of Reynolds's 1970s fame, his good ol' boy roles consisted of a private eye in *Shamus* (Buzz Kulik, 1973); a felon who goes undercover in *White Lightning* (Joseph Sargent, 1973) and *Gator* (Burt Reynolds, 1976); a felon footballer in *The Longest Yard*; and, perhaps most famously, a beer runner in the *Smokey and the Bandit* series. Each has the accoutrements of a cowboy: cowboy hat, shirt, boots, and the blue jeans with flashy belt buckle. He chews gum and has a cigarillo, toothpick, or cigar dangling from his lips as he wisecracks his way out of trouble. Reynolds's good ol' boys are young but just old enough—in their late thirties to forties—to have some life experience and know the tricks of their trade. He is a ladies' man, good-looking and charming, a bit rough around the edges but not a serious outlaw. In fact, this good ol' boy is narratively positioned as a white working-class hero who is sticking it to the system but does not carry the racist baggage of previous good ol' boys who strove to keep the white southern status quo (Nystrom 2009, 59). Reynolds's good ol' boys are quite the opposite of Clint Eastwood's steely eyed and stoic cowboys—they're rascals. They know their pursuits are ridiculous, but are nevertheless in on the joke and committed to getting the job done. Furthermore, Reynolds was decidedly apolitical, which granted him wide audience appeal.

The Good Ol' Boy Turns (Kind of) Serious

It is difficult to definitively pinpoint why Reynolds's star faded after 1983. It might have been that his brand of sexuality was no longer in demand, with the introduction of hard-bodied box-office stars like Arnold Schwarzenegger and Sylvester Stallone. It might be that Reynolds's project selection was poor, that he couldn't shake being typecast as a good ol' boy, or that the charm of the southern folk hero had simply dulled (Long 2017, 54). Interestingly, character roles contributed greatly to his comeback in the 1990s. He had a successful turn on television with the critically lauded *Evening Shade* (1990–94), then played the shady congressman in *Striptease* (Andrew Bergman, 1996). However, it was his turn as pornography director Jack Horner in *Boogie Nights* that marked his career comeback.

The film, a 1970s period piece, follows a young man's journey from bus boy to porn star. Reynolds plays the patriarch of a porn family, a director who fancies himself an auteur and approaches pornography as a narrative art form. Although Reynolds is no longer the sex symbol he was twenty years before, he brings a quiet, suave confidence to Horner, who mentors the young Eddie (Mark Wahlberg) to stardom. Though paunchy and now in his sixties, Horner proves his virility by beating down an overzealous man who is harassing one of his actors, Roller Girl (Heather Graham). Nonetheless, with a scarf tied neatly around his neck, his khaki shirt, and his frosted toupee, Reynolds exudes a mature performance that is a sharp departure from his wise-cracking, fun-loving good ol' boys (Stephens 1997, 11). He draws from a well of experience within, sharing a kinship with Horner. Both the actor and the character struggle with the sense that their prime has passed them by and feel they have artistic value to share with the world but are simply out of step with the way the world is changing (Reynolds and Winokur 2015, 200). At sixty-two, Reynolds demonstrates that he can still produce a great performance for the silver screen; however, the roles that followed only confirmed how tied Reynolds was to his 1970s good ol' boy persona. His appearances as Boss Hogg in *The Dukes of Hazzard*, Coach Nate Scarborough in *The Longest Yard*, and his portrayal of himself in *Archer* demonstrate that, "unlike any other of the stars of the 1970s, Reynolds came to represent—and get stuck in . . . the 1970s by being the only star to promise his audience the 1970s' key region, the south" (Long 2017, 56).

Embracing Vulnerability

The white male redemptive story is a popular film genre that centers on men who have become less virile and more vulnerable in their old age, both physically and emotionally. *The Wrestler* (Darren Aronofsky, 2008); *Crazy Heart* (Scott Cooper, 2009); and *Trouble with the Curve* (Robert Lorenz 2012) give aging stars Mickey Rourke, Jeff Bridges, and Clint Eastwood, respectively, redemptive tales, and each film pairs the aging male lead with a younger woman because so many of their youthful mistakes involved hurting the women or girls in their lives. This is also true of Reynolds's Vic Edwards in *The Last Movie Star*, which features the aging star coming to terms with the consequences of his good ol' boy style of masculinity on his body, his career, and his personal life. Rifkin crafted the script specifically for Reynolds with the desire to showcase his ability to bring vulnerability to the role, believing it was a strength of Reynolds that hadn't previously been fully realized (Reynolds 2018). In tandem, the film's title and poster magnify Reynolds's star image to market the film as though it were biographical. Furthermore, the film opens on a young Vic Edwards as a late-night talk-show guest who is telling a tale of his first screen test with self-deprecating charm. In actuality the footage is of a young Burt Reynolds, effectively blurring the lines between the character and the actor from the very start. The next shot shows present-day Vic in close-up. In stark juxtaposition to Burt's/Vic's previous youthful energy, his face is now weathered, sunken, his hair grayed, his skin no longer bronzed. The camera then tracks out to reveal he is sitting in a veterinary waiting room with his dog atop his lap, cane in hand. His faithful friend, Squanto, is about to be put down. Afterward, Vic heads home, and it's clear this faded star now lives an isolated, quiet life in a modest house. The man who once walked with breezy ease is now bent over, weighed down with pain and a lifetime of regrets.

Vic learns over lunch with his agent, Sonny (Chevy Chase), that he has been invited to a film festival in his honor in Nashville. Though hesitant at first, he decides to accept the invitation, believing that it is a prestigious ceremony that Robert DeNiro and Clint Eastwood have previously attended. Vic begins to suspect that the festival is more amateurish than they have let on. He is seated in economy class during his flight and is picked up by a punkish, half-dressed young woman in a junky car. As it turns out, Lil (Ariel Winter) is the sister of the festival's organizer, Doug

(Clark Duke), and is doing him a favor by being Vic's driver. However, she is too wrapped up in her own personal drama to care that Vic is put off by the whole charade. When Vic arrives at the bar to attend the festival, he is met with the cheers of millennial fans who worship him and are quite frankly surprised that he actually showed up. After being forgotten for so long, it's jarring to have cellphones shoved into his face, like the cameras of old. The attention sends him into a spiral because it is a reminder of how successful he once was. When they screen one of Vic's old films, he ducks out to the bar and gets drunk, his old movies too painful to watch.

The next morning, Vic decides to head home but abruptly changes his mind in the car and asks Lil to instead take him to Knoxville. As Lil makes a hard turn, he suddenly finds himself taken off-road and hangs on for dear life as he sits shotgun with his younger self, who is actually a younger Burt Reynolds as the Bandit from *Smokey and the Bandit*. As the scene plays out, old Vic is taken aback by the antics of his younger self as they speed to evade Smokey. When old Vic suggests they slow down or pull off to the side of the road, he is brushed off by the arrogance of his younger self, who simply responds, "Cute." The older and wiser Vic tries to reason with young Vic as they cruise along in the famous black Trans Am: "Vic, take it easy, I may be old, but I'm not ready to die yet." However, young Vic continues on with a carefree laugh, while old Vic tries again to talk some sense into him—"What the hell is the matter with you? We could have been killed. You think you're gonna live forever?"—to which young Vic replies, "Uh-huh." This daydream allows elderly Vic to try and stop his younger self from making the mistakes he made as a young man, but also offers him the opportunity to face his regrets. The use of a scene from *Smokey and the Bandit* underscores Reynolds's regret that he missed out on serious projects by taking on so many good ol' boy roles. He would reflect in his memoir, "When I started, I was faking it, and I hid my fear behind cockiness. The ambition came later. It wasn't until I was close to forty that I wanted to be respected as an actor" (Reynolds and Winokur 2015, 262). The satisfaction of substantive material was important to Reynolds, but the critical recognition of his talent was also a concern. Therefore, the good ol' boy way of living meant that a man kept everything bottled up inside. Likewise, Vic Edwards has lived a long time hiding his vulnerable side within a shell of masculinity that required him to grin and bear it. Reynolds could also relate and, in fact, hinted at this even at the height of his fame in a 1978 interview: "The guy on *The Tonight Show*, for me, is a character. It's one of many people I do. But I have to get geared up to be him" (McBride and Riley 1978, 21). Therefore, his disclosure on late-night television blurred the distinction between his sense of self and performative image. This not only affected his own health, but also his relationships with women.[1]

Additionally, a major regret for Vic is his treatment of his first wife, Claudia (Kathleen Nolan). He shares with Lil that, though he was married five times, Claudia was the woman who stood by his side when he was struggling to break through, but he ultimately left her behind when he found fame and fortune. This remark prompts the second interaction between young and old Vic, highlighting his regret. Old Vic is now on the Cahulawassee River, dressed in a plaid shirt and fishing vest. He leans back in the boat with a fishing pole as he watches his younger self, this time Reynolds's Lewis Medlock from *Deliverance*, try to shoot a fish using a bow and arrow. Amused, old Vic remarks, "It was fun while it lasted, huh, Vic? We had some great times—you and me. We got to do things that most people just dream about." Young Vic agrees, still focusing on catching a fish. Old Vic then asks, "Where'd it all go, man? What does any of it mean? After all these years, I still can't figure it out—what the game's about." Young Vic/Lewis offers wisdom beyond his years: "Survival—who has the ability to survive, that's the game." Old Vic agrees, adding, "I took it for granted. I thought I had it all figured out. I look in the mirror now and I have no idea who that person is staring back at me." Taking a beat, he admires the good looks of his younger self. Young Vic/Lewis is in his early thirties and at his physical peak, his biceps bulging in his black rubber vest as he lines up his shot. Old Vic then concludes, "You know, time is like this river, no matter what you do or don't do, no matter how much you think you can beat it, it all keeps rushing by." Young Vic agrees before finally shooting his fish: "You don't beat it . . . you don't beat this river." Young Vic celebrates, as the older man sighs, lamenting his mistakes.

The revelations on the river throw Vic into self-pity. The next morning, Lil wakes to find Vic on the hotel floor, disheveled, as though he hasn't slept. When she asks if he's okay, he responds without looking at her: "I've

1. Loni Anderson and Sally Field reflect on their relationships with Burt Reynolds in the documentary *I Am Burt Reynolds* (2020) and memoir *In Pieces* (2018), respectively.

watched everyone I've ever cared about die. One by one, they seem to just disappear on me. It won't be long before I disappear, too." After he explains to Lil that the reason why he wanted to go to Knoxville was to say goodbye, they make the drive to visit Claudia at her nursing home, only to find that her dementia has progressed beyond her ability to remember him. Vic, however, finds the good ol' boy within, and, with Lil's help, they break Claudia out and take her to the spot where he had proposed, so that he can make amends. In doing so, he redeems the biggest mistake of his youth, which gives Vic the courage to return to the film festival and finally accept his award. His speech reveals a man who has come to terms with his regrets: "What have I really achieved in this lifetime? Well, I had a hell of an act one. A pretty shitty act two, and I screwed up most of act three, I made certain of that. But thanks to you . . . you've helped me to see maybe it's not too late for my Hollywood ending." At the height of Reynolds's good ol' boy fame, he feared that the work he was doing would not be critically appreciated. He stated: "I hope to God I'm still alive when the AFI salutes me" (McBride and Riley 1978, 19). Though that didn't happen, the fictional International Nashville Festival award in *The Last Movie Star* represents the celebration that Reynolds deserves from the fans who love and appreciate him most. In the final scene of *The Last Movie Star*, Vic proudly admires the trophy atop his mantel, then breaks the fourth wall by looking directly into the camera and giving viewers his signature smile, assuring them that both Burt and Vic are going to be okay. Like in the film, Burt Reynolds ends his memoir on a redemptive note: "As I look back, I'm proud of my accomplishments and disappointed by my failures. I always wanted to experience everything and go down swinging . . . And there's one thing they can never take away. Nobody had more fun than I did" (Reynolds and Winokur 2015, 263).

Burt Reynolds's good ol' boy star image skyrocketed him to fame in the 1970s, and he would reign as box-office king five years in a row, from 1978 to 1982, according to the annual *Top Ten Money Making Star Poll* (Long 2017, 38). During this time, he skillfully blended the action and comedy genres, a novelty for the era. Reynolds began his career as a young man of the South set on having the time of his life. However, by the time he wanted to be taken seriously as an actor, Hollywood had moved on from his brand of southern good ol' boy rascal, and during the 1980s Reynolds's star faded among the backdrop of bad film choices and personal troubles. The 1990s, though, turned out to be more promising for a comeback as

Reynolds garnered critical acclaim on television and received a Golden Globe win and an Oscar nomination for *Boogie Nights*. His final comeback attempt twenty years later, *The Last Movie Star*, would be his swan song. The role allowed Reynolds to draw on his own regrets and wisdom to impart on the role of Vic Edwards, a star who is also decades past his Hollywood peak. The intertextuality of Reynolds's star image in *The Last Movie Star* and his interaction with the movie footage from two of his biggest films, *Deliverance* and *Smokey and the Bandit*, add a sense of verisimilitude to Vic's redemptive journey by way of Reynolds's own notable films. The incorporation of the soulful wisdom of Lewis Medlock and the rascal of the Bandit represents the duality of Burt Reynolds's career: the serious role with depth that Reynolds desperately wanted to repeat, and the fun star-making role that would make him a star but would ultimately define his career. He shines in his sincerity and vulnerability in *The Last Movie Star*. It is bittersweet that Reynolds passed away before he could mount his next great comeback, but his last film is an ode to the good ol' boy in all its glory and flaws and gives every ounce of signature Burt Reynolds charm.

Works Cited

Anderson, Paul Thomas, dir. 1997. *Boogie Nights*. Burbank, CA: New Line Cinema. iTunes.

Long, Christian, B. 2017. "Burt Reynolds Brings the New South to Hollywood." In *The Imaginary Geography of Hollywood Cinema, 1960–2000*, 33–56. University of Chicago Press.

McBride, Joseph, and Brooks Riley. 1978. "*The End* Is Just the Beginning." *Film Comment* 14 (3) (May–June): 16–21.

Nystrom, Derek. 2009. "*Deliverance*, an Allegory of the Sunbelt." In *Hard Hats, Rednecks, and Macho Men: Class in 1970s American Cinema*, 59–78. Oxford University Press.

Reynolds, Burt, and Jon Winokur. 2015. *But Enough About Me*. Penguin Random House CloudLibrary.

Reynolds, Burt. 2018. "Burt Reynolds." Interview by George Pennacchio. *Off the Red Carpet*, ABC7, April 4, 2018. podcast, 13 min.

Rifkin, Adam, dir. 2017. *The Last Movie Star*. New York: A24. iTunes.

Stephens, Chuck. 2017. "The Swollen Boy: Paul Thomas Anderson's *Boogie Nights* and Diggler Days." *Film Comment* 33 (5) (September–October): 10–12, 14.

PART IV

AGING STAR BODIES

13

VIVECA LINDFORS'S AGING NUDE BODY IN *TABOO*

Saki Kobayashi

When *Good Luck to You, Leo Grande* (Sophie Hyde, 2022) was released, media attention concentrated on the leading star Dame Emma Thompson baring her sixty-three-year-old body to play a middle-aged woman seeking real sexual satisfaction (Sperling 2022, C1). Although expressing admiration for Thompson's bravery, such reactions epitomize how old women's bodies and sexuality onscreen are yet-to-be-broken taboos today.

Considering this, it is conceivable that the challenge experienced by a female actor embodying a sexually active aging woman was far bigger in the 1970s. Viveca Lindfors took on that challenge. Lindfors, the highest-paid female film star and renowned sex symbol in Sweden in the 1940s, performed full-frontal nude scenes in *Tabu* (*Taboo*, Vilgot Sjöman, 1977) as the amorous bisexual artist Sirkka Lind. The film, her comeback to Swedish cinema at fifty-six after an absence of almost three decades, presents a curious encounter between Lindfors's younger and older selves.

During her heyday, she portrayed passionate, sensual, norm-breaking heroines, and the Swedish media celebrated her sex appeal while sometimes making vulgar jokes about her. After moving to the United States in the mid-1940s, Lindfors worked in theater, film, and television for five decades, successfully gaining a reputation as a respected actor. While Lindfors gradually grew into a performer whose acting skills were as appreciated as her beauty, her face started to show signs of aging by the 1960s: her full lips and cheeks became thinner, her cheekbones more conspicuous, her eyes more sunken. A decade later, her drooping mouth corners and nasolabial folds created a distinctive, slightly grumpy look of the old Lindfors, which made a stark contrast to the seductiveness of her younger self.

Because of *Taboo*'s status as an art film that challenged sexual norms, the generous exposure of Lindfors's aging body here could have been interpreted as the established actor's artistic audacity. The director Sjöman, one of the flag bearers of the Swedish New Wave in the 1960s, was (in)famous for pushing the boundaries of filmic representations of sexuality with films such as the internationally well-known *Jag är nyfiken-gul* (*I Am Curious (Yellow)*, 1967). In *Taboo*, he tackled what was then regarded as various kinds of sexual aberrations—for example, homosexuality, transvestitism, exhibitionism, BDSM (bondage, discipline, sadism, and masochism), and necrophilia—again causing a scandal in Sweden.[1]

However, due to the film's graphic depictions of sex, the majority of critics dismissed it as pornographic trash, and, consequently, the nude body of the aging former sex symbol was seen as a mere part of the film's "grotesquery" (Schildt 1977, 22).[2] One of the reviews stated, for instance, that the audience reacted with "giggle, yawn, [and] groan" and "a few coarse comments on the naked Viveca Lindfors" (*Expressen* 1977, 28). Although the media had made teasing comments about her excessive sensuality even in her younger days, what made Lindfors in *Taboo* mockable was most likely her age.[3] As Rebecca Feasey's study on Sharon Stone shows, a female star who has established an image as a femme fatale incarnating "youthful beauty and sexual danger" can be greeted with "hostility and derision" when she reproduces that image in her middle age (2012, 109–10). The veteran star Lindfors could not escape such stigmatization.

What is noteworthy, however, is the approval of Lindfors's performance by the gay magazine *Revolt mot sexuella fördomar* (Balaceanu 1977, 7; Falk 1977, 9): her character was praised by critics Michael Balaceanu

1. The film presents an outdated conception of sexual aberration.

2. Translations from Swedish to English are mine.

3. Lickå Sjöman, a twenty-eight-year-old who plays the heroine in *Taboo*, performs nude scenes that are as daring as Lindfors's. However, the media did not mock her nudity but highlighted how she overcame shyness during filming, whereas it commented on Lindfors's nudity in either a dismissing or sensationalizing way. This contrast suggests that the nude body of Lindfors as well as her acting effort was underestimated solely because of her age.

and Johan Falk as an embodiment of emancipation.[4] The contrast between the reactions of the gay magazine critics and the mainstream suggests the film's camp quality. In *The Cinema of Camp*, Jack Babuscio defines camp as "elements in a person, situation, or activity that express, or are created by, a gay sensibility," which is in turn defined as "a creative energy reflecting a consciousness that is different from the mainstream; a heightened awareness of certain human complications of feeling that spring from the fact of social oppression" ([1977, 1978] 1999, 118). In light of this, I argue that Lindfors's performance expresses a gay sensibility because of its subversive nature vis-à-vis the cultural and cinematic norms that oppress an older woman's body and sexuality. To demonstrate my claim, this chapter will examine how Lindfors's aging body is presented as an attractive sexual object and an active sexual subject in one of her nude scenes in *Taboo*. My analysis will deal with not only the representation of the character Sirkka but also the way Lindfors embodies that character. This is because the concentration on "a fictional character" or "the effect of camerawork and picture editing, sound recording and editing" in analyses of screen performances leads "the work of the individual actor to be discounted." (Krämer and Lovell 1999, 5). To elucidate the norm-breaking power of her performance as Sirkka, however, it is essential to foreground the fact that Lindfors as an actor actively contributes to the creation of the meaning of her body by using it.

From Sex Symbol to Respected Actor

At the age of twenty-one, Lindfors had a breakthrough with her third film *Tänk, om jag gifter mig med prästen* (*Imagine If I Marry a Vicar*, Ivar Johansson, 1941). In it she plays a young teacher who has an affair with a vicar and becomes a single mother. As a result of this success, Lindfors starred in two films in Italy and then attained stardom back in Sweden with a hit film, *Anna Lans* (*The Sin of Anna Lans*, Rune Carlsten, 1943), a cliché-ridden melodrama about a provincial girl's hardships in the city.

4. It is worth noting that while Lindfors's performance met with sympathy, the magazine responded unfavorably to *Taboo*, in line with the socialist homosexual organization Homosexuella socialister, which denounced the film as a promoter of prejudice.

Her prominence in Sweden led Lindfors to sign a contract with Warner Bros. in 1946. Though publicized as a new Greta Garbo or Ingrid Bergman, she yielded only a mediocre result, since the American studio cast her against type in roles of rather demure women. Dissatisfied, she returned home to play the title role of *Singoalla* (Christian-Jaque, 1949), a costly Swedish-French coproduction released in three different language versions. However, she soon went back to the United States, which became her permanent home, signed with Columbia, and later became a freelance actor. Her career in theater also flourished, starting with her debut on Broadway in 1952. The title role of the stage production of *Anastasia* in 1955 became one of her greatest critical successes.

Lindfors stayed prolific on screen, too, gradually establishing herself as a capable supporting actor in mainstream American films and television programs as well as playing leading roles in independent and international productions. One of her screen career highlights was the adaptation of Jean-Paul Sartre's *No Exit* (Tad Danielewski, 1962), which won her and costar Rita Gam a Silver Bear for Best Actress at the Berlin Film Festival. While Lindfors's gradual success abroad was reported in the Swedish media, it wasn't until she toured with a theater performance of *Brecht on Brecht* in 1963 that she regained substantial public attention. Her comeback with *Taboo* fourteen years later was publicized as a welcome return prior to the film's release because it was the first time since *Singoalla* that she appeared in a Swedish film. Two years later, Lindfors was featured in *Linus eller Tegelhusets hemlighet* (*Linus and the Mysterious Red Brick House*, Vilgot Sjöman, 1979), which became her last Swedish film. She lived in the United States for the rest of her life, until she died in Sweden during her tour of a theatrical production in 1995.

Norms of an Aging Woman's Body

Taboo was not Lindfors's first nude performance. Prior to her breakthrough in *Imagine If I Marry a Vicar*, she performed skinny dipping in *I paradis . . .* (*In Paradise*, Per Lindberg, 1941), a now lost romantic comedy with a backdrop of the summer Stockholm archipelago. Also, *Imagine If I Marry a Vicar* included a seminude scene where she was seen in black underwear, and a scene in *Brödernas kvinna* (*Brothers' Woman*, Gösta Cederlund, 1943) suggested her nudity by the shadow on the wall contouring her body. Because the young Lindfors's curvaceous body was an essential element of her image, the aging nude body of Lindfors in *Taboo* created a visual connection with that of her younger self that would simultaneously sharpen the contrast between them.

In Western culture, women's bodies have been valued differently depending on their age: A woman's body where "youth and shapeliness signify allure and the decency of regularity" is idealized and romanticized, whereas an older woman's body is characterized by "wrinkles, gray hair, and untoned muscle" and lack of "proportion and harmony" (Frueh 1999, 213–14). A young female body is privileged not only aesthetically but also sexually: In contrast with the young body bestowed with "femaleness as an invitation to sex," the older one is associated with "nurturance and warmth safe from—because sterilized of—sex" (214). Thus, an old female body is desexualized to compensate for deficiencies in beauty and sexual attractiveness.

Film as a cultural institution has promoted these norms about women's bodies. The fact that an older female body is overwhelmingly underrepresented compared to a younger counterpart testifies to how film reinforces "stereotypical notions of older women's bodies as not worth looking at" (Gravagne 2013, 66). Furthermore, film can actively marginalize and stigmatize an older woman's body as neither a desirable sexual object nor an active sexual subject when it is visible onscreen. As discussed by Pamela H. Gravagne and E. Ann Kaplan, even films from the early 2000s that appear to acknowledge the aesthetic value or sexual agency of an older woman's body eventually comply with these norms by implying the need of juvenilization/beautification of her body or avoiding too much focus on it (2013, 78–80; 2012, 23–28). In this light, Lindfors's performance in *Taboo* seems ahead of its time insofar as her aging nude body is presented without any beautifying manipulation but nevertheless is neither desexualized nor devalued. However, this strategy could not be achieved within mainstream aesthetics but only by appropriating camp.

Lindfors's Performance as Camp

Taboo is narrated from the perspective of the young heroine Sara, who engages in a romantic relationship with Kristoffer, a young lawyer ostensibly supporting the rights of those whom he calls "borderline people," regarded as "sick" by society because of their sexual behavior. The romance ends when it is discovered that his advocacy is motivated by an egoistic attempt to come to terms with his own homophobia and sexual frustration originating from his failed relationship with his mother. Lindfors's Sirkka is one of the "borderline people," a bisexual artist specializing in sexually provocative works, who also has an undefinable relationship with Kristoffer. Sirkka makes her first appearance in the film when Sara and Kristoffer visit her party for male transvestites with whom she has a cordial relationship.[5] In this sequence, Lindfors performs the most daring nude scene in the film.

The relaxed atmosphere of the party becomes sexually charged, at first in a playful way, when Sirkka begins to dance to mellow music playing on the radio. Sara and Kristoffer join her. The three hold and peck each other on the mouth, while Sirkka's gaze is directed at Sara, signaling her desire for the young woman. Sirkka then picks the male transvestite Margareta as her next dance partner, covers Margareta's eyes with a shawl and caresses her body, including the buttocks and the crotch.[6] This gesture triggers Sirkka's exhibitionist impulse: Encouraged by the radio now playing an upbeat, joyful tune she cries, "Yahoo!" and removes her shirt and pants, revealing her bare skin. Making a quick turn, she hops onto a step to flaunt her body to the diegetic audience, the male transvestites and the young couple. Over the next three minutes, as she dances, the camera captures her nude body in long and medium shots from the front, back, and side, allowing the audience to thoroughly observe it.

Although Lindfors's body is well proportioned, the less elastic skin, cellulite, and saggy breasts reveal the differences from her younger body. However, what highlights her aging even more are the frequent close-ups of her face, revealing deep wrinkles around the mouth and between the

5. The film uses the term "transvestites" to ambiguously refer to male transvestites, both homosexual and heterosexual, and trans women. Most of the people invited to Sirkka's party are, according to her, "real guys" or "hetero," but at least one of them is said to want gender affirmation surgery, which suggests that this character might be a trans woman. Insofar as the people with different gender identities are lumped together in one single category ("transvestites"), the film reflects the lack of knowledge about this issue.

6. Margareta is a self-admitted heterosexual male transvestite. However, Sara calls Margareta "a woman" and uses the pronouns "she/her" to refer to the character. Therefore, I follow that designation in my analysis.

eyebrows. The aging of the face is a more striking contrast with Lindfors's younger face—chubby cheeks and a full-lipped mouth—than the contrast between her old and young body, therefore amplifying the aging of the body. Lindfors's face, separated from the body, defines her body more than the body itself does. This complicated relationship between Lindfors's aging face and body is worthy of attention in relation to Susan Sontag's argument that women are split into a body and a face. While her body more directly arouses a man's desire, a woman's face creates her identity "in defiance of the laws of simple sexual attraction" ([1972] 1997, 22). Sontag understands that a woman, by devoting herself to the physical care of her face, transforms it into a mask that hides "what she doesn't want it to show" and represents what she wants it to show (23). Lindfors's aging face, by contrast, uncovers the unwanted.[7] However, it paradoxically confirms the dominant role of a woman's face in defining her. Thus, ironically, Lindfors's body in *Taboo* is, because of her face, emphatically marked as an old woman's body, which is supposedly deprived of sexual attraction and agency.

Despite this fact, however, her body is consistently presented as a desired object. The shots of the dancing Sirkka are intercut with reaction shots of her diegetic audience fixing their gaze on her, establishing the relation between the looking and the looked-at. Interestingly, due to the genders of her diegetic audience, Sirkka's body is objectified in the way it defies the "'double-double standard'" (Gravagne 2013, 65) of women's aging that devalues older women "not only in relation to men but also in relation to their younger counterparts" (quoted in Gravagne 2013, 65). The transvestites' gaze can be construed as both envious and lustful: Sara's voices her admiration and Kristoffer's conveys his heterosexual desire, which is not questioned at this point. Therefore, Sirkka's body is desirable and attractive from the perspectives of a man, men-as-women, and a young woman.

At the same time despite being objectified, Sirkka is capable of expressing her own agency as a sexual subject, as a desiring subject, because she derives pleasure from being looked at. Lindfors's face again plays an important role here. As a part of the spontaneous choreography,

7. In her autobiography, Lindfors divulges her dislike of the wrinkles on her face while defending her "hanging breasts" as a result of breast-feeding (1978, 70–71).

Sirrka/Lindfors quickly shakes her head from side to side, grins, opens and closes her mouth as if she experienced a facial spasm. While these close-ups of Lindfors communicate Sirkka's ecstasy, her exaggerated facial expressions can be read as a parody of sexual pleasure, which makes this whole scene comic. The way Sirkka/Lindfors handles her aging body also contributes to the impression that the character taking active sexual pleasure is also *playing with* it. When one of the transvestites walks past her, Sirkka/Lindfors lifts her saggy breasts as if to show them off, which causes obvious embarrassment.

Lindfors's performance as Sirkka presents four basic features of camp named by Babuscio: "Irony," "Aestheticism," "Theatricality," and "Humour" ([1977, 1978] 1999, 119–28). Her exaggerated facial expressions and gesticulations to enact the character's joy is in line with camp's aestheticism, which emphasizes "style as a means of self-projection, a conveyer of meaning, and an expression of emotional tone" (122). This exaggeration can also be related to camp theatricality that often involves overemphasized sexual role-playing (123–24). By exaggerating the mature woman's ecstasy, Lindfors emphasizes that her aging body *is* a sexual being just as it used to be in a "natural" way in her youth. Needless to say, the humor of her performance strengthens its camp quality.

Furthermore, the scene is imbued with irony. Toward the end of her dancing, the playful expression of Sirkka's sexual agency shifts to a more serious invitation to a direct physical sexual contact. Sirkka/Lindfors gradually stops her grinning and directs a predatory stare at Kristoffer. Lured by Sirkka's sexual magnetism, he kneels down in front of her, holds her lower torso, and kisses her abdomen, moving toward her crotch. Sirkka/Lindfors closes her eyes in what seems to be an expression of real sexual excitement and embraces the young man. This "incongruous contrast" of "young man/old(er) woman" is highlighted because of the presence of Sara, Kristoffer's young lover, feeling jealousy toward her older rival (Babuscio [1977, 1978] 1999, 119). The fact that Sirkka, a middle-aged woman whose body is supposed to be desexualized, is privileged as a desirable sexual being and free from frustration in contrast with Sara, a young woman who is less desired and more frustrated, constitutes the irony of this scene. Furthermore, considering that Sirkka is privileged in the circle of "borderline people," not among "normal" folk, confuses "the 'normal,' 'natural,' 'healthy' heterosexual order of things" even more (119–20).

Lindfors's performance also encourages thinking about "the serious"—in this case, the cinematic—norms of older women's bodies (Babuscio [1977, 1978] 1999, 128). In the middle of her dancing, Sirkka shouts: "Set free your lust! Any pleasure is not a taboo!" On a superficial level, this simply justifies the character's exhibitionist pleasure. However, does the "taboo" only refer to that? From the film audience's perspective, is the actor exposing her aging body on screen not as outrageous as the character's striptease in the diegetic world? This issue invites another question: What is "pleasure" about, and whose is it? What is at stake here is the pleasure the film's audience might elicit from looking at Lindfors's aging nude body. Laura Mulvey famously argued that mainstream narrative cinema has traditionally offered visual pleasure by constructing a woman, and, for that matter, predominantly a young woman like Sara, as "a passive image of visual perfection" (1975, 16). By contrast, Lindfors's strikingly self-conscious performance "encourages an affectionate involvement" of the audience and thereby makes their voyeurism controlled by the object itself, Sirkka/Lindfors (Babuscio [1977, 1978] 1999, 123). Then, is it not this pleasure, which the film's audience is encouraged to derive from looking at an older woman, an "imperfect" beauty and erotic object, that is suggested as a taboo in contrast with the "normal" visual pleasure?

Considering the mainstream reception of Lindfors's performance, it is questionable whether the film succeeded in breaking this taboo. But the acknowledgement of the taboo-/norm-breaking power of this performance came from gay critics, demonstrating that, thanks to a gay sensibility, the aging nude body of Lindfors was transformed into the symbol of liberation from sexual oppression of all kinds.[8] "Viveca Lindfors' Sirkka . . . is open and uncomplicated and seems to be completely free from prejudice. . . . Imagine if pretty well every one of us could be a little more like her and show the same open-mindedness and lighthearted attitude" (Falk 1977, 9).

8. Two gay magazine critics (Balaceanu and Falk), two women, a film critic, and a sex educator, left positive, but very short, comments on Lindfors. However, another female critic criticized Lindfors's performance for failing to portray the character realistically. Furthermore, the positive comments about the film by two female audience members interviewed by a newspaper did not deal specifically with Lindfors. Therefore, it is difficult to evaluate how her appearance in the film was accepted by women.

After more than four decades, what message can Lindfors's aging nude body communicate to the audience? As mentioned at the beginning of this chapter, the destigmatization of older women's bodies is still much needed. In that sense, the comeback of the 1940s Swedish sex symbol in the late 1970s can and should be reevaluated as a challenge to the persistent cinematic norms relating to women's age and sexuality. Although largely remembered as a film that scandalized mainstream critics, *Taboo* challenges cinematic norms governing the presentation of aging female bodies because of the presence of the character Sirkka. At the same time, Lindfors's courageous performance proved almost exceptional in liberating mature women from the pernicious restrictions and double standards of age appropriate sexual behavior.

Works Cited

Babuscio, Jack. [1977, 1978] 1999. "The Cinema of Camp (AKA Camp and the Gay Sensibility)." In *Camp: Queer Aesthetics and the Performing Subject: A Reader*, edited by Fabio Cleto, 117–35. Edinburgh University Press.

Balaceanu, Michael. 1977. "70-talets debattfilm?" *Revolt mot sexuella fördomar* 8 (3): 7–8.

Falk, Johan. 1977. "Varför så negativt?" *Revolt mot sexuella fördomar* 8 (3): 8–10.

Feasey, Rebecca. 2012. "The Ageing Femme Fatale: Sex, Stardom, and Sharon Stone." In *Aging, Performance, and Stardom: Doing Age on the Stage of Consumerist Culture*, edited by Aagje Swinnen and John A Stotesbury, 109–27. LIT Verlag.

"Fniss, gäsp, stön: I salongen med Tabu." 1977. *Expressen*, February 18, 1977.

Frueh, Joanna. 1999. "Monster/Beauty: Midlife Bodybuilding as Aesthetic Discipline." In *Figuring Age: Women, Bodies, Generations*, edited by Kathleen Woodward, 212–26. Indiana University Press.

Gravagne, Pamela H. 2013. *The Becoming of Age: Cinematic Visions of Mind, Body, and Identity in Later Life*. McFarland.

Kaplan, E. Ann. 2012. "The Unconscious of Age: Performances in Psychoanalysis, Film, and Popular Culture." In *Aging, Performance, and Stardom: Doing Age on the Stage of Consumerist Culture*, edited by Aagje Swinnen and John A Stotesbury, 17–37. LIT Verlag.

Krämer, Peter, and Alan Lovell. 1999. "Introduction." In *Screen Acting*, edited by Alan Lovell and Peter Krämer, 1–9. Routledge.

Lindfors, Viveca. 1978. *Viveka . . . Viveca . . .* Bonnier.

Mulvey, Laura. 1975. "Visual Pleasure and Narrative Cinema." *Screen* 16 (3): 6–18.

Schildt, Jurgen. 1977. "Gud bevare aktörerna—men vem ska bevara Vilgot Sjöman." *Aftonbladet*, January 29, 1977.

Sjöman, Vilgot, dir. 1977. *Tabu*. In *"Svenska kultklassiker: Raggare!"; "Chans"; "Miss and Mrs. Sweden"; "Smutsiga fingrar"; "Stenansiktet"; "Tabu."* Stockholm: Studio S Entertainment, 2016. DVD.

Sontag, Susan. [1972] 1997. "The Double Standard of Aging." In *The Other Within Us: Feminist Explorations of Women and Aging*, edited by Marilyn Pearsall, 19–24. Westview.

Sperling, Nicole. 2022. "Baring It All Onscreen at 63, Despite Her Fear." *New York Times*, June 15, 2022.

14

SEX AND POLITICS

Aquarius and Sonia Braga's Star Image

PEDRO GUIMARÃES

She is a mixture of Marilyn Monroe and Eleanor Roosevelt.

—*Moon over Parador* (Paul Mazursky, 1988)

When *Aquarius* (Kleber Mendonça Filho, 2016) debuted in Brazil, the film's screening quickly turned into a moment of national catharsis. The audience shouted slogans, defending Dilma Rousseff, who had just been fraudulently impeached and removed from the post of president. When Clara learns that a developer intends to force her out of her seafront apartment in Recife, where she has lived for decades, in order to build a luxurious multistory building, she decides to fight back. At the Cannes International Film Festival, where the film was shown in competition, the director, lead actor, and the film's crew held up posters denouncing the coup.

Brazilian political columnists and scholars drew parallels between Clara, played by aging star Sônia Braga, and the country's troubled president.[1] Here were two powerful, mature women confronting political and economic opposition in the form of misogynistic exploitation and a massive campaign to degrade their lives and reputations. While feces are deposited on the stairs of Clara's apartment building, stickers were pasted on cars with fake images of Roussef in erotic poses. These parallels generated a heated debate and garnered the film both national and international

1. For further analysis, see Reis 2018.

attention. *Aquarius* also brought one of the country's most fascinating and successful stars back into the forefront of Brazilian cinema at the age of sixty-six, twenty years since Braga had a major presence in film and television.[2]

Braga's casting provides an opportunity to analyze the updating of her star image. The concept of the star text includes filmic and parafilmic elements: privileged character types, aesthetic preferences for acting, advertising and speeches of celebrities in the press, the actor's personal engagements in social causes or policies. The star text encompasses the systematized manifestation of discourses about the persona of the star and the public image of the actor created from the films and their intimate life, which determine their reemployment in subsequent films. Braga's star text appears to be built on the principles that established the star system during the golden era of classic American cinema. Using the term "star discourse," Richard De Cordova states that "private and professional become two autonomous spheres that can be articulated in paradigm. . . . The real hero behaves just like the reel hero," and that "the private life of the star was not to be in contradiction with his/her film image. . . . The two would rather support each other" (1991, 27). Edgar Morin discusses the reciprocal contamination between the actor's image and their characters: "The star is more than an actor incarnating characters, she is incarnated in them and they are incarnated in her" (1972, 37).

Therefore, it is highly important to understand Clara's character in an intrinsic relationship with the actor who plays her. This chapter will demonstrate how *Aquarius* draws directly upon many of the aging star's previous screen roles and her former image, as well as Braga's political positions. I will begin by briefly outlining some of the main aspects of her career prior to 2016.

Brazil's Dark Export

Despite being born in the south of Brazil—in the state of Paraná, a region with a great number of German and Italian immigrants—Braga

2. Between 2000 and 2015, Braga mostly appeared in television series and films made for TV. She did make a number of films that were released in cinemas, usually in supporting roles, none of which had the cultural impact of *Aquarius*. It is this film that restored her to the forefront of Brazilian cinema.

was notable for the representation of women from the Brazilian northeast, predominantly Black women. Stephanie Dennison argues that her body suggests a racial mixture: "With her black wiry hair, wide hips and dark skin, she stands out . . . as physically one of the most Africanized of Brazil's successful white actresses" (2006, 137). Braga might best be characterized as the brunette who "frequently fills the role assumed by the mulata in other arts" (Dennison 2007, 138), even though she does not necessarily conform to the stereotypes associated with Black Latina women, such as an exaggerated sensuality and a devouring sexual appetite. Dennison writes: "For many (including those who work in her publicity machine), Braga is the archetypal morena, a term meaning a dark-skinned or dark-haired 'white' woman, but which is often confusingly also used as a euphemism for mulata (mixed-race). Mulata in turn was until recently frequently used to mean black. Both Morena and mulata have sexual as well as racial connotations" (2007, 163).

Yet, in Brazil, the brunette often evokes upper-class characters—that is, a direct descendant of the Portuguese bourgeoisie that emigrated to the country during the time of colonization. It is this embodiment of the brunette that marked Braga's first film role in *A moreninha* (Glauco Mirko Laureli, 1970). Years later she also appeared in the title role in *Mestiça, a escrava indomável* (Lenita Perroy, 1973) as an enslaved woman of indigenous origin who awakens love in a white bourgeois man, revealing how effectively she could portray women of very different social classes. Black or brown, Braga's physical belonging to a class of women of marked African or indigenous origin is emphasized in *Aquarius*, when the young entrepreneur Diego (Humberto Carrão) states unequivocally that he respects Clara's social status despite her darker skin. Although disguised as admiration, this remark is used by the young man to belittle Braga's character and makes the racial dimension central to the film's narrative. Interestingly, although Clara's family is presented as being typically white and middle-class, Braga embodies the subaltern, immigrant, dark-skinned woman, like so many characters that she played in the past.

Braga's acting destiny was determined by her intersection with the imagination of the Brazilian northeast, predominantly that of Jorge Amado, one of the most translated Brazilian writers abroad, openly communist and known for creating characters of strong and sensual women from the Brazilian northeast. In *Dona Flor e seus dois maridos* (*Dona Flor and

Her Two Husbands, Bruno Barreto, 1976), adapted from Amado's novel, she portrays a housewife so devoted to her dead husband that she has sex with his corpse. A resounding success at the box office, this film launched Braga as a sex symbol, both inside and outside Brazil. She became associated "with the transgressive and liberated mood of the period of opening, and this must be one of the reasons why she became such a popular movie star" (Shaw and Dennison, 2007, 166).[3] The film, along with the previous year's telenovela *Gabriela* (Walter Avancini, 1975), helped create the image of a woman always ready for sex, an image that would also define Braga's offscreen persona.[4] Later she starred in another film directed by Barreto, *Gabriela* (1983), an international production with Marcello Mastroianni that confirmed her presence in foreign markets.

Along with *Dona Flor and Her Two Husbands*, *Kiss of the Spider Woman* (Hector Babenco, 1985) became Braga's best-known film outside Brazil, one that definitively transformed her into a sensual, elegant, and idealized woman with an image drawn from European and Latin melodrama and espionage films, built on the detailed and passionate descriptions of the prisoner Molina (William Hurt). Braga's character embodies the dreams of the imprisoned man, part panther-woman/vampire-woman, part cabaret singer à la Marlene Dietrich. Over the next three years, Braga's public image circulated within a wide and diverse international market, among art house and mainstream audiences.

Braga became the best-known Brazilian star outside Brazil since Carmen Miranda.[5] When Braga emigrated to the United States fifty years after Miranda, she experienced a similar kind of national stereotyping that included being used to represent a dangerous sensuality, often being required to play characters driven by unbridled sexual desire, such as in *The Rookie* (Clint Eastwood, 1990), in which she appears primarily to seduce, kill, and be killed.

3. The term "period of opening" refers to the political changes following the end of the twenty-one-year military dictatorship in Brazil.
4. Braga played the title character in this telenovela based on Amado's novel. According to Shaw and Dennison, "Gabriela is one of Jorge Amado's archetypal mixed-race females from the North-East: cinnamon-coloured, devastatingly sexy without even trying, a free spirit and dirt-poor" (2007, 164).
5. Miranda's move to the United States was part of the Good Neighbor policy of cooperation between the two countries in the late 1930s.

Inevitably, perhaps, Braga returned to Brazil in the nineties, where she became increasingly involved with environmental causes, which included a personal and professional connection with actor Raul Julia, with whom she acted in *The Burning Season* (John Frankenheimer, 1994), a biopic of the environmentalist leader Chico Mendes, who was killed for defending the Amazon rainforest. She also became the symbol of Loucos Varridos, a project to collect garbage on the beaches of Rio de Janeiro and elsewhere. One of her most important films of this period was *Tieta do Agreste* (*Tieta of Agreste*, Carlos Diegues, 1996), where she played a woman from a repressive rural background who returns home twenty years after being barred by her father for exploring her sexuality. She is now a rich woman, having worked as a prostitute in São Paulo. Based on a novel by Amado, the film deals with the environmental destruction and the impoverishment of local populations caused by commercial tourism along the beaches and mangroves of the northeast. Interestingly, while in the novel the character Tieta does not want to get involved in the fight between the businesses from the south of Brazil and local authorities and small defenders of the peaceful life of the village, when played by Braga in the film she is transformed into a staunch defender of the environment.

The women Braga enacts have something in common (with the exception of Flor): long flowing, sensual black hair. Braga is the brunette version of Veronica Lake and Catherine Deneuve, whose hair became an authorial mark and an element of recognition of their characters, a true "hair-desire" (*chevelure-désir*), as Alain Bergala describes the hair of Luis Buñuel's leading women (2011, 16). Significantly, the first part of *Aquarius* is titled "Clara's Hair." Here, the character appears with very short hair due to her undergoing cancer treatment. But, later, when she is older, Clara once again flaunts the power of the black mane, which she curls and ties into a bun, a gesture that also appears in other characters she has played. Her hair becomes a symbol of strength with which she will fight against her opponents, like a female Samson.[6]

Amado is not the only writer who created sensual women roles for Braga. Another Brazilian novelist contributed greatly to the construction

6. President Dilma Rousseff also suffered from cancer at a mature age, an event that was highly publicized years before she became president, when she also appeared with short hair.

of her persona as a carnal woman: the playwright and chronicler Nelson Rodrigues. In *A Dama do Lotação* (*Lady in the Bus*, Neville de Almeida, 1978), adapted from the writer's tale, Braga plays a frigid married woman who discovers sexual pleasure with strangers on public transportation in Rio de Janeiro. She avoids her husband but gives herself to unknown bus drivers, conductors, and other men in sex scenes that expose Braga's body. The film was hugely successful at the box office, and critics were reminded of Catherine Deneuve's character in *Belle de jour* (Luis Buñuel, 1967). *Lady in the Bus* reveals the urban side of Braga's sensuality in the so-called *pornochanchadas*: erotic comedies of manners that display the female body in a systematic and fetishistic way.[7] Alberto da Silva remarks that in another of these *pornochanchadas*, *Eu te amo* (*I Love You*, Arnaldo Jabor, 1981) Braga portrays a kind of Latin femme fatale along the lines of the women of the American cinema of the 1950s, with her "sexuality at once fascinating and frightening for the male character" (2014, 4).

Connecting with Her Younger Screen Self in *Aquarius*

Many aspects of Braga's star image and previous screen roles resurface in *Aquarius*, a film in which environmental issues take center stage. As Clara, she stands up to a developer when he tries to force her out of her apartment so that a luxurious multistory building can be built. Yet *Aquarius* is not just about her fight with the construction company's owners; it is also a story of female bonding. A feeling of empathy develops between Clara and her "crooked" aunt Lucia (Thaia Perez) after the older woman's seventieth birthday party, during which her risqué behavior comes to light, along with her pioneering work as a lawyer and the political persecution she suffered during the military dictatorship. The film forges political links

7. The same year Braga also starred in the telenovela *Dancin' Days* (Gilberto Braga, 1978). She plays a woman who gets out of prison after many years and tries to regain the love and attention of her teenage daughter, who had been raised by her sister and rival. Set at the time when disco was popular, Braga performs numerous scenes dancing in the nightclub, wearing scanty clothes and showing much physical vigor and sensuality. As an ex-convict, she faces prejudice from the elitist society of Rio in her effort to regain her place as a mother. Filho remembered the dance scenes of the telenovela when he staged Clara's dancing alone in her apartment and facing the discrimination of the local power.

between the private and the public spheres. Moreover, the powers that try to suffocate Clara are similar to those that have suffocated Brazilian society, most evidently since the deposition of President Dilma Rousseff but also historically as a result of the growing evangelism and reactionary ideas. It is this world that forces Clara to take a stand, just as Sônia Braga had done as an environmentalist in the 1990s.

Clara is an unusual character in Brazilian cinema for two main reasons: gender and age. First, given her social and political positions, she could be seen as a female actualization of the intellectually engaged characters of Cinema Novo, a movement notable for representing lower social classes that had been absent from the screen until then. Some films problematized the figure of the left-wing middle-class male intellectual facing a crisis, such as *Terra em Transe* (*Entranced Earth*, Glauber Rocha, 1967) and *O Desafio* (*The Dare*, Paulo César Saraceni, 1966). It is not by chance that these films appeared immediately after the coup d'état suffered by the Brazilian democracy in 1964, in which, according to Ismail Xavier, "the pain of defeat, of mourning" prevails (2012, 186). In a similar blow to the Brazilian democracy caused by President Roussef's impeachment, it is symptomatic that a character resurfaces as a woman. The second characteristic that separates Clara from other female characters in Brazilian cinema is that she is a woman over sixty who maintains a romantic and active sex life. This is notable when, after watching a group of people having sex through a crack in the door, she calls a male prostitute to satisfy her own desires. She indulges in a daring sex encounter with a man thirty years younger than herself, exposing her body in the process. The sex taboo of the elderly is dismantled here as Clara reprises an erotic moment that Braga often portrayed throughout her career. Both the press and moviegoers in Brazil were not alarmed by the sight of a mature woman maintaining an active sexual life. Braga facilitated this acceptance given her various similar appearances in films and soap operas.

Aquarius is an important work of contemporary Brazilian cinema because of its political connotations and the intense reaction it generated at home and abroad. However, as this chapter has demonstrated, it is also significant as a comeback vehicle that revived Sônia Braga's star image by drawing together various threads from her cinematic career.

Works Cited

Bergala, Alain. 2011. "Qu'est-ce qu'un grand cinéaste de la chevelure?" In *Brune/Blonde: La Chevelure Féminine dans l'Art et le Cinéma*, edited by Alain Bergala, 14–27. Cinémathèque Française/Skira Flammarion.

Filho, Kleber Mendonça, dir. 2016. *Aquarius*. São Paulo: Imovision, 2017. DVD.

Garcia Reis, Octávio. 2018. "'Vai ter luta?': *Aquarius* e algumas narrativas do cenário político brasileiro no prégolpe de 2016." *Ilhas Literárias Magazine*. https://www.ufrgs.br/ppgletras/coloquiosularquipelagos/artigos.html.

Da Silva, Alberto. 2014. "Sônia Braga: la beauté latine de la 'vraie femme brésilienne' des années de la dictature." *Mise au point* 6. https://journals.openedition.org/map/1748.

DeCordova, Richard. 1991. "The Emergence of the Star System in America." In *Stardom: Industry of Desire*, edited by Christine Gledhill, 17–29. Routledge.

Dennison, Stephanie. 2006. "The New Brazilian Bombshell: Sônia Braga, Race, and Cinema in the 1970s." In *Remapping World Cinema, Identity, Culture, and Politics in Film*, edited by Stephanie Dennison and Song Hwee Lim, 135–43. Wallflower.

Morin, Edgar. 1972. *Les stars*. Paris: Seuil.

Shaw, Lisa, and Stephanie Dennison. 2007. *Brazilian National Cinema*. Routledge.

15

"TONIGHT, I'M GONNA RETURN THE FAVOR"

Wesley Snipes's Punishment and the Challenges of the Black Action Star Comeback

Clem Bastow and Glen Donnar

The vulnerability of the aging action star is redoubled in the figure of the former star seeking a comeback in an industry that seemingly either no longer values or needs them. Reminiscent of the action genre trope of being "used (up)" by anonymous, distant others, redundancy for the former action star centers on perceptions of having passed one's use-by date. After a decade starring in direct-to-video (DTV) releases and completing a three-year prison sentence for tax evasion, from 2010 to 2013, Wesley Snipes began his Hollywood comeback in the third installment of *The Expendables* franchise (2010–14) in 2014. Snipes's previous standing as the preeminent 1990s Black action star and this later association with geriaction (a recent cycle of Hollywood action films that has revitalized the careers of aging stars from their mid-fifties to seventies) frame his comeback. Snipes's role in *The Expendables 3* (Patrick Hughes, 2014) playfully references his real-life imprisonment—he is rescued from long-term incarceration in its spectacular opening—and recalls his previous onscreen blockbuster with Sylvester Stallone in *Demolition Man* (Marco Brambilla, 1993), in which his character escapes after being unfrozen from cryogenic incarceration.

Crucially, Snipes also illustrates the difficulty of a late-career comeback for a former action star both ahead of his time—as the first Black

Marvel cinematic superhero, Blade—and after "doing time." Comebacks, especially those derided as derivative and insubstantial, are often taken as elegiac reflections on faded stardom and evidence of diminishing creative capacity. This diminished worth is redoubled in Hollywood action genre cinema, in which the routine repetition of tropes, themes, and catchphrases is popularly claimed to be without substance.

This chapter analyzes Snipes's comeback with a focus on three critically reviled films that emphasize intertextual "callbacks" to his former Hollywood action stardom and, less positively, to his later DTV works and legal struggles: *The Expendables 3* and "off-off-Broadway" lead roles in straight-to-streaming hybrid action/sci-fi/horror films *Armed Response* (John Stockwell, 2017) and *The Recall* (Mauro Borrelli, 2017). Snipes's comeback—whether his character is rescued, cast aside, or unable to escape his past—nostalgically recalls the aging actor's former stardom. While he has more recently delivered affected, flamboyant comic performances in *Dolemite Is My Name* (Craig Brewer, 2019) and *Coming 2 America* (Craig Brewer, 2020) that recall his 1990s comedies, this chapter will concentrate on comeback films that evoke the challenges Snipes faced in returning to the heights he held at the end of the 1990s, and that particularly call back to his roles as the outlandish villain Simon Phoenix in *Demolition Man* and the eponymous half-vampire in the *Blade* trilogy (Stephen Norrington, 1998; Guillermo del Toro, 2002; David S. Goyer, 2004).

The blurring or equation of star and character or lived experiences and roles has long been part of Snipes's star text, characterized by his infamous 1998 promotional interview for *Blade*, conducted "in character." Responding to a question about Blade's origin story, Snipes began, "He was transformed genetically after his mother was bitten by a vampire . . ."—turning his gaze slightly toward the camera, he continues as Blade—". . . who I'm still looking for to this day, can't wait to meet up with Daddy again." His playfulness gives the interview a camp charge, but Snipes's fluid melding of star and character personae typifies his star text.

Comebacks, especially those that recall rather than diverge from past roles, are often taken as evidence of lack and loss, melancholic and elegiac reflections on faded stardom and diminishing returns. The later work is often considered to be lesser than the star's most identifiable work—the comeback understood as diverting but, being financially motivated, ignominious and a career nadir. Any screen comeback plays on the cultural weight of a star's onscreen persona and the roles that established their star text, but Snipes's comeback was especially focused on both his existing body of work and his real-life tribulations. Snipes's lead roles in straight-to-streaming hybrid action/sci-fi/horror films could be viewed as not unlike those he made as his star waned previously. In a sense, his comeback required him to return to his DTV years of decline as penance and to reestablish his star image.

"You Make One Damn Mistake": The Pleasure of Breaking Out and the Coincidence of Star-Character in *The Expendables 3*

Snipes was the preeminent Black action star in the early 1990s. A martial arts expert, he "had the taut, wiry body and graceful movements of a dancer . . . fused with a quick-witted athleticism" (Bogle 2016, 368). His stardom rose "by sticking to unhinged characters who know no justice, no peace" (Williams Jr. 2014, 159), drawing on his Bronx upbringing. He gained notice as a ruthless Harlem drug kingpin in *New Jack City* (Mario Van Peebles, 1991), one of numerous roles as "outsider renegades" (Bogle 2016, 368) that revealed his range and daring. Atypically for an action star, Snipes's early career also includes numerous celebrated performances in smaller independent films such as *Jungle Fever* (Spike Lee, 1991); *The Waterdance* (Neal Jimenez, Michael Steinberg, 1992); and *One Night Stand* (Mike Figgis, 1997). As his action stardom grew, he starred in *Passenger 57* (Kevin Hooks, 1992); as the cop buddy of Sean Connery in *Rising Sun* (Philip Kaufman, 1993); and as the supervillain antagonist of 1980s action luminary Sylvester Stallone in *Demolition Man*. Between 1998 and 2004 he starred as the first Black superhero in the *Blade* trilogy, his presence within superhero cinema considered "inherently threatening to white patriarchy" (Gayles 2012, 286). Snipes's star image stood in marked contrast to the predominant whiteness of the action genre, a notion reinforced when his rogue cop character reminds the white terrorist in *Passenger 57* to "always bet on Black!" Bogle argues that Snipes brought a fascinating "new vigor and cultural demarcation to standard action films, elevating them to another level, infusing them with a new aesthetic" (2016, 369). Snipes both reanimates and parodies Black screen masculinity. Although his characters are often positioned, and even described by other characters, as frightening and feared, his macho posturing is often knowing and performative, even camp. However, in part associated with his legal action about his treatment in the final installment, and bad press relating to his alleged on-set behavior, his career waned over the second half of the decade with almost all his films between 2005 and *Brooklyn's Finest* (Antoine Fuqua, 2009) released direct-to-video. This decline reached its apparent nadir when he was jailed for three years in 2010 for tax evasion (charged in 2006), seemingly ending his career.

Snipes's comeback to the screen after jail begins via *The Expendables* franchise (2010–14), reuniting him with Stallone in *The Expendables 3*.[1] As well as being identified with Stallone, Arnold Schwarzenegger, and other aging action cinema luminaries, *The Expendables* franchise has also sought to rekindle or redeem the damaged careers of aging stars who have experienced scandal, including Mel Gibson and Snipes.[2] In the film, Snipes's character is rescued from imprisonment, the spectacular opening sequence reintroducing him and his seemingly ageless, undiminished movement to audiences after his real-life incarceration.

The Expendables 3 opens as the camera sweeps toward a heavily armored prison transport train, replete with half a dozen gun-toting guards riding on its roof. A guard, speaking Russian, makes an intercom call: "We have recaptured the fugitive. We're returning the prisoner now." As the guards prepare for the train's arrival at Denzali Prison, members of the Expendables, a team of aging mercenaries led by Barney Ross (Stallone), ready themselves for a raid. They board a helicopter and begin to pick the guards off one by one. They alight from the helicopter and board the train. After shooting the remaining few guards, they enter the jail cell at the heart of the train, and the object of the heist is revealed: "Doc" Death (Snipes). Wild-eyed and bushy-bearded, Doc's lethal danger is marked by his Hannibal Lecter–esque leather restraint. Exiting the cell, he stares with transfixed vengeance at an official portrait of his chief captor. Part of the pleasure in the sequence is to witness Snipes's resumed performance of the star self. The delay in introducing Snipes onscreen functions to build

1. Snipes was originally invited to take the role of Hale Caesar in the first installment of *The Expendables* (2010) but was unable to leave the United States.
2. In 2006, during an arrest for DUI, Gibson was recorded making antisemitic remarks; it later emerged that he had been verbally abusive toward his wife, Oksana Grigorieva, and former costars.

suspense before fans of action cinema can take pleasure in his return/appearance.

The viewer is pushed to wonder: Has Snipes still "got it" after all this time on the sidelines of Hollywood action cinema? This perception of the aging action star's agelessness or undiminished capacity is key to Snipes's action cinema comeback (Donnar 2022). In contrast to Stallone et al., Snipes's graceful athleticism seems undiminished by age, despite more prominent frown lines and a beard flecked with gray. Moving to the roof of the train, he hesitates as Ross dips the helicopter low to extract the team. As the score reaches a crescendo, two close-ups reveal Doc's knowing gaze at Ross, before Doc turns and sprints toward the front of the train. Doc swings down from the top of the train, swiftly disarms a waiting guard with a martial arts move, and steals his knife, which he throws to dispatch another guard. This immediately recalls his opening scene in *Blade*, in which, announcing his presence as a Black superhero, Snipes switches to hand-to-hand combat in a mixture of martial arts–inspired and professional wrestling–style moves and "is completely kinetic as he leaps, slices, kicks and punches his way through the film" (Gayles 2012, 286). Revealing Blade's iconic throwing glaive, in a moment of comic camp, Snipes flashes his trademark smile, as if acknowledging the weapon's coolness to the viewer. Returning to *The Expendables 3*, Doc then enters the engine compartment and incapacitates the driver, pushing the throttle to full and sending the train hurtling toward the prison gates. In contrast to Snipes's comic book–inspired fighting style in *Blade*, in which he regularly freezes after striking a killing blow, or pauses to reveal a new weapon, this sequence recalls Gallagher's observation that Snipes, like Jean Claude Van Damme, "moves with an eroticized sleekness or fluidity" (2006, 172).

The sequence also symbolically rights a previous cinematic wrong, as the viewer and action genre fan will recall that it was Stallone's character who incarcerated Snipes in *Demolition Man*. Snipes's Simon Phoenix, introduced snorting cocaine in his hideout, is immediately identified with Black urban culture, his garish striped pants and flashy black and yellow leather jacket giving him a "street" edge. Phoenix is captured by supercop Spartan (Stallone), but not before framing his "good cop" nemesis for the deaths of dozens of hostages when the building explodes. Both men are deemed to be equally violent, and both are incarcerated in the

Cryo-Penitentiary. Upon escaping from deep freeze three decades later, Phoenix is "activated" by a subliminal message from Dr. Cocteau (Nigel Hawthorne) as he uses a Compu-Chat information kiosk to begin searching for firearms, carrying out Cocteau's evil bidding. His ensuing, gleefully violent rampage through the now-sedate streets of San Angeles in 2032 is accompanied by musical cues that pastiche the sounds of rap music: needle scratches and breakbeats. Phoenix is not just a maniac, as the San Angeles police so often call him—he is Black, a relic from "the urban wars of the late 20th century," the alternate history of contemporary USA (beginning in a dystopian 1996) described by Compu-Chat. In *The Expendables 3*, then, the opening sequence reframes Snipes's cinematic history while also winking at his real-life travails.

As is typical in intergenerational examples of geriaction (Donnar 2016), most of the physical action is performed by the characters of slightly younger, more agile star bodies, such as Kellan Lutz or Jason Statham. Snipes's perceived agelessness is supplemented by rapid editing and the use of a stunt double shot either from behind or in extreme long shot. The cycle additionally amplifies the self-reflexive engagement with the genre's most famed hypermasculine action star images and filmographies that had assumed prominence by the early 1990s. The transition to multigenerational, multinational star ensembles for these aging action stars not only accords with the ascendance of the multiprotagonist format in contemporary action cinema, but also signals deep-seated anxieties about aging stars' capacity to perform, waning audience drawing power, and declining star value. Nostalgia not only relates to previous action narratives, tropes, and characteristics, but also "the phenomenological force of the star body's past performances in comparison to their present iteration" (Purse 2017, 164). Geriaction offers nostalgic narratives of star identities that resist outward decline and stars/characters who reassert threatened cultural-professional worth.

Snipes's character is again marked as excessive, out of control, and hyperviolent, typical of the Black screen masculinity he embodied early in his career in *New Jack City*. When Lee Christmas (Jason Statham) pleads with Ross, "Hey, forget this maniac!"—recalling Snipes's Demolition Man role as "maniac" super criminal Phoenix—Ross refuses, shouting, "I'm not leaving him!" The camera pushes closer to Snipes as Doc's eyes narrow in fury, then he jumps free and onto the helicopter at the last moment, the train and the prison explode, and the Expendables' helicopter flies away from the carnage as its occupants whoop in celebration. The sequence, which both presents the star's return—recasting his *Demolition Man* relationship with Stallone—and nostalgically recalls his preexisting star image and downfall, offers additional pleasure for audiences who recognize the repeated allusions to Snipes's real life. Doc wryly states that he was jailed for tax evasion (just like Snipes) and discusses what he will do now that he is back, an original member who has been replaced as the "knife guy" by Christmas. Snipes's self-reflexive, knowing support role is, given the film's ensemble nature, akin to a cameo. Snipes's appearance in *The Expendables 3* recalls Ernest Mathijs's observations about cameos, which "add pleasurably intertextual and reflexive dimensions to a movie. A cameo stands out as a punctuated moment because of the extratextual connotations it produces but also because of its role within the narrative. It is often an odd moment, hanging in time, pausing the progress of the story and inviting the viewer to ponder some tangential implications of the story's consequences" (2013, 146).

After his rescue, the Expendables alight the helicopter on an abandoned airstrip, and Doc questions why it's taken "eight damn years" to improve his situation. Ross explains, "You were in a black ops prison that doesn't officially exist. I just got the location." Doc exhales—"Eight years. What a waste of a life. . . . You make *one* damn mistake"—and we feel the weight of what Snipes lost in being ahead of his time, and then *doing* time, as a Black action star. Beyond being a trope within *The Expendables* franchise, this self-referential blurring of the lines between reality and fiction is a hallmark of Snipes's performances, drawn from his "improvisational comedy background" (Cumming 2021). Doc's dialogue also points back to Snipes's 1990s career zenith. Snipes's performance in *Demolition Man* is an example of the interracial male bonding/rivalry tradition examined by Ed Guerrero (1993). Discussing the success of Phoenix's pathological violence in achieving the megalomaniac white overlord's aims, Dr. Cocteau approvingly observes: "People are terrified of you." Looking almost directly into the camera, Phoenix/Snipes knowingly replies: "What's new? People have always been terrified of me." Bogle argues that these films ignore America's complex and contradictory interracial dynamics (2016). Guerrero further observes that they seek to contain "the socially charged and vexed issue of race relations on screen," while functioning to constrain

Black talent (1993, 128). Snipes's presence in *The Expendables 3*'s ensemble cast represents change, however minor, in the dominant mode of action genre works.[3] Although standing in marked contrast to the more mature character played by Stallone, the mise-en-scène also presents Snipes as Stallone's onscreen equal: as Doc and Ross walk across the tarmac, they mirror each other's stroll and have the same height and muscle bulk. The sequence elevates subtext to text: as Doc returns from the wilderness of incarceration, so too does Snipes seemingly announce his return to Hollywood action in emphatic style.

"The System Has Judged Us Deserving of Punishment": Doing Penance in the Straight-to-Streaming *Armed Response*

Snipes's comeback was consigned to support roles, with the underwhelming exceptions of the straight-to-streaming *Armed Response*, a sci-fi/horror/action hybrid with themes of war, and the box-office failure *The Recall*, a sci-fi/action/horror hybrid. Much as in *The Expendables 3* and Spike Lee's *Chi-Raq* (2015), Snipes is part of an ensemble cast but does take a producer's credit. These roles rely heavily on memories of his star text, particularly his performance as the antihero Blade. The films recall the genre hybridity of *Blade*, but ultimately return him to his period of DTV decline.

The fallen star attempting a comeback may need to take roles in lower-budget films to both reestablish their place in popular culture and add commercial weight or audience appeal to a film without studio backing. Snipes's presence in *Armed Response* and *The Recall*, in essence, returns him to the period immediately before his incarceration, a star who, punished by "the system" for his alleged difficulty on-set, must be content to pay his dues on the B-movie circuit, a well-worn path for actors whose star is on the wane and heading toward theatrical oblivion. However, this commercial imperative is often lost in the discursive response to such roles, which is often one of disappointment at diminishing returns. Adam Graham's review of *Armed Response* typified the critical reaction, given the impact of Snipes's role in *The Expendables 3*: "He could perhaps be a

3. *The Expendables* franchise had already established that Stallone was first among equals within its ensemble casts, including Chinese martial arts star Jet Li and Black actor and former NFL linebacker Terry Crews.

star again . . . , if only someone would give him the right vehicle. *Armed Response* is not that vehicle" (2017).

Armed Response, in which returned American soldiers are punished by a rogue AI "lie detector" system for crimes committed in Afghanistan, is set in a disused maximum security private prison. Locating the film in a penitentiary references Snipes's complicated star image. Midway through the film, Gabriel (Dave Annable), designer of the now-sentient AI system, discovers that it has been murdering the crew, not the Afghan warlord the AI had summoned to the prison. "The system has judged us deserving of punishment," he says. "The question is why?" The camera stays with Snipes's Isaac in a moment of metatextual import: Isaac knows why the AI has decided to enact vengeance, as the viewer later discovers that he led his team to carry out war crimes. The viewer also understands that other systems deemed Snipes to be deserving of punishment: both "the system" that incarcerated him for tax evasion, and the Hollywood system that returned him to the lowly place his action stardom was in prior to his absence.

Armed Response is a production of WWE Studios Inc., the narrative film and television arm of the global professional wrestling conglomerate. Its films, generally DTV or streaming, operate as star vehicles for WWE wrestling talent. They also tend to utilize Hollywood stars in minor ensemble roles—a broader shift within action cinema that Snipes had vehemently resisted during the filming of *Blade: Trinity* (David Goyer, 2004)—to give their productions a "Hollywood" veneer, their star presence effectively constituting part of the mise-en-scène. Much of the film's tension is associated with the audience's desire to see Snipes and costar former WWE champion Seth Rollins fight onscreen. These hopes go unanswered. More limiting even than the absence of action, the script gives Snipes little to do from a dramatic perspective. Snipes does engage in some combat during Isaac's brief climactic tussle with Gabriel, but Isaac is quickly overpowered when Gabriel chokes him using the prison's visitor room phone cord.

Snipes's role in *Armed Response* also recalls his association with villainy in action cinema. In his peak years and his comeback, Snipes embraced a range of action cinema roles, including antiheroes, and showed a penchant for playing outsized villains across science fiction and horror hybrids. This embrace both facilitates his action cinema comeback and complexly reinforces *and* transcends long-established constraints on Black screen masculinity (Bogle 2016; Guerrero 1993), as do references—direct or implied—to his real-life incarceration. However, any impact Snipes makes as part of his faltering comeback rests largely on the audience's disappointed anticipation of a return to the glory of his prior action star text.

"Goddamn Reporters": Spectacularization of the Comeback Star and a Reputation near Ruined in *The Recall*

The Canadian American film *The Recall*, which blends alien abduction tale and survivalist thriller, received a limited cinema release in 2017, as much an "opportunity for the film's Canadian investors to pose for pictures with Wesley Snipes on an ad hoc red carpet" as its use of the fledgling Barco Escape widescreen format (Semley 2017)—again, the former star serving as Hollywood window dressing. Credited only as "The Hunter," Snipes's survivalist character's initial intensity in *The Recall* calls back to *Blade*, while his outsized performance recalls his role as Simon Phoenix in *Demolition Man*. As Paul McDonald observes, the "spectacularization of the star" is especially resonant in moments "staged precisely to display the star attraction," from advanced marketing through to the star's entrance in the narrative (2013, 184). Snipes's introductions often associate him with masculine spectacle and frame him as a star, regardless of the status of his character as hero or villain, or whether he is a lead, support, or cameo. In *The Recall*, Snipes's character appears seemingly out of thin air, startling Brendan (R. J. Mitte), who has been snooping around with a camera at a semiabandoned gas station—a horror trope. "Keep yappin', see what happens," he warns the terrified youth, subverting the generic expectation of the audience by issuing a one-liner more befitting an action hero than the harbinger figure in a sci-fi/horror hybrid. His performance again hints at Snipes's real-life travails: Seeing Mitte's camera, the seemingly deranged loner sniffs, "Goddamn reporters—haven't you taken enough already?" The Hunter later reveals his trashed reputation as a former astronaut who was grounded and then ostracized after he attempted to explain his mistreatment at the hands of alien abductors, but the line has metatextual impact, considering Snipes's own treatment at the hands of the press. This metatextual quality continues moments later, as Brendan and his friends drive away. He tells them, "Dude, this hillbilly was, like, crazy strong. His hands, he had kung fu action grip or something."

The comeback star does not have to work at revealing any other aspects of his character because the audience quickly recognizes him and attaches a series of expectations to the character, particularly from his role as Blade. *Blade* epitomizes McDonald's "spectacularization of the star" (2013, 184) in Snipes's introduction as the eponymous vampire hunter, a half-human, half-vampire "daywalker." In the film's opening sequence, set in an illegal rave called "Bloodbath," a vampire's unsuspecting human date attempts to flee amid a feeding frenzy. Crawling to the edge of the dance floor, his gaze meets the unblemished combat boot of a mysterious figure dressed in black leather. The camera tilts up, introducing the figure's high-tech tactical gear. A series of reaction shots from the gathered vampires concludes with one whispering, "Jesus, that's *him*," before the sea of revelers parts in slow motion to reveal Blade, who begins killing vampires, using a pump-action shotgun. Snipes later totes a shotgun as the Hunter again, which prompts the viewer to consider the accumulated weight of his action star text.

The Hunter later takes the surviving teens to his cabin to recuperate, where he explains his personal history: While working as a shuttle astronaut in the late 1990s, he was abducted by aliens and experimented upon, leaving him scarred and with strange powers. The aliens also implanted memories that revealed that "the visitors" have been adjusting humans' genetic code for millennia. When one of the teens accuses him of withholding this information from humanity, he says: "I told everybody. They told me I was having a transformation of my sense of reality." Transcending the outlandishness of the plotline, his monologue, delivered in sober seriousness, recalls the response to Snipes's accusations of mistreatment and exclusion during the making of the final *Blade* film. The camp frisson of Snipes's earlier action roles in films like *Demolition Man* only returns when he reveals his plans to the teens: "The visitors took everything from me," he says, before switching into a groove and singing, "so, tonight, I'm gonna return the favor!"

Snipes's starring presence in *Blade* was groundbreaking in the specific context of the Marvel Cinematic Universe, and superhero cinema more broadly. It is bittersweet to view *Blade*, considering Snipes's later tribulations in making the *Blade* series, and his ensuing legal battle with the production team following the release of *Blade: Trinity* haunts his presence in low-budget comeback vehicles. Snipes's complaint became lost in media coverage focusing on a white costar's claims of his allegedly outrageous, even violent, behavior on the set of *Blade: Trinity*. Addressing these accusations years later, Snipes spoke frankly: "The presumption that one white guy can make a statement and that statement stands as true! Why would people believe his version is true? Because they are predisposed to believing the black guy is always the problem" (Hattenstone 2020).

Although he was an executive producer of each of the *Blade* trilogy films, Snipes's lawsuit against *Blade: Trinity*'s writer-director, executive producer, and studio New Line is illustrative of the limits of his creative control. The lawsuit alleged that "the real purpose of *Blade III* was to set the stage for spinoffs featuring other cast members [. . . and] intentionally hired only white people, leading to feelings of isolation and exclusion by Snipes" (Shprintz 2005). Snipes's difficulties recall Richard Dyer's commentary on the presence of Black stars within the action movie's "white ghetto": "Entering and being in white space can be profoundly intimidating," however at ease stars like Snipes or Danny Glover may appear within it on screen (2000, 20). Returning to the Hunter's assertion that "they told me I was having a transformation of my sense of reality" highlights how Snipes's star text is characterized by an "out of time" quality. In contrast to Snipes's experience of exclusion during the making of *Blade: Trinity*, greater diversity and inclusion efforts are now a key commercial imperative of major studio filmmaking. The planned *Blade* reboot by Marvel Studios, with Oscar winner Mahershala Ali taking over as the eponymous dhampir, will be written by Stacy Osei-Kuffour—the first Black woman to write a Marvel film—and directed by Pakistani-born director Bassam Tariq.

Snipes's comeback nostalgically recalls the aging star's former stardom, whether as characters rescued, ostracized, or haunted by the past. His comeback suggests that it is possible to kickstart a stalled career if the comeback star is willing to compromise at least temporarily, whether in accepting the ensemble casts and multiprotagonist formats Snipes had resisted during his ascendancy, or by appearing in low-budget B-films. In the years since these early comeback roles in action cinema, laboring tirelessly under his motto "I reject your reality and assert my own" (Hattenstone 2020), Snipes has delivered numerous camp and acclaimed turns in comedy and streaming dramas, winning numerous critics' association awards. While the role as Blade marked his career zenith, Snipes became an outlier within the later Marvel Cinematic Universe. Although Snipes will be replaced by a younger star, the long-mooted MCU reboot of *Blade* means that a new generation may rediscover his ground-breaking work as they explore the origins of Blade. Perhaps he will not stay an outlier and will come back from the dead yet again.

Works Cited

Bogle, Donald. 2016. *Toms, Coons, Mulattoes, Mammies, and Bucks: An Interpretive History of Blacks in American Films*. Bloomsbury.

Borrelli, Mauro, dir. 2017. *The Recall*. Los Angeles, CA: Freestyle Digital Media, 2017. DVD.

Brambilla, Marco, dir. 1993. *Demolition Man*. Burbank, CA: Warner Home Video, 2011. Blu-Ray.

Cumming, Ed. 2021. "Wesley Snipes: 'They Made It Very Seductive to Do Action Movies.'" *Independent*, March 6, 2021. https://www.independent.co.uk/arts-entertainment/films/features/wesley-snipes-interview-coming-2-america-b1812861.html.

Del Toro, Guillermo, dir. 2002. *Blade II*. Burbank, CA: Warner Home Video, 2012. Blu-Ray.

Donnar, Glen. 2022. "The Art of Making Do: Ageing Recent-to-Action Stars in Hollywood-Style French Action Cinema." In *Gender and Action Heroes*, edited by Steven Gerrard and Renée Middlemost, 21–33. Emerald.

Donnar, Glen. 2016. "Narratives of Cultural and Professional Redundancy: Aging Action Stardom and the 'Geri-Action' Film." *Communication, Politics & Culture* 49 (1): 1–18.

Dyer, Richard. 2000. *Only Entertainment*. Psychology Press.

Gallagher, Mark. 2006. *Action Figures*. Palgrave Macmillan.

Gayles, Jonathan. 2012. "Black Macho and the Myth of the Superwoman Redux: Masculinity and Misogyny in *Blade*." *Journal of Popular Culture* 45 (2): 284–300.

Goyer, David, dir. 2004. *Blade: Trinity*. Burbank, CA: Warner Home Video, 2012. Blu-ray.

Graham, Adam. 2017. "Review: 'Armed Response' Is No Snipes Comeback Vehicle." *Detroit News*, August 3, 2017. https://www.detroitnews.com/story/entertainment/movies/2017/08/03/movie-review-armed-response-wesley-snipes-comeback-vehicle/104275876/.

Guerrero, Ed. 1993. *Framing Blackness: The African American Image in Film.* Temple University Press.

Hattenstone, Simon. 2020. "Wesley Snipes on Art, Excellence, and Life after Prison: 'I Hope I Came out a Better Person.'" *Guardian*, November 2, 2020.

Hughes, Patrick, dir. 2014. *The Expendables 3*. Santa Monica, CA: Lionsgate Films, 2014. DVD.

Mathijs, Ernest. 2013. "Cronenberg Connected: Cameo Acting, Cult Stardom, and Supertexts." In *Cult Film Stardom: Offbeat Attractions and Processes of Cultification*, edited by Kate Egan and Sarah Thomas, 144–62. Palgrave Macmillan.

McDonald, Paul. 2013. *Hollywood Stardom*. Wiley-Blackwell.

Norrington, Stephen, dir. 1998. *Blade*. Burbank, CA: Warner Home Video, 2012. Blu-ray.

Purse, Lisa. 2017. "Confronting the Impossibility of Impossible Bodies: Tom Cruise and the Ageing Male Action Hero Movie." In *Revisiting Star Studies: Cultures, Themes, and Methods*, edited by Sabrina Qiong Yu and Guy Austin, 162–86. Edinburgh University Press.

Semley, John. 2017. "The Recall Offers Little More Than a Theatre-Technology Gimmick." *Globe and Mail*, June 1, 2017.

Shprintz, Janet. 2005. "Snipes Throwing Legal Blade at *Trinity* Team." *Variety*, April 20, 2005. https://variety.com/2005/biz/news/snipes-throwing-legal-blade-at-trinity-team-1117921445/.

Stockwell, John, dir. 2017. *Armed Response*. Los Angeles, CA: Saban Films, 2017. DVD.

Williams, Roland Leander, Jr. 2014. "Good Buddy." In *Black Male Frames: African Americans in a Century of Hollywood Cinema, 1903–2003*, 143–67. Syracuse University Press.

16

"I'LL BE BACK"

Linda Hamilton and the Return of Sarah Connor in *Terminator: Dark Fate*

CHRISTA VAN RAALTE

On a motorway bridge in Mexico, two young women prepare to defend themselves against a terrifying, dual-bodied assassin: a machine sent from the future to kill them. Suddenly, a station-wagon screeches into view, and out steps their savior, accompanied by emphatic Foley, as her combat boots hit the ground. Starting at those boots, the camera tilts up, and then the film cuts to reveal a sixty-three-year-old Linda Hamilton clad in fatigues and a bulletproof vest, reprising her iconic role as Sarah Connor—now a seasoned warrior and armed to the teeth. Having disabled the enemy with a lethal combination of sangfroid and firepower, she strides off to finish the job, but not before turning to her astounded audience to deliver the franchise's signature catchphrase: "I'll be back!"

The Return of an Icon

Linda Hamilton's return to the *Terminator* franchise after an absence of thirty years represents one of Hollywood's most dramatic comebacks. It is one, moreover, that is significant in terms of the ways in which age and gender are performed in the Hollywood action film. Dubbed "geriaction," the recent spate of films featuring aging action stars has proved something of a boy's club—the last refuge of the old guard, as women increasingly encroach on the male-dominated territory of the action film (Crossley and

Fisher 2021, 132).[1] Hamilton joins a tiny band of female usurpers within this subgenre, playing a part in the wider cultural landscape that echoes the impact of her previous performance in the role.[2]

Sarah Connor, played by Hamilton in *Terminator 2: Judgment Day* (James Cameron, 1991), has earned an iconic status in Hollywood history and also in feminist film criticism.[3] Popular critics obsessed about the intensive training Hamilton undertook in preparation for the role, constructing both her body and her skills as unnatural (Brown 1996, 59). As the poster girl for Yvonne Tasker's concept of "musculinity," meanwhile, Hamilton/Sarah became a focus of academic debate about the female action lead. For some she was effectively a man in drag—wearing her built body as an armor and adopting masculine traits at expense of maternal ones (Jeffords 1993, 249–50; Cornea 2007, 163); others argued that binary theoretical constructs of gender risk undermining the transgressive, revolutionary potential of the role (Brown 1996, 52–71; Hills 1999, 38–50).

Following the short-lived rise of the hardbody heroines in the late 1980s and early 1990s, typified by James Cameron's *Aliens* (1986) and Ridley Scott's *Thelma and Louise* (1991), Lisa Purse describes an evolution of the female action lead that is far from consistently progressive. From her brief moment in the cinematic sun, she moves into television, where her image and activities are normalized, no longer coded as "inappropriate," then returns to the big screen as an eroticized figure, before settling into what Purse describes as an "accommodating, allegedly 'positive' post feminism" (2011, 83). A similar pattern can be traced in the female leads of the *Terminator* franchise, unfolding through the successive films together with the TV series *The Sarah Connor Chronicles* (Warner Bros., 2008–9). Yet the ghost of Linda Hamilton's Sarah Connor haunts all these texts—either in the imagery or in the narrative—preparing the ground, one might say, for the return of the real Sarah Connor.

1. A term helpfully defined by Crossley and Fisher in their special issue on the subject, which explores the subgenre from a number of perspectives (2021, 132).
2. The most prominent, perhaps, being Helen Mirren in *RED* (Robert Schwentke, 2010) and *RED 2* (Dean Parisot, 2013).
3. She also played the role in the first film of what became the franchise: *The Terminator* (James Cameron, 1984).

Dark Fate (Tim Miller, 2019) is the sixth of the Terminator films, but in effect presents itself as a sequel to the first and second films in which Hamilton/Sarah evolved from terrified waitress to determined survivalist—mother of a future messiah, John Connor, destined to save humanity from the rule of the machines.[4] In this latest reboot a Terminator (Arnold Schwarzenegger) has murdered the young John, and a grief-stricken Sarah has spent the three decades since hunting and exterminating successive Terminators, then drinking until she blacks out. Back in the future, meanwhile, a new savior arises, referred to only as "the Commander." Again, the machines send a Terminator back in time, the terrifying Rev-9 (Gabriel Luna) who can not only shape-shift but also split himself in two. Again, the humans send back a protector, the human "augment" Grace (Mackenzie Davis), a soldier injured in battle and rebuilt with enhanced capabilities. The focus of their respective missions is Dani (Natalia Reyes), a young factory worker in Mexico City.

It quickly becomes apparent that Grace will not be able to protect Dani on her own. Partly because, being only one enhanced human, she is outnumbered by the duplicating Rev-9, and partly because she has a fatal flaw: she is built for short bursts of hyperactivity, after which she slumps and requires medication to revive her. Fortunately, Sarah appears in her hour of need—powerful, determined, and extremely experienced. Together they set out for Texas to locate a mysterious helper, who turns out to be none other than the Terminator who killed Sarah's son. In completing his last mission, he has eliminated the future that sent him and, with it, his programming. Seeking a new purpose in life, he has adopted the unlikely name "Carl" and the even more unlikely trade of curtain fitter; he has discovered family and something akin to love and has set out to make amends for his former crimes. Sarah is deeply suspicious of Carl, but agrees to join forces to defeat the new enemy.

As the narrative progresses, it is revealed that Dani is not, in fact, another Sarah, the mother of the future savior; she is herself destined to become that future savior, the "Commander," who will build an effective

4. The time-traveling conceit at the heart of the *Terminator* myth allows for endless reboots with a gleeful disregard for continuity. A number of themes and tropes are carried forward from the intervening films, however, including the theme of age introduced by Schwarzenegger's friendly but grizzled Terminator in the fifth film, who pointedly describes himself to a young Kyle as "old—not obsolete!"

resistance to the rule of the machines. Eventually Grace and Carl sacrifice themselves to protect Dani, and Sarah once again becomes the lone mentor and protector of the last best hope of humanity.

Constructing the Aging Action Heroine

In *Judgment Day*, Hamilton/Sarah adopted what were considered a masculine physicality and a masculine skill set. Similarly, in *Dark Fate*, she appropriates a number of the traits and tropes that are the stock in trade of the male geriaction heroes. Josephine Dolan discusses how Hollywood contrives to render its older male stars "hard and firm," and its older female stars "hard and smooth" (2013, 227–36). Hamilton is most definitely aligned with the former: the famously muscular arms are on display but her face looks characterful, lived in, in sharp contrast with the Rev-9, who is uncannily smooth, both inside and out. Hamilton/Sarah also appropriates some of the positive attributes of masculine maturity, such as authority and experience, which Lennart Soberon argues make the male geriaction star in many ways the apotheosis of patriarchy (2021, 157). Like her male counterparts she brings to this new text a wealth of what Soberon calls "heroic capital" (156), highlighted by a crowd-pleasing deployment of intertextual tropes and jokes.

At the same time, there are differences in how the aging female star "does" action cinema. Sarah's aging body, for example, is not offered as a site of vulnerability. Soberon argues that male geriaction stars frequently draw on their age to supply that element of vulnerability and victimization so essential to the construction of the action hero (2021, 156). For Sarah, however, this comes from emotional rather than physical trauma: the loss of her son, which is repeatedly referenced, especially in terms of her difficult relationship with Carl. Another difference is the way in which the construction of Sarah's character draws on the cultural trope of the "crone." A mainstay of folklore, this figure represents the older woman as social outsider, often attributed sinister or supernatural characteristics, at best feared as a "wise woman," at worst reviled as a witch or hag. Over the past quarter-century, however, feminists across a range of disciplines have reclaimed this term from its pejorative cultural origins, reappropriating it to highlight the revolutionary, if often unappreciated, potential of the older woman in terms of her prophetic wisdom, outspoken truth-telling, freedom, and disregard for social conventions—qualities represented, if not always appreciatively, in diverse cultural texts and contexts (Segal 2013, 210).[5] These qualities bring a degree of fallibility and humor to Hamilton/Sarah's character in *Dark Fate*, but they are also weaponized to reinforce the agency and status of the female geriaction star. Indeed, it can be argued that she needs all the help she can get, given the cultural odds stacked against her.

Kathleen Woodward argues that ageism is "entrenched in feminism itself," and that postfeminism is no better, being overwhelmingly preoccupied with the concerns of young women (1999, xi). At the very least, older women are neglected; at the worst, they are vilified. Woodward argues that the "youthful structure of the look" dominates western culture (2006, 162), where age is too often negatively contrasted with youth, offering women in particular "no possibility of transcending the reductive role" (165). By way of response to these tendencies, Anne Jerslev, writing on older female CEOs in TV dramas, posits an edgy and decidedly postfeminist sensibility of "cool" as a challenge to the youthful structure of the look, with elegant dresses and big statement necklaces representing a refusal to become invisible (2017, 72–79). No attempt is made to disguise Sarah's age in *Dark Fate*. On the contrary, the fact that she has been chasing Terminators for the past thirty years is a key plot point, and, while she looks very good in the role, there is no question that she looks her age. Like Jerslev's CEOs, however, Sarah is not only unashamedly visible as an older woman, but devastatingly cool—albeit replacing elegant heels and frocks with combat boots and a flak jacket, and big statement necklaces with big statement firearms. Her positioning alongside the two younger women, Grace and Dani, serves not to age or diminish her in comparison but to emphasize the criticality of her role. In fact, it is not despite but because of her age that she is essential to this team and to this film. Her age is, in effect, her superpower.

Age as Superpower

Besides her combat skills, an impressive arsenal of weaponry, and her preexisting iconic status as a kick-ass heroine, Hamilton's Sarah brings

5. These include writers working in such diverse areas as self-help (Kenton 1998, 225–27); marketing (Stevens, Maclaran, and Kravets 2020, 1106–11); and cultural studies (Rountree 1997, 211).

some very particular qualities to her role on account of her age. She draws on extensive experience, together with a dogged dedication and staying power that has been reinforced rather than diminished by her years in the field. Notably, as a heroine she benefits from a quality particularly pertinent in a war against machines: her humanity, which is explicitly defined by her fallibility and mortality. These qualities are underpinned by some of the disruptive and transgressive tendencies of the postmenopausal "crone."

From her first appearance, when she comes to the rescue of Dani and Grace, Sarah exudes experience, and the authority it brings: she moves quickly but calmly from one weapon to another, clearly knowing her enemy only too well. Later, when she picks up the younger women as they blunder out of the pharmacy (which they have just held up to get medication for the failing Grace), she again assumes control and manages to hang on to it, even when physically challenged by a revived and decidedly imposing Grace. Quickly, albeit reluctantly, Grace recognizes that she needs Sarah's insider knowledge of this world, from her understanding of how the Terminator will be able to use mobile phones and police communications to track them, to her well-placed contacts able to supply them with a range of military grade hardware at a moment's notice. Sarah's experience and authority are contrasted with Dani's initial lack of either. This comparison is highlighted by Sarah's original assumption that Dani is in effect a young reincarnation of herself, telling Grace, when asked why she cares what happens to Dani: "I was her."

Sarah's sheer staying power is evidenced by her thirty years as a hunter of Terminators across fifty states and is in sharp contrast to Grace's turbo-tuned metabolism. It is reminiscent of the dogged endurance of Schwarzenegger's character in *Terminator Genisys* (Alan Taylor, 2015), a reboot of the first film in which Sarah has been raised by a friendly Terminator after her parents are killed. She and her human partner, Kyle, are sent ahead into the future to complete a complex game plan devised by the Terminator. Meanwhile he, for technical reasons, has to go the long way around, living through all the years they skip and preparing the ground for their mission. In *Dark Fate*, it is Sarah who has gone the long way around, and Grace who has simply appeared out of nowhere, ready for the final battle. The Sarah of *Judgment Day* was likened by some to a Terminator due to her driven, uncompromising, and arguably dehumanized characterization. In *Dark Fate*, a mature Sarah's relentless sense of mission is clearly represented as a strength that has kept her going all this time and will continue to do so, making her a formidable Terminator hunter. Despite the trauma of her son's death, she has continued to fight for the survival of humanity and will continue to protect and mentor Dani after her other protectors are gone. Sarah has come to represent humanity's dogged, almost timeless, resistance to the rule of the machines—the structuring logic of the franchise.

Sarah's humanity is also closely associated with her age in the film. This is partly because her age in itself speaks to her mortality,[6] the ultimate fragility that marks out the humans from the machines.[7] Yet it is also because of her own very human journey in the film, from grief and despair toward reconciliation and renewed hope. In this respect Sarah is contrasted with Schwarzenegger's Terminator (a.k.a. "Carl"), who, despite his efforts to blend in and his increasing understanding of the human condition, is most definitely not human himself. This is the subject of several wisecracks—including one by Sarah who wonders why Carl's partner has not noticed that he never sleeps and weighs four hundred pounds. Catherine Summerhayes argues that the first two films present Sarah as a key point of identification for the audience as the representative of humanity among the machines: the only significant adult human who remains in her own timeline (2007, 39). In *Dark Fate* she shares this position with Dani. As the narrative progresses, Carl and Grace (neither fully human nor native to the current era) are increasingly framed together, while Sarah and Dani are likewise aligned. Ultimately, only Sarah, wise, experienced, reliable, and entirely mortal, is fit to mentor the woman who will emerge as humanity's future leader.

Finally, the transgressive qualities of the "crone," as well as misplaced social assumptions about the older woman, become part of Sarah's armory. While the prophetic Sarah Connor of *Judgment Day* was considered dangerously insane and then incarcerated, the older Sarah Connor of *Dark Fate* is presented as merely eccentric, with her insistence on having saved the world and on keeping her phone in a chip packet. Prophecy and

6. An idea I have explored in more depth elsewhere (van Raalte 2021, 144–54).

7. The importance of the distinction between human and machine is foreshadowed in the early scenes of the film, set in the factory where Dani works and where robots are making people gradually redundant.

nonconformity are traits traditionally tolerated in older women as harmless, providing a form of camouflage for those who are anything but. Thus, when Sarah is, briefly, captured at the border detention center en route from Mexico to Texas, her age and the social assumptions it brings are weaponized. The guards mockingly congratulate Sarah on being wanted in fifty states but make the mistake of treating her as something of an oddity rather than a threat. In the only direct reference to her age throughout the film, they joke about taking her to the senior living quarters—immediately before finding themselves overpowered by their prisoner as she makes her escape. Unlike Helen Mirren's Victoria in *RED* (Robert Schwentke, 2010), who self-consciously affects a very British, positively demure gentility to distract opponents from her lethal qualities, Sarah does nothing to deliberately mask her identity or underplay her powers: it seems she does not need to.[8] The film narrative exploits the wry humor of the situation, as is so often the way with the action genre, extradiegetically, without its characters' conscious collusion.

Sarah's fractious relationship with Schwarzenegger's Terminator ("Carl"), whom she insists on referring to as "It," is also characterized by a disruptive quality ascribed to the crone (and also without consciousness of the comic effect): she tells the truth, however uncomfortable. Thus on learning of his new identity Sarah announces, "I'm never gonna fucking call you 'Carl'!" She also tells him to his face that she intends to kill him once their mission is over. Perhaps most important of all, the crone is free and able to make her own choices. Just as Carl, no longer preprogrammed by the machines of a nonexistent future, is free to find his own purpose, so Sarah is no longer beholden to the biological imperative. No longer a mother, or a walking womb in waiting, she is free to choose her new role as Dani's mentor and to embrace the philosophy repeated like a mantra in every iteration of the franchise: "There is no fate but what we make ourselves."

Linda Hamilton's comeback as a female geriaction star, I would suggest, embodies imagery and discourses every bit as contentious as those raised by her previous performances, with as much productive potential for feminist film criticism. The manner in which she usurps her male

8. One is put in mind of the much-quoted line from *V. I. Warshawski* (Jeff Kanew, 1991): "Never underestimate a man's ability to underestimate a woman."

costar's trademarks, from the sunglasses to the Foley-enhanced footsteps, to the deadpan one-liners, can be read as a direct challenge to the primacy of the male geriaction star. Just as her performance in *Judgment Day* helped to redefine the parameters of the female action lead, so her role in *Dark Fate* helps to open up new opportunities to explore the disruptive potential of aging femininity in the action film.

The majority of older action stars may still be male; however, the younger female stars who have been slowly but surely infiltrating the action genre show no sign of stopping, as they move into their forties, fifties, and beyond. Thus recent years have seen Angelina Jolie returning to an action role in *Eternals* (Chloe Zhao, 2021) at the age of forty-five, and Salma Hayek, in *The Hitman's Wife's Bodyguard* (Patrick Hughes, 2021) at fifty-five, reprising her 2017 role with considerably more firepower.[9] Meanwhile, Charlize Theron, at forty-seven, has two action sequels in development at the time of writing, provisionally entitled *Atomic Blonde 2* and *Old Guard*, the latter also to feature the forty-two-year-old Veronica Ngo alongside a fifty-one-year-old Uma Thurman.

Something has shifted in social perceptions of which roles are appropriate for older women. The journalist Judy Gerstel relates how, interviewing the forty-two-year-old Sigourney Weaver after the release of *Alien 3* (David Fincher, 1992), she asked about the possibility of a fourth film. The star answered: "It would be pushing the limits of my belief to have this character save the day yet again," casting doubts, which the journalist shared, on her potential, postmenopause, to carry off a role of this kind (Gerstel 2019).[10] By way of contrast, when Linda Hamilton, after *Dark Fate*, was asked the equivalent question, her concern was not about the capability or plausibility of an aging Sarah Connor but simply the quality of the film: "Only if there's something really viable in the script and story and characters, would I ever consider doing it again. Otherwise, it's just diminishing returns, isn't it?" (Reyes 2020).

It is, moreover, clear from her remarks that Hamilton understands very well the wider cultural impact of a powerful cinematic performance. Indeed, it could be argued that her refusal to play a dying Sarah in the third

9. In *The Hitman's Bodyguard* (Tom O'Connor, 2017).

10. Although, of course, she did go on to make *Alien: Resurrection* (Jean-Pierre Jeunet, 1997) at forty-seven.

film did much to support her cinematic legacy. Critics and fans alike speculate as to whether the franchise can recover from *Dark Fate*'s disappointing box office (notwithstanding many of the best reviews for the franchise since *Judgment Day*)—whether Hamilton/Sarah, true to the catch phrase, will "be back." Perhaps this is the wrong question to ask, for, in an important cultural sense, it can be argued, she never went away.

Works Cited

Brown, Jeffery. 1996. "Gender and the Action Heroine: Hardbodies and the 'Point of No Return.'" *Cinema Journal* 35 (3): 52–71.

Cornea, Christine. 2007. *Science Fiction Cinema: Between Fantasy and Reality*. Rutgers University Press.

Crossley, Laura, and Austin Fisher. 2021. "Geriaction Cinema: Introduction." *Journal of Popular Film and Television* 49 (3): 130–35.

Dolan, Josephine. 2013. "Firm and Hard: Stardom, Gender, and the Troubling Embodiment of 'Successful Aging.'" In *De-Centring Cultural Studies: Past, Present, and Future of Popular Culture*, edited by Patricia Bastida-Rodriguez and Jose Igor Prieto-Arranz, 217–47. Cambridge Scholars.

Gerstel, Julie. 2019. "Why Women over 60 Are the Action Heroes of the Future." Everything Zoomer, July 22, 2019. https://www.everythingzoomer.com/arts-entertainment/2019/07/22/action-heroes-women-over-60/.

Hills, Elizabeth. 1999. "From 'Figurative Males' to Action Heroines: Further Thoughts on Active Women in the Cinema." *Screen* 40 (1): 38–50.

Jeffords, Susan. 1993. "Can Masculinity Be Terminated?" In *Screening the Male: Exploring Masculinities in Hollywood Cinema*, edited by Steven Cohan and Inna Rae Hark, 245–62. Routledge.

Jerslev, Anne. 2017. "The Look of Aging: Agelessness as Post-Feminist Cool? The Aging Female CEO in Contemporary US TV Series." *MedieKultur* 33 (63): 68–84.

Kenton, Leslie. 1998. *Passage to Power: Natural Menopause Revolution*. Random House.

Miller, Tim, dir. 2019. *Terminator: Dark Fate*. Los Angeles, CA: 20th Century Studios, 2020. DVD.

Purse, Lisa. 2011. *Contemporary Action Cinema*. Edinburgh University Press.

Reyes, Mike. 2020. "Linda Hamilton Thinks Box Office May Have Finally Killed the *Terminator* Franchise." Cinema Blend, January 30, 2020.

https://www.cinemablend.com/news/2489354/linda-hamilton-thinks-box-office-may-have-finally-killed-the-terminator-franchise.

Rountree, Kathryn. 1997. "The New Witch of the West: Feminists Reclaim the Crone." *Journal of Popular Culture* 30 (4): 211.

Segal, Lyn. 2013. *In Our Time: The Pleasures and the Perils of Aging*. Verso.

Soberon, Lennart. 2021. "Too Old for This Sh*t: Aged Action Heroes, Affect, and 'the Economy of Exertion.'" *Journal of Popular Film and Television* 49 (3): 155–67.

Stevens, Lorna, Pauline Maclaran, and Olga Kravets. 2020. "Reclaiming the Crone: Reimagining Old Age and Feminine Power." *Advances in Consumer Research* 48:1106–11.

Summerhayes, Catherine. 2007. "Just a Woman Among the Cyborgs: Sarah Connor in *Terminator 2: Judgment Day*." In *Women Willing to Fight: The Fighting Woman in Film*, edited by Silke Andris and Ursula Frederick, 38–54. Cambridge Scholars.

Tasker, Yvonne. 1993. *Spectacular Bodies: Gender, Genre, and the Action Cinema*. Routledge.

van Raalte, Christa. 2021. "Reflections on Mortality: The Imagery of Mirrors in Clint Eastwood's *Gran Torino*." *Journal of Popular Film and Television* 49 (3): 144–54.

Warner Bros. Television. 2008–9. *Terminator: The Sarah Connor Chronicles*. Los Angeles, CA: Twentieth Century Fox Television.

Woodward, Kathleen, ed. 1999. *Figuring Age: Women, Bodies, Generations*. Indiana University Press.

Woodward, Katherine. 2006. "Performing Age, Performing Gender." *NWSA Journal* 18 (1): 162–89.

CONTRIBUTORS

CLEM BASTOW is an independent scholar. They completed a PhD in the School of Media and Communication at RMIT, Melbourne, Australia. Their dissertation examines the creative intersections of critical autism studies, screenwriting practice, and Hollywood action movies. They are the author of a nonfiction book, *Late Bloomer: How an Autism Diagnosis Changed My Life* (2021), and coeditor of *Someone like Me* (2025). They have also published book chapters on feminist cinema, voice in television screenwriting, and screen media piracy. They work as a screenwriter and neurodiversity consultant for film and television.

STUART BELL is a PhD candidate in the department of Film Studies at King's College London, UK. His dissertation examines costar pairings in contemporary francophone cinema, with particular emphasis on aging stars. He is the editor of *Moving Impressions: Essays on Art and Experience* (2021), *On Feminist Films* (2024), and *French Cinema: Stars and Histories* (forthcoming).

WILL DODSON is adjunct assistant professor in the department of Media Studies at University of North Carolina Greensboro, USA, where he teaches rhetoric, literature, film, and media studies. He is the series coeditor of *The Anthem Series on Exploitation and Industry in World Cinema* and the coeditor of *American Twilight: The Cinema of Tobe Hooper* (2021). His current books in progress are *Teen Comedies and the Crisis of Masculinity* and the coauthored *Alien Invasion TV from the Cold War to QAnon: Paranoia and Conspiracy Culture on the Small Screen*. He has published articles on Tod Browning, Jess Franco, Hugo Haas, and Shirley Jackson, and various film genres.

GLEN DONNAR is senior lecturer in the School of Media and Communication at RMIT, Melbourne, Australia. He is the author of *Troubling Masculinities: Terror, Gender, and Monstrous Others in American Film Post-9/11* (2020) and the coeditor of *Asian Celebrity Cultures and Digital Media* (2023). He has published articles on stardom and celebrity and popular cultural and screen representations of men and masculinity in film and television. He is completing a monograph, *Ageing Masculinity in Hollywood Action Film.*

LISA DUFFY is an independent scholar. She completed a PhD in the department of Film Studies at Queen Mary University of London. Her dissertation examines gender and sexuality in the fantasy spaces of classical Hollywood musicals. Her research interests include screen musicals and the signifiers of star personae (Barbra Streisand's makeup and Judy Garland's voice). She has also published an article on camp constructions of Disney witches.

JENNIFER LOUISE FIELD is a PhD candidate in the department of Humanities at York University, Toronto, Canada. Her dissertation examines the depictions of interracial intimacy on 1990s movie posters. Her research interests include the study of film paratext (posters and trailers) and star studies. She has published a book chapter on the Civil Rights Movement.

LUCY FISCHER is Distinguished Professor Emerita of English and Film Studies at the University of Pittsburgh, USA. She is the author of *Cinematernity: Film, Motherhood, Genre* (1996); *Sunrise* (1998); *Body Double: The Author Incarnate in the Cinema* (2013); *Cinema by Design: Art Nouveau, Modernism, and Film History* (2017); *Emotion Pictures: Cinema and Feelings* (2023); and *The Cinema of Converging Lives: Complex Films in Theory and Practice* (forthcoming). She is the editor of *Stars: The Film Reader* (2004); *Art Direction and Production Design* (2015); and *Recollecting Collecting: A Film and Media Perspective* (2023); and the coeditor of *Teaching Film* (2012).

PEDRO GUIMARÃES is associate professor in the department of Media and Communication and the Graduate Program in Multimedia in the

Institute of Arts at UNICAMP, Brazil, where he teaches film studies. He is the coauthor of *Helena Ignez, actrice expérimentale* (2018) and the coeditor of *Douglas Sirk, o príncipe do melodrama* (2012). He has published articles on film genres, Brazilian cinema, Isabelle Huppert, and Vivien Leigh.

LEON HUNT is senior lecturer in the department of Arts and Humanities at Brunel University London, UK, where he teaches film and television studies. He is the author of *British Low Culture: From Safari Suits to Sexploitation* (1998); *Kung Fu Cult Masters: From Bruce Lee to Crouching Tiger* (2003); *Cult British TV Comedy: From Reeves and Mortimer to Psychoville* (2013); and *Mario Bava: The Artisan as Italian Horror Auteur* (2022). He is the coeditor of *East Asian Cinemas: Exploring Transnational Connections on Film* (2008) and *Screening the Undead: Vampires and Zombies in Film and Television* (2014).

SONY JALARAJAN RAJ is assistant professor in the department of Communication at MacEwan University, Edmonton, Canada, where he teaches film studies and is coordinator of the Film Studies Program. He is a professional journalist turned academic who has worked in different positions as a reporter, special correspondent, and producer in several news media channels (BBC, NDTV, Doordarshan, AIR, and Asianet News). He is the editor of *Journal of Media Watch*. He was the recipient of a Reuters Fellowship and is a Thomson Foundation Fellow in Television Studies with the Commonwealth Broadcasting Association Scholarship. He has published articles on Asian cinema, Indian cinema, gender and sexuality, and culture studies.

SAKI KOBAYASHI is a PhD candidate in the Department of Media Studies at Stockholms universitet, Sweden. Her dissertation analyzes the stardom of Viveca Lindfors from a transnational perspective to explore the notion of Swedishness and the star-making machinery. Her research interests include female stars in classical Swedish cinema. She has published an article on Eva Dahlbeck. From 2018 to 2019, she worked as a curatorial assistant at the National Film Archive of Japan in Tokyo.

DAISUKE MIYAO is professor and Hajime Mori Chair in Japanese Language and Literature in the department of Literature at the University of

California, San Diego, USA, where he teaches film studies. He is the author of *Sessue Hayakawa: Silent Cinema and Transnational Stardom* (2007); *The Aesthetics of Shadow: Lighting and Japanese Cinema* (2013); *Cinema Is a Cat: A Cat Lover's Introduction to Film Studies* (2019); and *Japonisme and the Birth of Cinema* (2020). He is the editor of *The Oxford Handbook of Japanese Cinema* (2014) and the coeditor of *Transnational Cinematography Studies* (2017).

GLORIA MONTI is associate professor in the department of Cinema and Television Arts at California State University, Fullerton, USA, where she teaches film studies. Her research interests include Hollywood cinema, Jean-Luc Godard, feminist film theory, and critical race theory. She has published articles and book chapters on Italian, French, and independent American cinema.

KRISZTA POZSONYI is an independent scholar. She completed a PhD in the department of Performing and Media Arts at Cornell University. Her dissertation examines the influence of television's postwar emergence as a mass medium on the circulation and work opportunities of female stand-up comedians as it (re)shaped the vaudeville-rooted circuits of live performance. Her research interests include television and film studies, performance studies, comedy studies, gender studies, and queer theory. She has published an article on teaching (with) humor in media courses.

MARTIN SHINGLER is an independent scholar, freelance writer, and editor. His research interests include film stars, screen performance, and melodrama. He is the author of *Star Studies: A Critical Guide* (2012); *When Warners Brought Broadway to Hollywood, 1923–39* (2018); and *Diana Dors: Film Star and Actor* (2022), and the coeditor of the BFI Film Stars book series from 2010 to 2019. He has published articles on Bette Davis.

GABRIELLE STECHER is lecturer in the department of English at Indiana University, Bloomington, USA, where she teaches digital composition, intensive writing, and honors courses. Her research interests include narratives about women artists, primarily from the nineteenth century to the present. She has published articles on Elizabeth Taylor, Disney artist Mary Blair, and adaptations of Victorian novels in classical Hollywood cinema.

ADITH K. SURESH is research assistant in the Department of Communication at MacEwan University, Edmonton, Canada. He holds a master's degree in English language and literature from Mahatma Gandhi University, India. He has published articles and book chapters on horror cinema, gender studies, and South Asian cultural studies.

CHRISTA VAN RAALTE is associate professor in the Media Production department, Faculty of Media and Communications, at Bournemouth University, UK, where she teaches film and television studies and is the head of the Centre for Excellence in Media Practice (CEMP). She is the lead author on a report: *Where Have All the PMs Gone?: Addressing the Production Management Skills Gap in UK TV* (2024) and the coeditor of *Action Heroines in the Twenty-First Century: Sisters in Arms* (forthcoming). She has published articles, book chapters, and industry-facing reports on constructions of gender in science fiction and action films, narrative strategies in complex TV, as well as working conditions and management practices in the film and television industries.

INDEX